How to Master
A Great
Golf Swing

How to Master A Great Golf Swing

Maxine Van Evera Lupo
Illustrations by Dom Lupo

TAYLOR TRADE PUBLISHING
Lanham • New York • Toronto • Oxford

Published by Taylor Trade Publishing
An imprint of The Rowman & Littlefield Publishing Group, Inc.
4501 Forbes Boulevard, Suite 200, Lanham, Maryland 20706

Distributed by NATIONAL BOOK NETWORK

Library of Congress Cataloging-in-Publication Data

Lupo, Maxine Van Evera
    How to master a great golf swing / Maxine Van Evera Lupo : illustrations by Dom Lupo.
        p.   cm.
    Includes index.
    ISBN-13: 978-1-58979-350-7
    ISBN-10: 1-58979-350-1
    1. Swing (Golf)   I. Title.
GV979.S9L87   1992
796.352'3—dc20   92-109
                                                          CIP

Manufactured in the United States of America.

My special appreciation and heartfelt thanks
to all of those who encouraged and supported me in
my effort to help those who play golf
help themselves play better.

Contents

Foreword

During the mid-1970s I began working with professional and amateur golfers, peripheral to my clinical duties in the Navy Medical Service Corps. In helping players chase their golfing dreams it became very apparent to me that peak performance could only be achieved through a complex interaction of proper mental focus and sound swing mechanics.

Searching for golfing excellence is often a mysterious and somewhat mystical pursuit—a thrilling adventure of trying to master concentration, focus, imagery, and tactile feel, all while performing a complicated sequence of technically correct body movements. In searching for excellence we meet the golf swing, a creature with a mind of its own that can lead us on a nerve-wracking emotional journey that ranges from joy and euphoria to agony, frustration, suffering, and despair. Such is the game we play! It tempts us with an addictive web that never lets us know with certainty when our next exhilarating payoff will arrive.

Understanding swing mechanics and how they cause an object with dimples and no smile to do strange and unusual things (i.e., go hard left, hard right, too low, too high, too fast, too slow) falls within the realm of the professional golf instructor. In 1983 I met Maxine, myself an avid golfer in search of better swing mechanics. Not only was I introduced to her teaching brilliance on the lesson tee, but far more important, I was blessed with a lifetime of warm friendship and by the marvelous gift of her wise and good counsel. I also found her original guidebook *How to Master a Great Golf Swing*, a valued reference tool in my pursuit of game improvement. In this reissue of her innovative step-by-step instructional guide, present-day golfers of all ability levels will find many "pearls of wisdom" outlined in a clear, concise approach to fifteen key fundamentals of the basic golf swing. Maxine's insights can become wonderful companions on the exciting journey of mastering the golf swing. In conjunction with dedicated practice and sound individualized instruction, this book can enrich the reader's knowledge of proper fundamentals and provide a solid foundation for capturing the magical essence of creative shot making.

There are no easy ways to gain complete mastery of the golf swing, no simple short cuts to achieving consistent peak performance in the game of golf. To appreciate this all we have to do is watch the weekly trials, tribulations, and struggles of the most talented players in the world on the men's and women's professional golf tours. However, after enjoying this book, after all the learning and studying, and after all the practice and play, I hope you are able to capture the true spirit of the game that Maxine so effectively taught me—

"Believe" mightily,
"Hope" joyfully,
"Hit" divinely . . .

. . . but most of all have fun and enjoy the game.

—Dr. Jay Brunza

Chapter One

Understanding the Basic Golf Swing

The golf swing is structured on the natural tendency and physical ability of an individual to swing, throw, or hit conceivably anything. Although everyone who plays golf employs this ability to some degree, many players still play badly more often than they play well. As a result, many hundreds of books have been written on golf to help dedicated students play better.

Bobby Jones wrote in 1959, for instance, that golf was not taught the way it is learned; that it was taught as a science but learned as a game and that teaching and writing had become far too technical and complicated. "What the game needs most," he wrote, "is a simplification of teaching routines which will present a less formidable aspect to the beginner and offer to the average player a rosier prospect of improvement." Regardless of Bobby Jones's admonition to teachers and writers to keep it simple, however, golf still remains frustrating for players.

Although knowing how to swing a golf club is accepted without question as a skill necessary for playing, still buried under a cloud of misconception is the belief that too much thinking about it complicates performance. Nothing could be more inane. Because of this, golf should be taught as a science because its difficulty does not necessarily lie with golfers who think too much or with teachers who teach golf as a science, but with players who play it as a game without first learning it as a science.

Here's why: Science is defined as "knowledge of facts and laws arranged in an orderly system." Similarly, the art of teaching golf evolved from a study of sequential movements that employ both shifting the weight and turning in a natural swinging-hitting action. Ultimately then, a sound method of teaching a "basic" swing developed. Regardless, however, most golf swings are not patterned after this prototype that makes the golf swing work because most golf swings are self-taught and self-developed.

Rather than learning from time-proven guidelines, too many players have first taken up the game with the object of just hitting the ball and then continued the practice until bad habits formed. The result is that very few golfers ever know what either does or doesn't make the golf swing work. What most golfers need, therefore, is not giving up the game, continuing to play badly, or simplification in teaching, but a greater effort toward learning.

Although independent actions within the golf swing are all fairly natural, such as shifting the weight to accommodate swinging and hitting, problems occur because the golf swing itself, as a whole, is not natural. In 1981, for instance, Sam Snead, famed for his "natural" golf swing, wrote, "I'd like to have a quarter for every shot I hooked with my natural grip before I developed the unnatural grip that let me hit them straighter." And Ben Hogan acknowledged that there is absolutely "nothing natural" about the golf swing. A natural swing can be developed, though, by learning how to establish and swing through positions that promote coordination.

Unlike more natural movements such as those found in tennis or baseball, the body turns rotationally in golf while the arms swing upright with the hands together—movements that are natural in themselves but unnatural in golf. As a result, a "basic" swing evolved as a series of fundamental positions and movements that coordinate and can be "built" in practice to serve as a self-help method for improving personal performance. The following pages present these fundamentals in sequence. You'll learn what they are, their purpose, how to apply them, where they are located in the swing, and how they affect each other. Learning about this golf swing as taught by teachers who teach "knowledge of facts and laws arranged in an orderly system" is the most important self-help "tool" for improving personal performance.

Playing well within their own ability motivates golfers at all ages and levels of proficiency to improve for personal satisfaction. How far you progress is not always a matter of inherent ability but often the ability to establish or adjust those parts of your own golf swing that are not fundamentally correct by comparing your swing with basics. Even more important, however, is that while you're learning the use of fundamentals you'll be learning to help yourself—and helping you help yourself is the purpose of this book.

Chapter Two

Learning To Use Fundamentals

Anyone can play golf and, with practice, can play consistently well. Many golfers fall victim to self-imposed problems and frustration in golf, however, because they have not developed a sound golf swing based on fundamentals.

One dictionary defines a fundamental as "a principle, rule, law, etc., that forms a foundation or basis, essential part, indispensable, underlying." A golf fundamental, then, may be defined as "a position or movement that is essential to building a strong foundation for a sound, repeating golf swing."

The combination of inaccuracies that cause problems in golf is neither prevented nor corrected by doing a few things right. You prevent problems by doing most things right and correct them by mastering specific positions or movements that relate to specific problems.

Understanding and applying these basic positions and movements help individual golfers improve personal performance and proficiency in two ways: (1) by learning how to establish positions initially that promote coordination, thereby avoiding problems; and (2) when problems do occur, by knowing how to correct or adjust those parts of the swing that are not fundamentally correct by comparing their swing with basics. Without fundamental guidelines as points of reference, however, it is difficult to establish correct positions, keep the swing intact, or analyze and correct swing problems.

Building a basic golf swing is the same as building a prefabricated house. Each must be built on a strong foundation with sections built independently that are strong enough to give strength to the whole. Units or sections of the swing, although always part of the whole, are the grip, position of address, backswing, downswing, and follow-through. These units are then connected with fundamental procedures such as "the waggle" and forward press that tend to promote good timing and rhythm—and all are developed in the learning stage by simply connecting the units in sequence.

All golfers use some fundamentals, whether they are aware of them or not. While they may use some, however, most golfers can improve their swing considerably by learning to use more fundamentals more effectively. Since each golfer and each golf swing is unique and not everyone uses fundamentals in exactly the same way, not all golfers can improve or correct their swing by using the same fundamentals. Therefore, in both teaching and learning, *learning which fundamentals affect each individual swing is the key to self-improvement.* The following chapters help you understand and achieve that goal for more enjoyment of golf.

PART I
The Grip

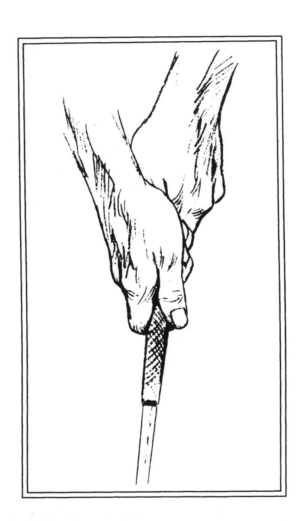

Chapter Three

Analyzing the Grip

An accurate grip is the most basically important ingredient in a reliable golf swing, contributing about 60 percent to its overall efficiency. Difficulty in other sections of the swing can frequently be traced directly back to the grip, because an incorrect hand position may have restricted the *ability* of muscles in other parts of the body to perform correctly. This inability of the other muscles gives the false impression that the difficulty lies somewhere other than in the grip.

Because the grip is so basic, golfers initially develop one that seems comfortable but does not necessarily contribute to the swing as it should. *Initial* comfort in golf may not always imply correctness; therefore, a study of the contribution the hands make to the swing, both separately and as a unit, can benefit even experienced golfers who presume their grip is correct.

The Vardon, or overlapping, grip—named after British champion Harry Vardon—positions the little finger of the right hand over the left forefinger, and it is rarely disputed as being the most popular put-together formula. The interlocking grip, where the left forefinger is locked in between the last two fingers of the right hand, is equally effective. This book refers to the more common overlapping grip throughout, but the principles applied refer to all golf grips, including the less common 10-finger grip.

The obvious purpose of establishing the grip is to enable the hands to work together as a closely knit unit. However, establishing the grip and actually completing the grip are not exactly the same. Because the right hand is positioned lower on the club than the left, extending the right arm to complete the grip exerts a muscular influence on other positions. Unless firmly secured, these other established positions may then inadvertently be changed.

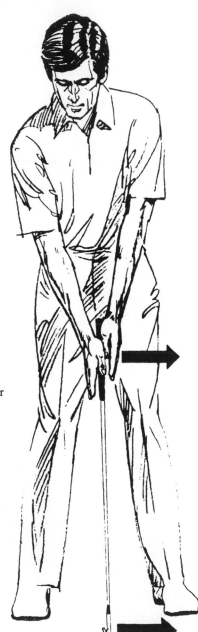

Aligning the hands and clubface square to each other helps return the clubface to square when the hands hit through the ball.

FIGURE 2

To promote full understanding, Part I presents a study of the grip itself, studying each hand separately as well as together. Part II then separates the hands while introducing fundamentals that position the clubhead, feet, and lower body *before* the right arm moves to position the right hand.

Before we actually begin studying the grip, look at your hands and study their natural action. Although alike, they oppose each other, working independently yet together through muscular control.

Use either hand to toss a soft object (such as a wad of paper) up in the air and hit it to the left with the palm of your right hand. Notice that your hand automatically pulls back with a little wrist action to slap or hit the object for distance. To hit the paper in the same direction with the *left* hand, however, you use the back of your hand, employing a natural firm-wristed "batting" effect, striving to hit the object straight rather than far. Both hands hit squarely at impact, however, and the same natural use of the hands is employed in the swing; through the grip you impart this action to the clubhead. The left-hand grip allows the left arm to keep the ball on target with backhanded firmness, while the right-hand grip allows the hand to smack the ball for distance.

The essential function of the grip is to align the hands and clubface at address in a manner that will return the clubface to square at impact. Aligning the back of the left hand, the palm of the right hand, and the clubface all square to each other and to the target in the address position returns the clubface to square when the hands hit naturally back through the ball. (Figure 2) Once established square, the hands and clubface swing squarely together throughout the golf swing; therefore, the alignment of the thumbs in relation to the toe of the clubhead at address can be used as a guideline for swinging correctly as well as for establishing positions at address.

Top performance in golf is not determined by brute force but by coordination of muscles, and as awkward as it seems, the grip is devised to promote accuracy and coordination throughout the entire golf swing. Though it isn't *initially* comfortable, it soon becomes so with practice.

Golf clubs are only extensions of the arms, and the grip is a sensibly constructed tool for transferring power from the body to the clubhead through the hands. They must be positioned accurately, closely united, firm, and active in order for good hand action to coordinate with other swing movements. An accurate grip develops confidence by promoting accuracy and coordination in a sound *repeating* swing.

Top performance in golf is not determined by brute force but by coordination of muscles.

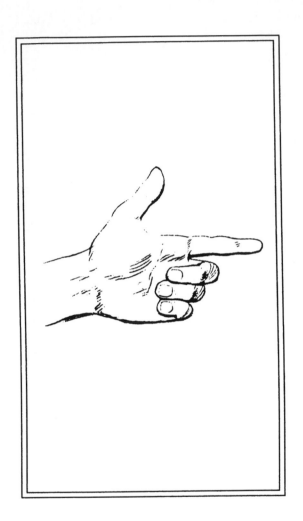

Chapter Four

Fundamental No. 1: The Left-Hand Pistol Grip

An accurate grip is the very foundation of an accurate golf swing. Although any method will teach the same left-hand grip as taught by the pistol grip, the pistol grip uses the hand's natural conformity to the shooting position to establish the grip more naturally.

The Procedure

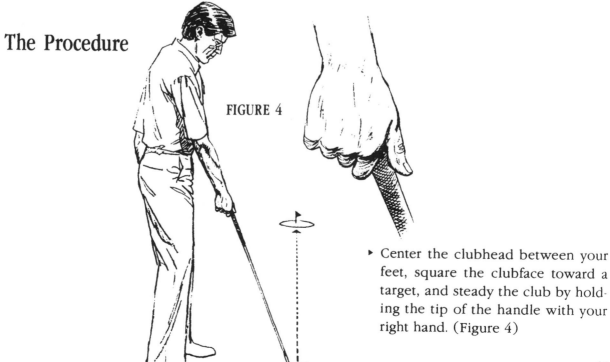

FIGURE 4

▸ Center the clubhead between your feet, square the clubface toward a target, and steady the club by holding the tip of the handle with your right hand. (Figure 4)

- Assume a shooting position with your left hand: point the forefinger straight ahead with the other three fingers in an open cupped position. Align the three fingers parallel to the thumb. (Figure 5)

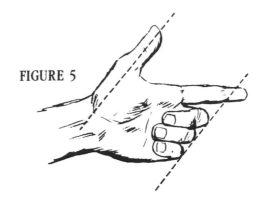

FIGURE 5

- Extend your left arm to aim the forefinger alongside and straight down the shaft. Square the back of the left hand directly toward the target and measure the top of the handle to the top joint of the thumb where the wrist breaks. (Figure 6)

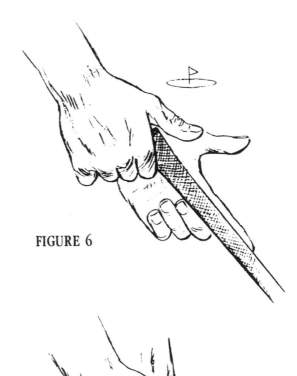

FIGURE 6

- Bend your wrist to cock your hand downward. The thumb, rather than the forefinger, will then aim alongside and straight down the shaft. The forefinger will point between your feet, toward your heels, and the knuckles of the cupped fingers will be parallel to the handle. (Figure 7)

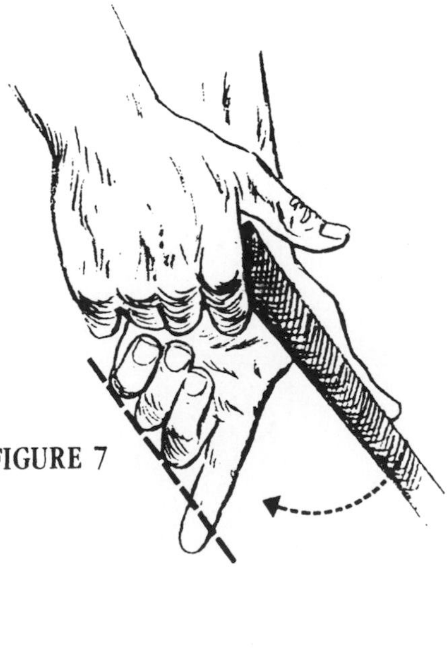

FIGURE 7

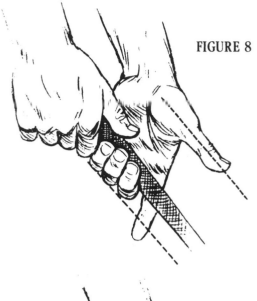

FIGURE 8

▸ Use your right hand to press the handle firmly down into the upper joints of the three cupped fingers and the base of the palm by pressing a small fold of skin from the palm down onto the last two fingers. (Figure 8)

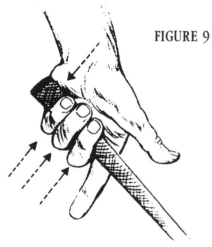

FIGURE 9

▸ Leaving the thumb and forefinger off the club, close your hand by gripping *up* with the fingers while pressing *down* with the heel pad of the hand. A tiny bit of muscle should extend over the tip of the handle. The gripping action of the hand will cock your left wrist inward. (Figure 9)

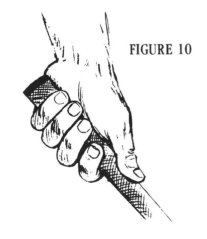

FIGURE 10

▸ Drop your thumb straight down on top of the handle and *lightly* curl the forefinger around the handle of the club. (Figure 10)

▸ Press down slightly with the flat pad of the end of the thumb. Although the thumb remains on top, firming the grip will pinch the base of the V formed by the thumb and forefinger together, and the line of the V should aim toward the right shoulder. (Figure 11)

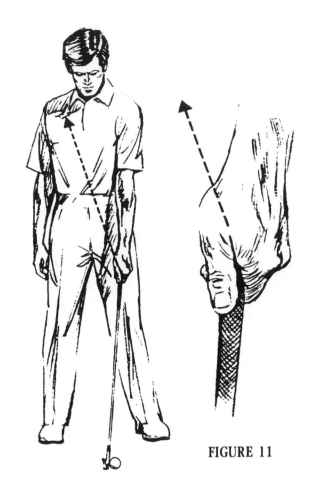

FIGURE 11

Importance of the Procedure

Mastering the left-hand pistol grip:

A. *cocks the hand into position so you can grip the club naturally while maintaining an upright posture*
B. *locks the club into position with a palm, three-finger grip*
C. *strengthens the left-hand grip*
D. *accurately positions the left thumb*
E. *removes the left-hand pincer fingers as a control factor in the swing*

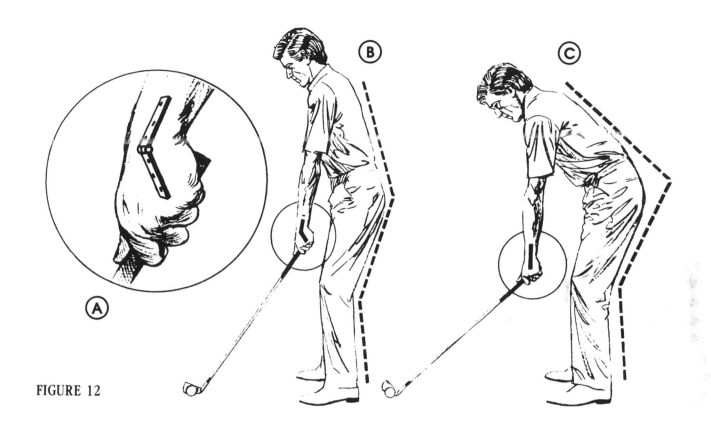

FIGURE 12

A: *Cocks the hand into position so you can grip the club naturally while maintaining an upright posture.*

"Hinging" the left hand downward at address angles the cupped fingers parallel to the diagonal line of the shaft, making it easy to grip the club naturally while keeping your posture upright. (Figures 12A and B)

Keeping your posture upright establishes important positions at address that promote such things as natural hand action and good footwork. Although their grip may be correct, golfers frequently establish positions that affect the swing adversely, often by leaning over too far and cocking their hands upward either to establish the grip or to position the clubhead. (Figure 12C)

Cocking the hands upward at address causes leaning over, and vice versa, frequently positioning the hands too low for good hand action; leaning over too far moves the weight toward the toes, making it difficult for you either to maintain balance or to shift your weight while swinging. The pistol grip, however, uses the natural angle of the left hand to establish correct positions.

Hinging the left hand downward (A and B) promotes accuracy at address and through the swing by preventing the body from leaning over too far to position the clubhead (C).

B: Locks the club into position with a palm, three-finger grip.

The backhanded batting action of the left hand uses natural muscular control to keep the ball on target, and a strong left-hand grip must be established to fortify the hand at impact. Strength combines with feel and maneuverability, however, when you secure the club with the muscular pad of the heel of your hand and *grip* the club with your fingers.

With the club secured at the base of the palm and the three fingers of your left hand firmly around the club, gripping *up* with the fingers and pressing *down* with the muscle of the heel of the hand firmly locks the club in place. Your left hand is firm and strong with the feel of the club in your fingers.

The basic palm-and-three-finger grip presses the skin at the base of the palm either upward or downward. Gripping the club correctly, by pressing the skin downward, generally forms two calluses at the base of the palm adjoining the last two fingers of the left hand. (Figure 13A) An incorrect and less comfortable grip presses the skin upward, forming calluses near the center of the palm (B). Developing calluses, although uncomfortable, is a necessary part of a strong golf grip.

At the top of the swing, momentum through the backswing is caught by the hands, causing a short pause at the top of the swing as the backswing shifts to the downswing. Unless your grip is strong at the start of the swing, momentum (all too often accentuated by a fast backswing) will force the left hand to loosen and drop the clubhead at the top as the downswing starts. (Figure 14) Since it is difficult to control the clubhead *with* the left hand, the right hand tightens and grabs the loose club. The left hand, in an effort to regain control, then closes very sharply and bounces the clubhead upward from the top of the swing. The two together, now in complete control, throw the clubhead *from* the top either down on top of the ball, into the ground behind it, or down sharply *under* the ball with the driver, which contributes to "skying," or hitting the ball too high.

C: Strengthens the left-hand grip.

Unless you're choking down on the club, which lowers the hands on the club for more hand and arm control, you can establish a stronger grip when you can feel a bit of the muscular pad of the heel of the hand pressing against the tip of the handle. (Figure 15) If the tip of the handle is in the palm or extends beyond this bit of muscle, the left-hand grip may not be as strong. You can test grip firmness by pulling back and forth on the club with the right hand.

FIGURE 13

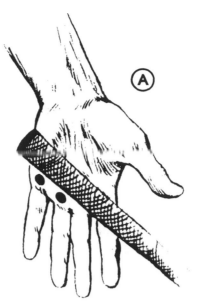

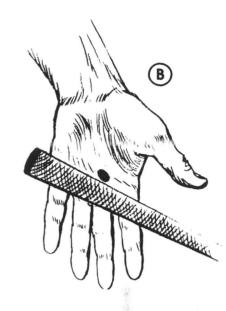

An accurate left-hand grip often forms two calluses at the base of the palm (A), whereas an incorrect grip forms calluses more toward the center of the palm (B).

FIGURE 14

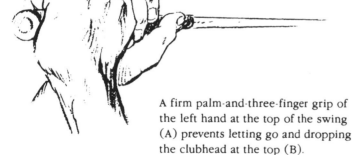

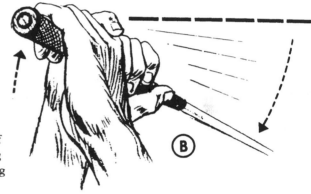

A firm palm-and-three-finger grip of the left hand at the top of the swing (A) prevents letting go and dropping the clubhead at the top (B).

FIGURE 15

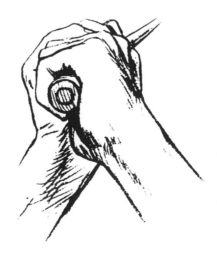

You get a stronger grip for full golf shots when a little of the heel pad of the left hand extends beyond the tip of the handle.

D: Accurately positions the left thumb.

Golfers frequently refer to a "long" or "short" left thumb position, describing its extension either up or down the shaft. Following this fundamental procedure positions the left thumb halfway between the two by simply dropping it on the club. Pressing down with the flat pad of the end of the thumb and pinching the base of the thumb and forefinger together strengthen the left-hand grip.

Drawing the left thumb up into a short thumb position creates a small triangular gap between the upper joint of the thumb and the club. This gives springy flexibility to the thumb and promotes feel in the hand by pressing the club more into the fingers. (Figure 16A) Extending the left thumb in a long thumb position eliminates the triangular gap and places the club more in the palm. Since this is a

FIGURE 16

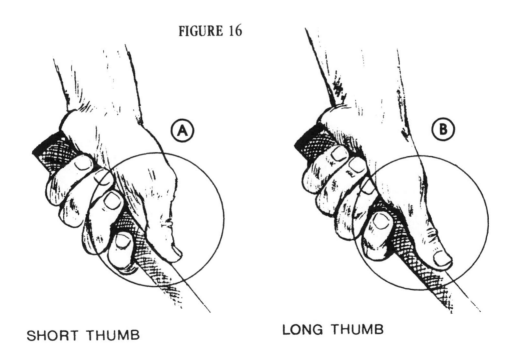

SHORT THUMB

LONG THUMB

Flexibility and feel are promoted with a short thumb (A), whereas clubhead control at the top of the swing may be improved with a long thumb (B).

somewhat stronger position, those with weak hands and those who consistently overswing or lose control of the clubhead at the top of the swing should try a longer thumb position. (Figure 16B)

Regardless of whether the left thumb is long or short (and you should experiment to see which gives more control), positioning the thumb straight down the shaft at address positions it directly *under* the shaft at the top of the swing, reinforcing the hand against letting go at the top and dropping the clubhead.

Through the backswing the left wrist is straight and the left hand hinges upward from the base of the thumb; consequently it is important to position the hand and thumb to work naturally, as well as correctly, through the backswing. Positioning the *hands* incorrectly causes inaccuracy through the wrist break.

E: Removes the left-hand pincer fingers as a control factor in the swing. The pincer fingers are the tips of the thumb and forefinger. Although their viselike strength may have everyday usefulness, they must not press tightly together in golf, for this will tighten outside rather than inside muscles of the arm, which causes tension and overcontrolling of the clubhead. To feel the muscular difference in your arm, first tighten only the last three fingers of your left hand (which are used to grip the club), then press just the tips of the thumb and forefinger together.

Pinching together the base of the V formed by the thumb and forefinger and lightly curling the forefinger around the club prevent you from creating tension in the hand, arm, and shoulder at address while still allowing your hand to be as strong as it should be. At the same time, the pincer fingers are prevented from helping your hands control the clubhead.

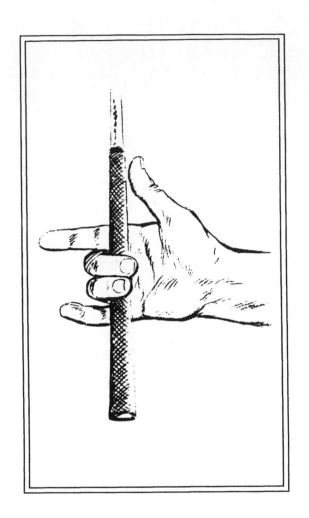

Chapter Five

Fundamental No. 2:
The Right-Hand Grip

Although the left-hand grip is established with the clubhead on the ground, it is easier to establish, strengthen, or check the right-hand grip for accuracy by lifting the clubhead off the ground.

The Procedure

▸ Square the clubface to the target with the left-hand grip, then lift the clubhead upward to position the right hand. Aim the back of the left hand and the palm of the right hand directly toward the target with your palms directly facing each other. The hands and clubface will then be square to each other and to the target. (Figure 18)

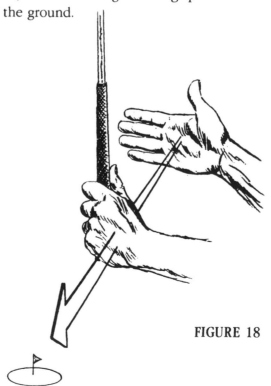

FIGURE 18

‣ Keeping the right palm open, place the two middle fingers of the right hand down firmly on the left forefinger and firmly press the handle into the two middle fingers at the base of the palm (A). The little finger of the right hand will then lie over the forefinger of the left hand (B). (Figure 19)

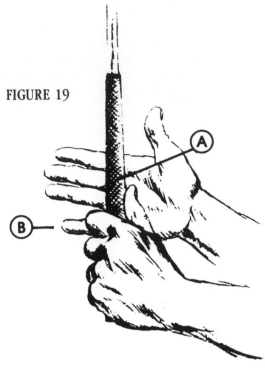

FIGURE 19

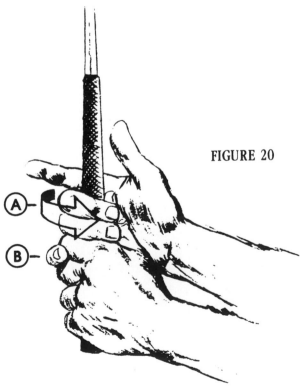

FIGURE 20

‣ With the thumb and forefinger still open, wrap the two middle fingers around the club and make certain your palms are still aligned. The tips of the two fingers should touch, but not overlap, the left thumb (A). Although the little finger falls naturally into place, it generally seats itself comfortably under the knuckle of the left forefinger (B). (Figure 20)

▸ As the club is gripped firmly in the two middle fingers, the upper joint of the "trigger" forefinger presses against the handle. Draw the right hand back a bit—with the palm still open (A)—and press the club to the right, pressing the handle even more firmly *under* the muscle pad and into this strong position (B). (Figure 21)

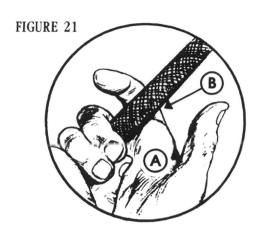

FIGURE 21

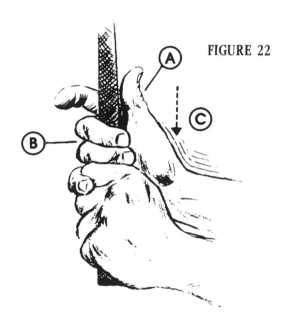

FIGURE 22

▸ Pinch the base of the thumb and forefinger together (A), keep the middle fingers firm (B), and draw the right hand down and over the left thumb (C). The thumb will fit snugly in the cup of the right hand. (Figure 22)

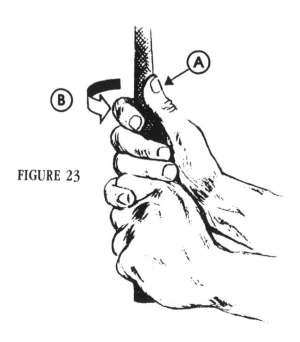

FIGURE 23

▸ Firmly position the right thumb slightly offset to the left on the club (A) and *lightly* close the forefinger (B). (Figure 23)

▸ The line of the **V** formed by the thumb and forefinger should aim between the chin and right shoulder. (See page 26, Figure 25A)

Importance of the Procedure

Mastering the right-hand grip:
A. *helps position the right hand naturally while keeping your posture upright*
B. *strengthens the grip*
C. *develops controlled right-hand power*
D. *accurately positions the right thumb*
E. *removes the right-hand pincer fingers as a control factor in the swing*

A: *Helps position the right hand naturally while keeping your posture upright.*

Placing the clubhead on the ground to establish the left-hand grip places the shaft at an angle that corresponds comfortably with the diagonal line of the hand. Holding the clubhead downward makes it easy to grip the club correctly because the handle lies diagonally across the base of the palm. When the hands are together and the grip is completed, however, the angle of the hands is not the same. Gripping the club in the two middle fingers with the little finger *off* the shaft results in the angle of the right hand being square rather than diagonal. (Figure 24A)

Because it is difficult to position a square hand on a diagonal handle without leaning over too far, raising the clubhead to establish the right-hand grip helps set your hand correctly, keeping your posture upright at the same time. (Figure 24B)

Lifting the clubhead off the ground in practice to position the right hand quickly develops a firm, comfortable feeling for securing the right-hand grip. So much so, in fact, that a large percentage of golfers, whether aware of it or not, "waggle" the clubhead off the ground while setting up to the ball, instinctively promoting both comfort and accuracy while securing the right-hand grip as part of the setup procedure.

B: *Strengthens the grip.*

The hands must be united closely throughout the swing to maintain control of the clubhead. Regardless of how sound the swing is, somewhere the hands might separate unless they are strong at address. Separation directs one hand or the other (usually the dominant right hand) through the hitting zone with enough force to overpower the other at impact. The result: you lose distance and accuracy and often the ball as well.

Positioning the two middle fingers of the right hand down firmly on the left forefinger positions the hands together. As the right hand completes the grip and the base of the thumb draws firmly against the left hand, the two middle fingers roll sideways and downward, drawing the right hand down even closer to the left. Extending the clubhead upward to position the right hand develops a strong, firm feeling—the same feeling that should be present with the clubhead on the ground.

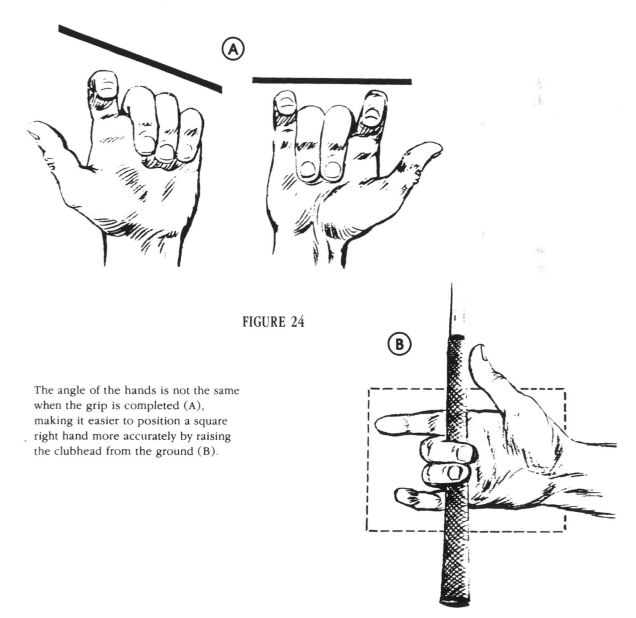

FIGURE 24

The angle of the hands is not the same when the grip is completed (A), making it easier to position a square right hand more accurately by raising the clubhead from the ground (B).

C: Develops controlled right-hand power.

The natural hitting ability of the right hand transfers into hitting power at impact. Right-hand power, however, which is dominant in right-handed golfers, must not be allowed to overpower the less dominant left hand, which is the reason for positioning the little finger *off* the club, on top of the left forefinger. (Figure 25A)

Although strengthening the grip by locking the hands together may appear to be the right little finger's major role, it actually serves another, albeit minor, purpose in both the overlapping and interlocking grip: the little finger is removed from the shaft for the more important purpose of *weakening* the stronger right hand.

Golfers occasionally refer to a "strong" or "weak" grip at address. These terms can be confusing because they refer more to positions at address than to actual strength or weakness. A so-called strong grip turns either hand more to the right; a weak grip turns either hand more to the left. But *strong* does not mean better with reference to the right hand, for positioning the right hand too far right positions it incorrectly under the shaft, thereby minimizing its effectiveness. (Figure 25C) Although too strong a grip is considered a hook or pull position, positioning only the right hand too strong results in poor hand action, which may cause slicing instead. A good check for right-hand accuracy is occasionally to place a tee in the V; the tee should point straight upward rather than outward. (Figure 25B)

A teaching professional may strengthen the grip of a child or an older person whose hands are not strong by placing all of the fingers, as well as the thumbs, on the club in a 10-finger grip. A regular

FIGURE 25

Positioning the right hand correctly (A) would position a tee in the V pointing upward (B) rather than outward (C).

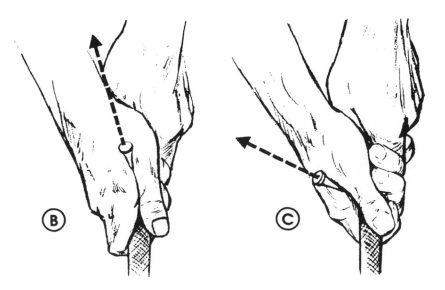

baseball grip (with the thumbs around the club) should not be mistaken for a 10-finger grip, however, because wrapping the thumbs *around* the club will weaken a golf grip.

At the same time that the right hand is weakened by removing the little finger, it is strengthened by finger control. Finger control promotes strong right-hand action through the impact zone, and the muscle pads of the hands play prominent roles in gripping with the fingers of both the left and right hand. Just as the heel pad of the palm of the left hand secures the club in the three fingers, you reinforce the right hand by pressing the handle firmly *under* the muscle pad at the base of the forefinger and gripping the club *in* the two middle fingers. This secures the handle in the fingers for strong right-hand action as your hands whip through the ball together.

D: Accurately positions the right thumb.

The right thumb is slightly offset at address for the reverse reason that the left thumb is more on top. If the *right* thumb is under the shaft at the top of the swing, just as the left, swing action stops too soon. Stopping swing action early by minimizing hand action shortens the backswing, whereupon the right hand bounces the clubhead back too fast, throwing the clubhead from the top and ruining the timing of a smooth, controlled swing. (Figure 26)

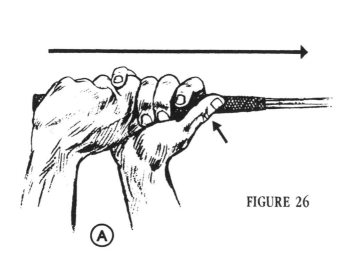
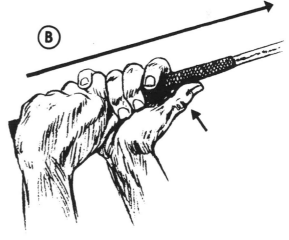

FIGURE 26

An offset right thumb at address positions the thumb offset at the top of the swing (A). When the right thumb is under the shaft (B), the clubhead bounces back too soon.

E: Removes the right-hand pincer fingers as a control factor in the swing.

When your forefingers are curled lightly around the club, both hands prevent the pincer fingers from controlling the clubhead. The forefingers should feel soft, as if you're handing a pencil to someone. (Figure 27) Lightly closing the forefingers turns them into "feel" fingers—a sort of sensory guide in the grip—but prevents the tips of the forefingers from joining forces with the thumbs to overcontrol the clubhead while swinging or to cause tension at address.

The feeling in the forefingers is similar to that of handing a pencil to someone.

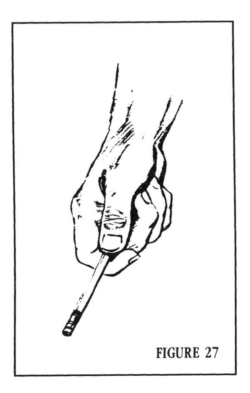

FIGURE 27

PART II
The Position of Address

Chapter Six

Analyzing the Position of Address

Addressing the ball correctly is the basic requirement for hitting an accurate golf shot. Unlike experienced, more proficient golfers, however, many golfers encounter problems throughout the swing because they have no procedure, guidelines, or checkpoints to follow for attaining important objectives.

Golfers who have only a general knowledge of objectives and fundamentals may feel almost uncoordinated when establishing the address position. It is not a matter of *being* uncoordinated, however, but of *feeling* uncoordinated by trying to attain unknown objectives with positions established at random.

The key to unlocking an uncoordinated feeling when setting up to the ball is the order in which you incorporate the fundamentals into the position to attain all of the essential objectives—alignment, posture, balance, weight distribution, ball position, and muscular tautness—which must be "programmed" into the address procedure. It is not easy, however, to attain any of these objectives—much less all of them—unless you first understand the objectives and then learn how to apply the fundamentals in sequence so that you reach your goals automatically.

Experience, feel, and confidence eventually replace the need to continue building the address position as described on subsequent pages. Building the swing is simply a learning technique to help you understand the golf swing better. If you learn the procedure and practice, you will eventually be able to set up knowledgeably with both confidence and accuracy by following *any* preferred procedure that still takes you to your goals.

Understanding the terminology that applies to setting up to the ball is an important part of golf. The *stance*, for instance, refers not only to the position of the feet at address but also to other basic positions and to the manner of standing and posture—standing *square*, *open*, or *closed*, for instance, as well as leaning over or standing upright.

The clubface, feet, knees, hips, and shoulders are described as being either square, open, or closed relative to each other and to the target line. Although the shoulders contribute to accuracy in the address position, they are not a major factor in establishing the target line in the building process. Other than the right shoulder being lower than the left (because the right *hand* is lower), the shoulders assume a square, open, or closed position similar to, and as a result of, other established positions.

The target line is established by two imaginary lines: a *line of flight*

28

To hit the ball straight, your feet, knees, hips, and shoulders must be square to each other and to the line of flight established by the clubface.

29

When the feet, knees, hips, or shoulders aim left of the target line, they are open. When the clubface aims to the left, however, it is closed.

30

When the feet, knees, hips, or shoulders aim right of the target line, they are closed. When the clubface aims to the right, however, it is open.

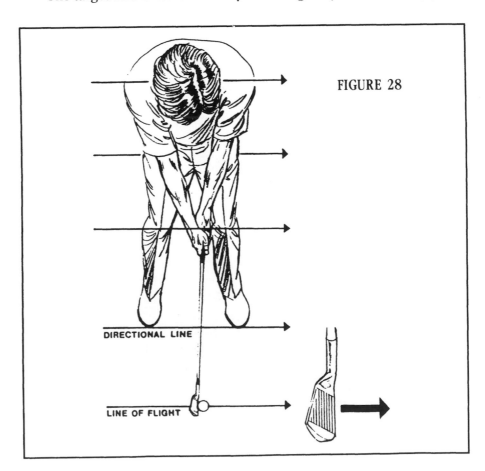

FIGURE 28

DIRECTIONAL LINE

LINE OF FLIGHT

established by the clubface, which is the line on which the ball and clubhead travel, and a *directional line* established by the feet and used for alignment. The directional line not only helps align the body correctly at address but also serves as an important guideline for swinging correctly throughout the golf swing.

To hit the ball straight, you must establish a square position of address in the basic swing. This simply means that you aim the clubface directly *down* a line of flight, directly *toward* the target, and your feet, knees, hips, and shoulders are aligned directly *to* the line of flight. (Figure 28)

The terms *open* and *closed* refer to positions aimed left or right of a line toward the target. When positions of the body and the clubface are aligned in the same direction, however, what opens positions of the body closes the clubface. For instance, when the feet, knees, hips, or shoulders aim left of the target line, they are open to the target, but when the clubface aims to the left, it is closed. (Figure 29) The reverse is true with positions aimed to the right of the target line: body positions are closed, but the clubface is open. (Figure 30)

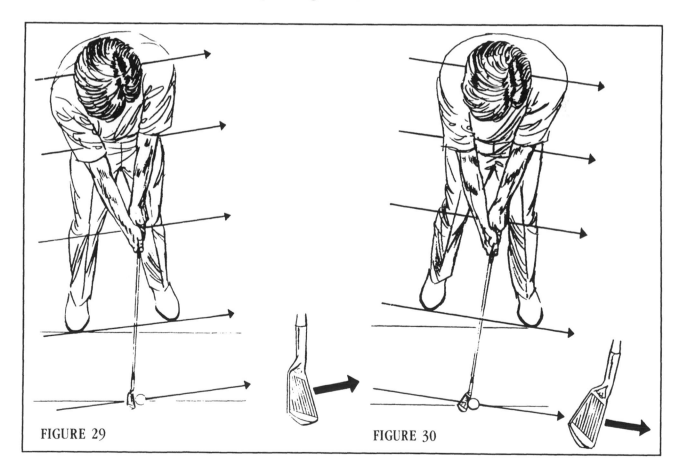

FIGURE 29

FIGURE 30

Open and closed positions combine in many ways to hit both intentional and unintentional shots. If you intentionally establish positions to manipulate the ball, you can curve the ball in flight at will. For example, you can combine an open stance with an open clubface to slice to the right or a closed stance with a closed clubface to hook the ball left. More often, however, you *un*intentionally establish *in*correct positions, causing the ball to be hit off-line. Trying to hit straight down the target line when the *stance* is closed, for instance, causes "blocking out"; you prevent yourself from turning through the ball and end up pulling the ball straight left or pushing straight right as well as slicing or hooking.

The clubhead has a tendency to move into the backswing on the line established by either the feet, the hips, or the shoulders. This clubhead path away from the ball helps determine the swing plane. In turn, the swing plane helps determine the angle at which the clubface strikes the ball. Because the clubhead generally returns the way it moves *into* the backswing, whether you hit the ball straight depends on whether you started a straight backswing—from a square address position with parallel target lines.

A square position of address enables the clubhead to start straight back on the line of flight and return squarely through the ball because the line of flight and the directional line are parallel to each other and both aim toward the target. Open or closed feet, hips, or shoulders, however, establish an angled directional line. Since the target lines are not parallel, the clubhead has no alternative but to start back on—and return *to*—an angle to *one* of the target lines. The ball will invariably be sliced or pushed right or hooked or pulled left. In a subconscious effort to return the clubface to the line of flight (which started on an angled directional line), golfers frequently "loop" the clubhead from the top back *to* the line of flight to still mis-hit the ball as the swing plane changes.

The average golfer should not be concerned with manipulating open and closed positions to finesse the ball intentionally but should avoid *unintentionally* establishing positions that lead to mis-hitting the ball. The need for hooking or slicing is almost nonexistent in the average golfer's game. To develop consistency it would be better to concentrate on the shot most difficult to teach or learn—the one straight down the middle—by establishing square positions.

Positioning the clubhead behind the ball is the switch that activates the mechanism of the swing. And since the clubface strikes the ball, squaring the clubface to the target is the first important alignment. The care and accuracy with which the clubhead is positioned determines the

Concentration is an important asset in golf and must not be wasted on something that can be relegated to fundamentals.

ability of other fundamentals to continue establishing a precisely accurate position, so clubface alignment is critical to the entire golf swing.

As positions are assumed, in sequence, the waggle—which is not a nervous gimmick but an important *part* of the swing—is used to feel positions into a secure, interlocking relationship with each other by firmly adjusting independent positions and blending them together. Except for relieving tension, however, no amount of waggling will benefit a golfer who is not establishing positions in sequence with specific objectives in mind. It is not difficult to waggle positions *out* of alignment if you're adjusting only to a comfortable position.

Learning and systematizing the procedure for addressing the ball correctly is not a mind-boggling experience, regardless of the number of fundamentals involved. Once you develop the procedure—*and* practice it—you won't be plagued by indecision about which step comes first; consistency and repetition will help you attain your objectives automatically.

When you can establish the position of address quickly and confidently because you *know* the positions are correct, your mind is free to concentrate on other areas of the swing that cannot be structured through a formulated plan. *Concentration is an important asset in golf and must not be wasted on something that can be relegated to fundamentals.*

The chapters devoted to addressing the ball present a comprehensive study of fundamental positions within the position of address, teaching the square position as the most dependable and teaching you how to eliminate doing the *wrong* thing by doing what is right. The process is an asset that no dedicated golfer can afford to be without.

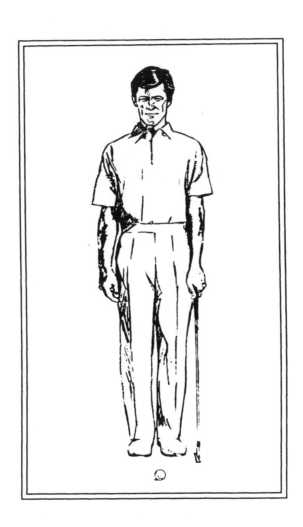

Chapter Seven

Fundamental No. 3: The Basic Position at Address

By following a fundamental procedure for setting up to the ball, you automatically achieve important objectives before the backswing starts and are used throughout the swing. The action seems so elementary, however, that just setting up to the ball is not always regarded as being fundamentally important. Alignment, posture, balance, weight distribution, ball position, and muscular tension must all be coordinated in the address position, however, and golfers who don't have a sound procedure to follow generally fail to attain *all* of these basic objectives.

Everyone who plays golf long enough eventually develops an individual, repeatable style or personal procedure for approaching and addressing the ball. You'll probably notice, however, that the "styles" of those without objectives seldom resemble each other. In contrast, knowledgeable golfers who practice and gain experience often resemble each other when setting up to the ball. Their experience has taught them that there *is* one basic method that works, so they instinctively use the fundamentals similarly to attain the same objectives. (See page 108, Figure 75.)

Establishing and understanding a rather elementary basic position is the first step in learning how to address the ball correctly.

The Procedure

Stand tall and straight, as if you're at attention, with your head back, chin in, feet together, and arms relaxed. Now pull in your stomach and tuck your hips under to pull your weight toward your heels.

Importance of the Procedure

Learning the basic position at address:
A. *promotes a balanced position by keeping your weight off your toes*
B. *establishes a square alignment of the feet, knees, hips, and shoulders*
C. *promotes an upright posture with the chin up*
D. *provides the foundation for a natural shoulder turn and pivot*

A: *Promotes a balanced position by keeping your weight off your toes.*
The strongest feeling in the feet occurs when they are positioned to spring forward with the weight toward the toes. Inexperienced golfers are sometimes tempted to establish this forward position, but it is not a good foundation for the swing.

A full golf swing generates tremendous momentum and, if given the opportunity, throws the body off balance. You maintain balance through the swing, however, by coordinating good footwork with the act of swinging and hitting as your weight shifts back and forth. Keeping your weight off your toes places your center of gravity toward your heels, promoting good footwork, strong legs, and a natural shoulder turn and pivot—all of which are needed to transfer weight and maintain balance while swinging.

Pulling the hips under moves the weight toward the heels, not to place your weight on the heels but to keep it off the toes. As you continue to build the address position using fundamentals, "sitting down" to the ball will flex the hips back so your seat protrudes a bit; and your weight moves slightly forward from this initial position. Meanwhile, however, it is good exercise for those who place their weight on their toes to feel it placed on the heels. Although the weight is not entirely on your heels at address, it definitely must *not* be on your toes.

To sense the feeling of a balanced position—and to compare

balance between the heels and toes—first separate your feet, flex, your knees, and extend your arms outward. Now swing your arms around while turning your body and shift your weight first right and then left. Exaggerate the movement, first with your weight on your toes, then with your weight toward your heels. It should be easy to determine that better balance is maintained with the weight toward the heels, which adds feeling to the balls of the feet and toes.

Swinging your arms around with your knees flexed helps your legs flow with the movement. As your hips and shoulders turn with the weight shift, your feet pull inward and your heels lift slightly off the ground. You easily maintain balance during this movement by using natural footwork to catch and hold the weight during weight transference for a strong, balanced swing.

Turning a golf club upside down and using the shaft as a stick to hit with—first with the right hand and then with the left—is an excellent practice exercise for developing the same feeling needed in golf to obtain the same natural results.

B: *Establishes a square alignment of the feet, knees, hips, and shoulders.* Standing at attention aligns your feet, knees, hips, and shoulders parallel to each other. Although nothing should occur to change this square alignment, the one position that can *inadvertently* change is the position of your hips; and your hips must remain square, with the knees parallel, to maintain the square directional line. Unlike your feet, which will retain their position, your knees and hips are easily influenced to change by the movement of other muscles as positions are established—particularly toward being turned open to the target line.

Muscular movement is directed toward the target when you're setting up to the ball. With the body structured so the hips swivel comfortably between the feet and shoulders, it is not uncommon for the hips and knees to slip into an open position. The shoulders may then want to go in the same direction. (Figure 32)

Open positions at address block both the shoulder turn and the pivot, whereupon the body sways laterally rather than rotationally as soon as the backswing starts. Although open positions often accompany each other, keeping the *hips* square helps you maintain the other positions.

It is not uncommon for the hips and knees to slip open at address, making it difficult to keep the shoulders square and to turn smoothly away from the ball as soon as the backswing starts.

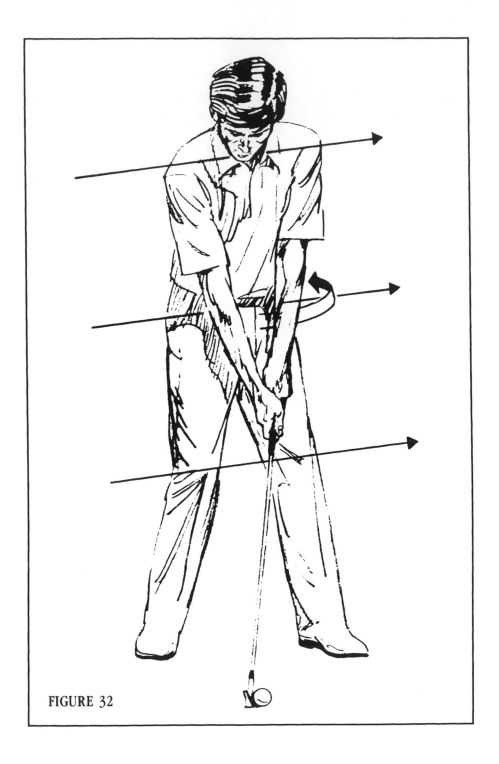

FIGURE 32

C: Promotes an upright posture with the chin up.

At address golfers appear to be leaning over or bending forward to position the clubhead, which in effect they do. But leaning over or bending too *far*, which is fairly common, affects the swing adversely by moving the weight toward the toes, dropping the chin too low, and positioning the hands incorrectly.

Tucking your hips under is simply a learning technique from which good posture evolves. By standing up straight and establishing good posture you allow the fundamentals to set the lower body first—before you lean over—by flexing your knees and sitting down to the ball while simultaneously releasing your hips to straighten your lower back, thereby keeping your posture upright in a strong, balanced position.

The familiar old (although outmoded and generally misunderstood) cliché "Keep your head down" continues to promote a chin-on-the-chest position, which makes it difficult to swing around a swing "center"; but following the address procedure for standing at attention correctly positions your head in line with your spine with your back straight and chin up—an important position established at address and maintained through the swing for balance.

D: Provides the foundation for a natural shoulder turn and pivot.

Although the shoulder turn and pivot are both natural movements, neither can be comfortably correct during the swing unless positions are correct at address.

The basic position of standing at attention provides a foundation for a natural shoulder turn and pivot by initiating good posture, balance, and alignment. Positions are square to each other and to the target line; your weight is more toward your heels than forward on your toes; and your chin is up rather than down. Following a later procedure for flexing the knees inward and sitting down to the ball only strengthens these early positions.

Positioning your chin too low restricts the shoulder turn as your shoulders turn *into* your chin throughout the golf swing; either your body sways laterally, your head is pushed up into the follow-through, or the backswing or follow-through is blocked as a result of the shoulder turn. Keeping your chin up, however, along with keeping your hips and shoulders square and knees parallel, enables your hips and shoulders to turn, rather than move laterally, as soon as the backswing starts. And you maintain good balance by keeping your weight off your toes.

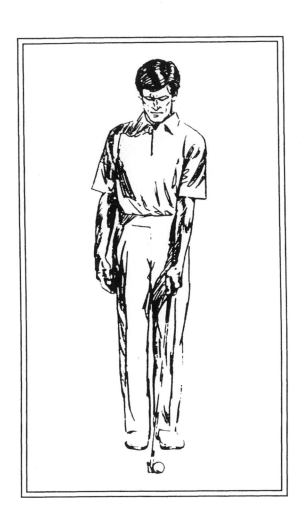

Chapter Eight

Fundamental No. 4: Positioning the Clubhead

The fundamental procedure for positioning the clubhead helps you attain the important objectives of alignment, posture, balance, weight distribution, ball position, and muscular tautness. It keeps your posture upright and maintains balance while you establish target lines, first by squaring the clubface to the target and then by squaring your feet and the rest of your body to the square clubface.

Although squaring the clubface to the target is the first important alignment, the first *movement* made at address is also important because it blends through the rest of the swing in a chain-reaction sequence.

The straight arm–shaft position is used to position the clubhead for the purpose of being changed as new fundamentals are added. Meanwhile, however, the position is an important beginning procedure for obtaining accuracy at address.

FIGURE 34
FIGURE 35

The Procedure

▸ Sight the target from behind the ball. (Figure 34)

▸ Lay a club on the ground, alongside the ball, on the target line. (Figure 35)

▸ Lay another club down just to the right of the ball, at an exact right angle to the other club, then pull it away from the other to leave a five-inch gap. (Figure 36)

▸ Standing upright and using only the left-hand grip to hold the club, straddle the end of the second club with your feet together and extend your left arm and shoulder in a straight arm–shaft "shaking hands" position to position the clubhead. (Figure 37)

▸ Still standing comfortably upright, adjust your feet along the club until you can lower and center the clubhead directly behind the ball—on the open slot—*with your hand ahead of the ball.* This squares the clubface to the target to establish a line of flight. (Figure 38)

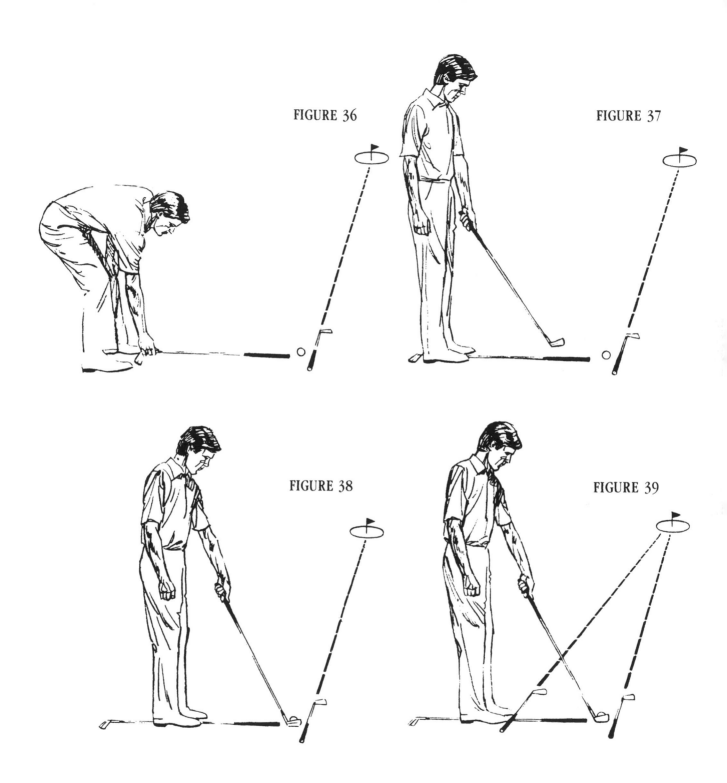

FIGURE 36

FIGURE 37

FIGURE 38

FIGURE 39

▸ Square your toes parallel to the line of flight, then lay a third club along the line of the toes to determine a directional line. The directional line will be parallel to the line of flight. (Figure 39)

Importance of the Procedure

Correctly positioning the clubhead:

A. *determines the target line*
B. *squares the clubface to the target to establish the line of flight*
C. *measures the swing radius*
D. *positions your hands and measures how far you should stand from the ball*
E. *positions your hands ahead of the ball with a straight left wrist*
F. *positions your head behind the ball*
G. *protects positions already established*
H. *develops a relaxed but strong position*
I. *helps square your shoulders at address*

A: Determines the target line.

Two lines establish the target line: a line of flight established by the clubface and a directional line established by your feet. The line of flight aims toward the target, and the lines are parallel to each other. To hit the ball straight, you must first square the clubface to the target

Lining Up to the Target

(1) Sight the target.
(2) Sight an intervening mark.

FIGURE 40

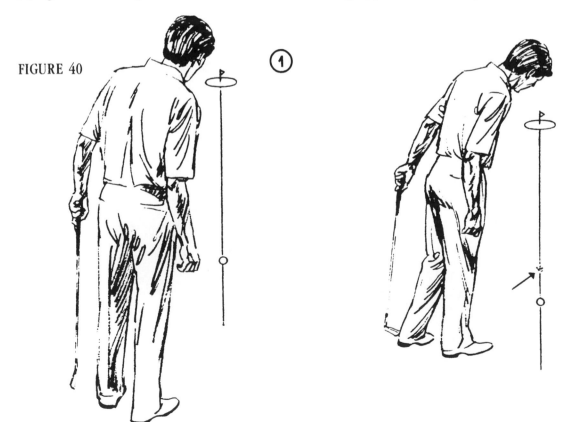

and then square your feet to the clubface. Although both lines form the target line, each line is independently important, both at address and through the swing.

Using alignment clubs is an excellent method for learning how to square up to the ball as well as for learning later how to swing the club correctly.

B: Squares the clubface to the target to establish the line of flight.
Aside from the grip, the basic requirements for hitting the ball straight are first determining the line of flight and then squaring the bottom (leading) edge of the clubface at a right angle to that line. It is not always easy at first to sight the target line and establish an accurate alignment, but practicing with alignment clubs helps you see the line more clearly and develop both subconscious and visual accuracy for consistently lining up correctly.

For more experienced golfers who understand basics but who still have trouble lining up correctly, these steps may be helpful:

1. Sight the target line from behind the ball. (Figure 40)
2. Locate a point *on* the target line a few feet in front of the ball.

(3) Square the clubface to the mark.
(4) Align the feet to the clubface.

3. Square the clubface to that point—either with or without the grip completed (whichever seems more helpful).
4. Complete the square alignment by squaring the feet to the square clubface.

C: Measures the swing radius.

The word *radius* is defined as "a straight line from the center to the outside of a circle," such as the spoke of a wheel. (See page 207, Figure 128.) The golf swing radius is the length of the left arm plus the length of the shaft. The radius is measured at address by extending the left arm in line with the shaft while the feet are together and the posture is upright. (Figure 41) Since the length of the radius determines the size of the circle, the golf swing radius determines the swing arc—or how large the circle will be.

The golf swing radius should never be larger or smaller than a comfortable extension of the left arm at address, first to build maximum clubhead speed with a maximum swing arc and second to return the clubhead to the exact location of the ball. Should the left arm be bent or extended too far at address, there will be physical leeway *through* the swing for the arms to adjust to a longer or shorter extension. Such discrepancies change the arc of the swing by either lengthening or shortening its radius, thus preventing the clubhead from returning accurately.

Once measured, regardless of how the hands are *re*positioned while completing the address position, the swing radius remains unchanged throughout the swing as the arms maintain extension— the left arm at address and through the backswing and the right arm into the follow-through.

FIGURE 41

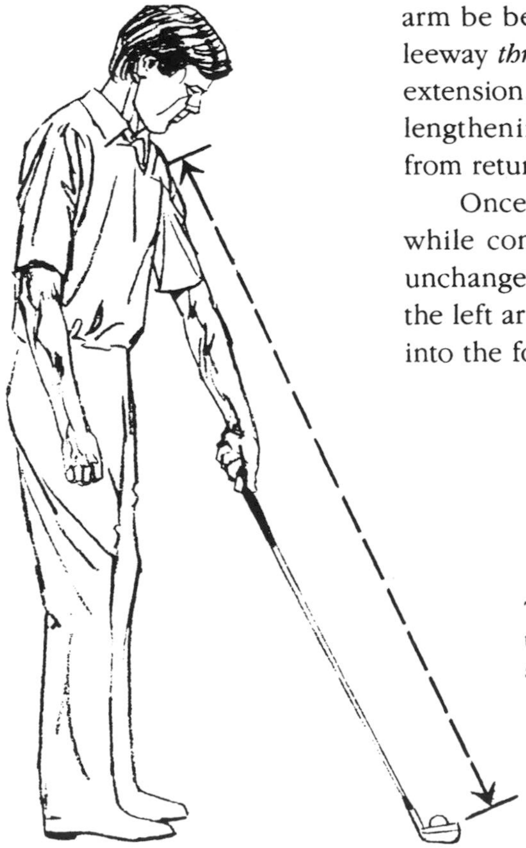

The golf swing radius is the length of the left arm plus the length of the shaft.

D: Positions your hands and measures how far you should stand from the ball.

Comfortably extending the left arm to position the clubhead—with your feet together and your posture upright—ultimately positions your hands naturally as well as correctly and measures how far you need to stand from the ball to use any club. The length of the shaft of different clubs positions the clubhead near or far by extending the distance for woods and shortening the distance for irons. The hands are positioned the same, however, from the driver through the wedge. (See page 73, Figure 56.)

Reaching too far by overextending your arms either moves your weight toward your toes or positions your hands too high, either of which cause swinging around the body—or swinging flat—and hitting the ball on the toe of the club. Since it is difficult to maintain balance with your weight on your toes, a common result is "casting," or throwing the clubhead outward from the top of the swing, which also causes "toeing." Combined with an open clubface, casting also results in shanking—or hitting the ball "dead right"—by hitting on the hosel, or the neck of the club.

By crowding your arms—not comfortably extending your left arm—you may either position the ball too close or your hands too low and may restrict your arms while swinging. You may then hit on the heel at impact as your swing adjusts the clubhead.

Positioning the ball correctly by positioning your arms, hands, and club correctly helps you avoid shots such as shanking, toeing, and heeling simply by following a basic procedure for setting up correctly to prevent establishing poor positions that lead to swinging incorrectly.

The hands are positioned the same, from the driver through the wedge.

E: Positions your hands ahead of the ball with a straight left wrist.

Extending your left arm and the shaft in a straight line while positioning the clubhead with just your left hand will eventually position both hands ahead of the ball with a straight left wrist. (Figure 42) Following this procedure prevents you from incorrectly positioning your hands behind the ball or having to adjust other positions, leading to inaccuracy, as a result of positioning the clubhead with the right hand. (Figure 43)

The position of the hands at address—either behind or in front of the ball—determines whether the clubhead is pulled or pushed away from the ball as the backswing starts. When positioned behind the ball, it is pulled; positioned ahead of the ball, it is pushed.

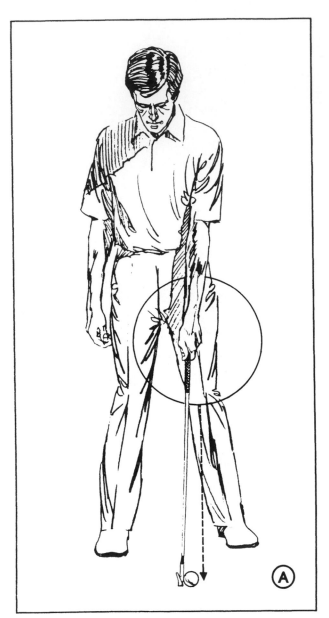
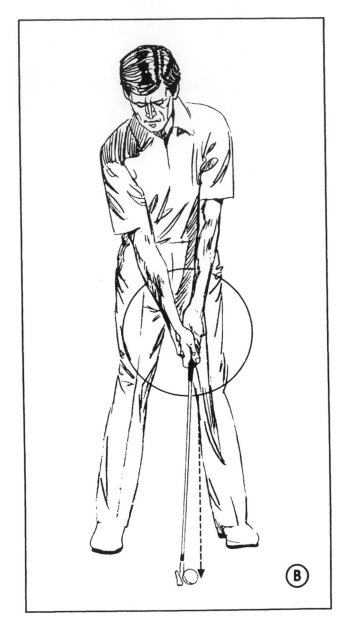

FIGURE 42

Positioning the clubhead with the left hand at address (Fig. 42) prevents you from incorrectly positioning the hands behind the ball, which occurs when you position the clubhead with the *right* hand (Fig. 43).

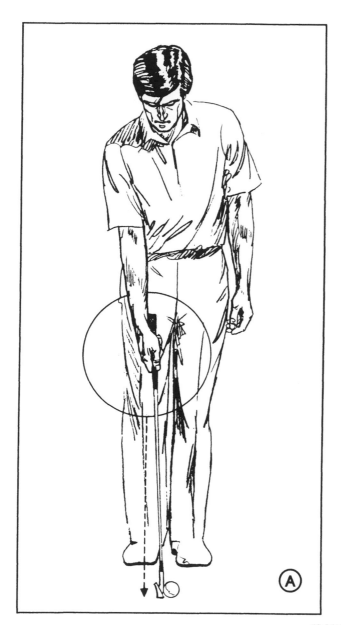

FIGURE 43

Pushing the clubhead away from the ball (without hand action) helps create clubhead speed by extending the left arm and promoting a big swing arc with a full shoulder turn. Pulling, however, wherein the hands start first, prevents a shoulder turn and pivot by pulling the body laterally with a fast backswing. Moving laterally, of course, causes your weight to move across the right foot, making it difficult to get *off* the right foot on the downswing and topping the ball as a result. If the weight transfers back to the left—which is essential but not too likely—a whipping action will occur to loop the clubhead from the top and change the clubface angle to open. Any number of mis-hit shots result from looping the clubhead from the top: slicing, pushing, toeing, even shanking the ball off to the right; or quick hand action may close the clubface at impact either to hook or to pull the ball left.

Muscles have a natural tendency to return to their original positions; consequently, when you position your hands behind the ball, they generally trail behind the clubhead back through the hitting zone. Rather than pulling the clubhead back through the hitting zone, your hands are forced to scoop the clubhead under the ball, causing you either to top or to skull the ball at impact with the leading edge of the clubface.

Both topping and skulling result in hitting grounders, or hitting the top half of the ball on the upswing, with either the bottom of the woods or the leading edge of the irons rather than on the clubface. Although the two are similar in results, there is a slight difference: topping refers more to adding power and hitting for distance with either woods or long irons, whereas skulling refers more to short irons and short shots to the green that need both loft and finesse. At any rate, however, positioning your hands forward, whether for long or short shots, is the best way to ensure that your hands will still be leading for *better* shots back through the hitting zone.

Your hands should be ahead of the ball at address for another reason: golf clubs are constructed with that position in mind. Golfers who are not aware of this not only will find it difficult to address the ball correctly but also will lose distance because the loft of the club is changed. Maximum distance with a five iron, for instance, will be changed to that of a six. (Figure 44)

Angling the shaft of the club forward (A) by positioning your hands ahead of the ball prevents a change in the loft of the clubface—the loft of the five iron, for instance, changed to that of the six (B).

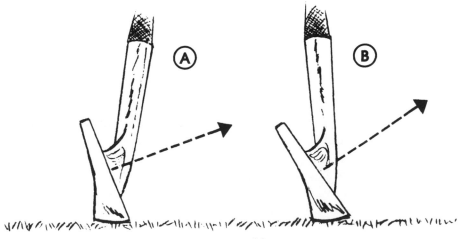

FIGURE 44

Angling the shaft of the club forward by positioning the hands forward makes it easier to establish other correct positions, one of which is the straight left wrist. The backhanded batting power of the left hand at impact can be implemented only with the left wrist straight from address into the follow-through. Again, however, the hands should not be *too* far forward, beyond the straight arm–shaft position, or "hooding" the clubface occurs while addressing the ball, which leads to "smothering" the ball at impact. (See page 117, Figure 79.)

F: Positions your head behind the ball.

Following the same address procedure for positioning the hands ahead of the ball positions the head behind the ball, where it should also be at impact. Maintaining the head position throughout the golf swing helps maintain the swing center, which in turn keeps the entire swing intact.

G: Protects positions already established.

Unless you are extremely familiar with what you're trying to accomplish, you'll have difficulty establishing a square alignment, positioning the ball correctly, keeping your posture upright, and distributing your weight correctly—particularly if your grip is firmly completed and your feet are positioned first. When you first approach the ball, you will tend to lean over at address with your weight on your toes and to establish poor positions that then need correction. (Figure 45) If you have difficulty establishing accurate positions, the left-handed, feet-together method for positioning the clubhead is an excellent procedure to follow when actually playing.

H: Develops a relaxed but strong position.

Comfortably extending the left arm to position the clubhead, while maintaining an upright posture and placing your weight toward your heels, not only measures the swing radius but also helps you develop a relaxed, strong position.

Muscles need to continue to stretch and wind up through the backswing, and they cannot work efficiently if they are strained beyond a comfortable firmness at address. Although your arms must be strong at address, they must also be free of tension to contribute to top performance. The right amount of "relaxed firmness" is initially provided in the straight arm–shaft position.

FIGURE 45

Following a basic procedure for setting up to the ball prevents you from establishing poor positions that position the ball or clubhead incorrectly.

I: Helps square your shoulders at address.

All of the foregoing benefits are derived simply by extending your left arm in a straight line with the shaft when positioning the clubhead. Keeping your hips square and letting your left shoulder move forward will then square your shoulders at address when your right arm is positioned. Keeping the shoulders entirely square as the left arm extends, however, establishes an open shoulder position in the final address position by enabling the right arm to pull the right shoulder ahead of the left as the grip is completed.

Just as open hips block the pivot as the backswing starts, open shoulders block the shoulder turn. Open shoulders *or* hips tend to start a lateral, rather than turning, movement as the clubhead leaves the ball.

Square shoulders at address help return the shoulders square at impact. Open shoulders, however, encourage the right shoulder to move forward from the top of the swing in an effort to return to the same open address position. You may prevent or correct coming over the top and swaying simply by keeping your hips square—with your weight toward your heels—and learning to let your left shoulder move forward in a "shaking hands" gesture as the left arm extends to position the clubhead.

Chapter Nine

Fundamental No. 5: Positioning the Feet

The importance of positioning the feet at address is frequently lost in a broader discussion of the stance as a whole. But discussing the overall stance position, which also includes posture, does not always reveal the benefits derived from positioning the feet, in particular, with deliberate accuracy.

Particularly in the cases of establishing alignment, weight distribution, and ball position (as emphasized in this chapter), *how* positions are established—that is, procedure—is often just as important as the positions themselves. In this case positioning the clubhead first and then separating the feet from the clubhead positions the ball correctly while allowing you to attain the other objectives.

While you should continue to use the five iron for instructional purposes, the fundamental procedure for positioning the feet applies to the use of all golf clubs.

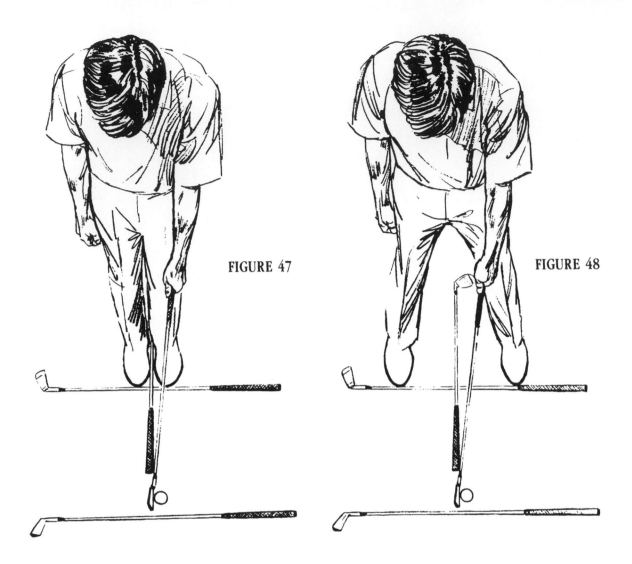

FIGURE 47

FIGURE 48

The Procedure

▶ Using the three alignment clubs, reestablish positions as described in Chapter 8. (Figure 47)

▶ Separate your feet by moving them the same distance from the vertical club. First move the left foot, *then* the right, to the width of the **shoulders**. Position the toes along the horizontal club (directional line), pointing straight ahead. The vertical club will be exactly halfway between your heels. (Figure 48)

▶ Keep your heels in place and angle your toes outward by moving your left toes four inches and your right toes one inch. The right foot will be closed in relation to the left as the left foot angles slightly open and moves a little off-line. (Figure 49)

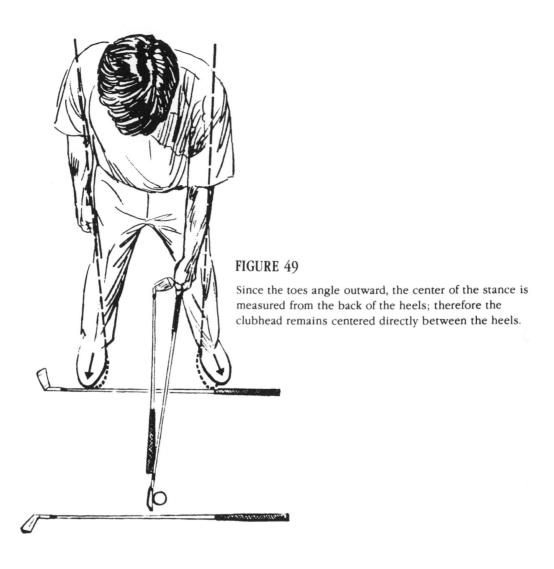

FIGURE 49

Since the toes angle outward, the center of the stance is measured from the back of the heels; therefore the clubhead remains centered directly between the heels.

Importance of the Procedure

Positioning your feet correctly:

A. *squares your feet to the line of flight to establish the directional line*
B. *protects positions already established*
C. *distributes your weight equally between your feet*
D. *determines the angle of the feet*
E. *determines the width of the stance*
F. *positions the ball correctly*
G. *provides guidelines for adjustments in playing short irons*

A: *Squares your feet to the line of flight to establish the directional line.*
Separating your feet with your toes parallel to the line of flight—
before angling your toes outward—squares your feet to the square
clubface, thereby establishing the directional line and completing the
target line. Although the line of flight and the directional line are the
same horizontally, establishing a line of flight with the clubface
before establishing the directional line with your feet is a far more
accurate procedure than positioning the feet first. Positioning the
feet first, before squaring the clubface, generally requires repositioning the feet, making it much more difficult to get a precisely accurate
alignment.

The target lines are used as guidelines both at address and
through the swing. Although the clubhead starts on the line of flight,
it quickly swings up and onto the directional line halfway through
the backswing. Unless the lines are parallel, it is difficult to learn to
swing the club correctly.

FIGURE 50

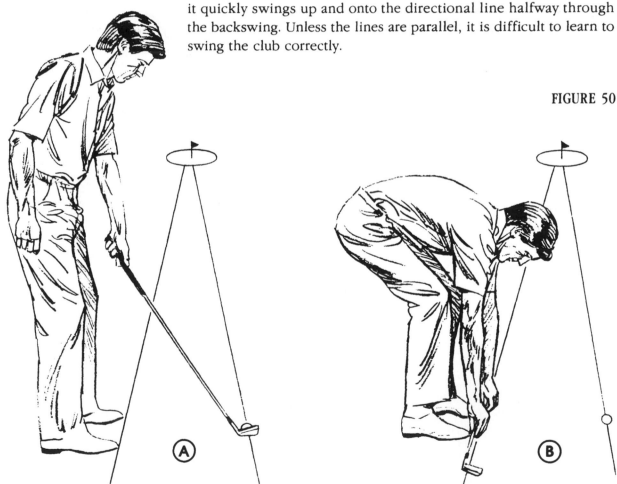

Checking the accuracy of alignment.

Using alignment clubs is an excellent learning technique. When they start sighting visually, however, even experienced golfers tend to drift toward lining up incorrectly with either the clubface or the feet. If you're hitting consistently right or left or your shots are just erratic, you can use a club to check your alignment even while playing golf.

Using the principle of receding parallel lines, wherein two parallel lines such as railroad tracks appear to meet in the distance, square the clubface to a faraway target (for the receding parallel-line effect), then square your feet to the clubface. (Figure 50A) Before setting the angle of your feet, lay the club down along the line of the toes. (B) Sight from behind the club, and if the shaft aims toward the target, both your feet and the clubface are aligned accurately. (C) If not, repeat the procedure and make corrections, then practice the new setup.

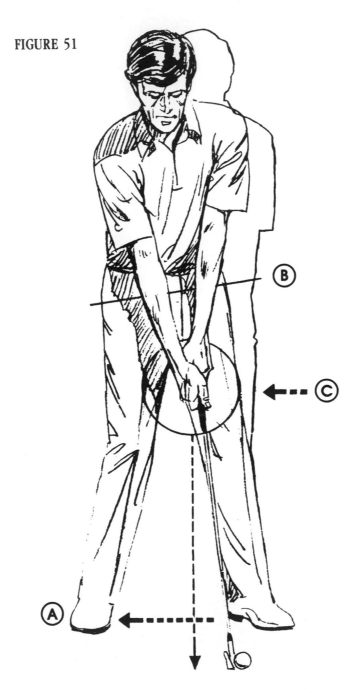

FIGURE 51

Positioning the right foot first (A) establishes a comfortable position from which the left foot may not move at all, establishing poor positions by pushing the hips open as the grip is completed (B) and positioning the hands behind the ball (C).

B: Protects positions already established.

A quick change in equal weight distribution and the position of the left hand and hips may occur if the right foot is positioned first. As your right foot moves to the right (A), your weight moves too. (Figure 51) With your weight then established on the strong right side, rather than the body shifting from what *feels* fairly comfortable, the left foot may not move at all. The feet just stay where they are, with the weight on the right. Since the clubhead is too far forward, however, rather than between the feet, one of two things occurs: either the right hand extends too far, which pushes the hips open (B), or the left hand moves closer to the right, behind the ball, so the right hand can grip the club more comfortably (C). Both hands are then positioned *incorrectly* and will pull the clubhead away from the ball rather than push it into the backswing.

First establishing then adjusting positions to produce accuracy makes it difficult to set up correctly. Along with other basics, however, positioning the left foot first is ample protection for distributing the weight evenly, keeping the hips and clubface square, setting the hands ahead of the ball, and positioning the ball and clubhead accurately.

C: Distributes your weight equally between your feet.

Good footwork is needed in golf to shift the weight to the right and then back to the left, and weight transference is easier when the weight is distributed equally at address. The keen feeling in the feet makes it easy to set up incorrectly, however, unless you position your left foot before positioning the right. Your weight can be almost entirely on one foot, but the feel of the other makes the weight seem equal.

The foot that is positioned first transfers weight in that direction, firmly establishing your weight on that foot. Being predominantly stronger than the left, the right side generally retains the greater percentage of weight if you position the right foot first—even when the left foot moves forward, whereupon it is difficult to get off the right foot on the downswing. When you position your left foot first, however, although your weight shifts to the left, the dominant right side pulls its share of weight back, automatically distributing your weight equally between your feet.

In any athletic endeavor that requires throwing or hitting, the weight shifts back and then forward with arm movement; so it is in the golf swing as the body turns away from the direction in which the ball is going. But weight transference is confusing to those who know that swaying, which moves the body laterally, is a disruptive force in the swing. To prevent swaying, golfers sometimes set the weight either left or right and try to keep it there. Swaying can be thwarted not by preventing the weight from shifting but by turning your hips and shoulders *as* your weight shifts back and forth.

Establishing the weight firmly on your left foot at address generally keeps it there while you swing, thereby weakening the swing by preventing a weight shift and changing the arc of the swing as your body lowers and rises. Worse yet, a reverse weight shift occurs as your weight kicks off the left foot onto the right as the downswing starts. Placing too much weight on your *right* foot at address has similar adverse results: it keeps your weight on the right as the downswing starts.

Problems such as a reverse weight shift cause other problems in golf: falling away from the ball, throwing the clubhead from the top, coming over the top, hitting behind the ball, topping, whiffing—any or all of which may be corrected just by distributing the weight more equally when stepping up to the ball and then practicing the correct weight shift.

D: Determines the angle of the feet.

Part of the difficulty encountered by golfers in establishing an accurate alignment stems from the fact that the word *square* is somewhat ambiguous with regard to the feet. Commonly referred to as *the stance* in golf, the feet themselves are square to the line of flight, but the *angles* of the feet are not. Although perfection is for experts, understanding the difference will help you establish positions more precisely.

The stance can be square, open, or closed as discussed in Chapter 6; but there are angles of the feet as well. (Figure 52) The angles of the feet are *closed*—or *square*—when the feet point straight ahead (A), and they are *open* when the toes angle outward (B). Although alignment is generally determined by the line of the toes, *precise* alignment of the feet to the target is determined neither by the angle of the feet nor by the line of the toes but rather by the alignment of the heels to the directional line.

An open stance, from a square stance position, angles the left foot open but also moves the left foot off the target line by positioning the heel off-line (C), whereas just angling the left foot open moves the toes off-line but keeps the heel in place to keep the stance

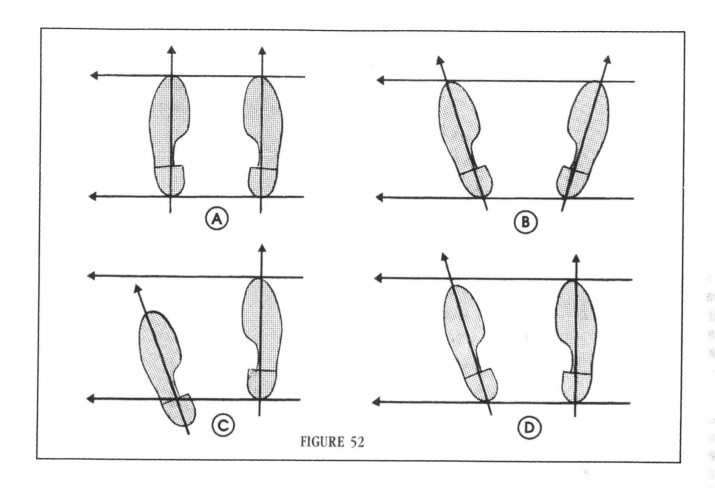

FIGURE 52

square (D). Because the left foot angles open in *relation* to the right, checking a square alignment before the angle is set is one of the keys to accuracy. (Figure 53)

The angle of the feet critically influences the swing by first restricting the backswing and then releasing the follow-through. The right foot is almost square to restrict the backswing as the weight shifts right, and the left foot is slightly open to release the follow-through as the weight shifts left. A thought to remember, however, when applying fundamentals is that nothing should be done to an extreme. There is always an exact "just right" position or movement that promotes coordination. Although the feet angle open or closed in relation to each other, neither foot should be entirely open nor entirely closed. Overestablishing positions and overcorrecting the swing are common mistakes in golf. Little adjustments make big differences, and *slightly* is a word used to encourage subtlety in both the physical and mental approach to the game.

Checking a square alignment before angling the left foot open is a key to establishing square positions and checking for accuracy.

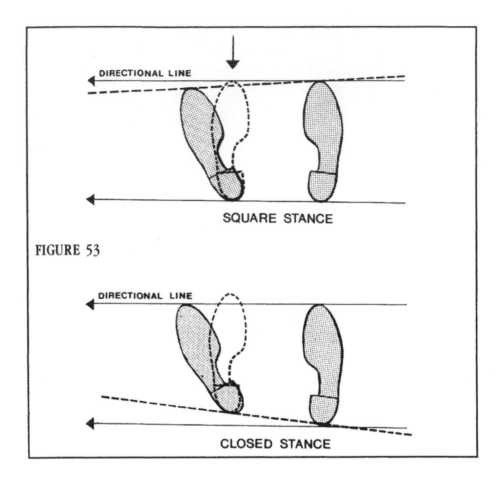

FIGURE 53

The Right Foot

A slightly closed—or almost square—right foot at address provides a variety of assets throughout the swing by restricting the backswing:

1. A slightly closed right foot promotes a full shoulder turn and pivot by preventing a lateral sway. Power in golf is generated by completing the shoulder turn so as to wind up the big back muscles between the shoulders and the hips. These torqued muscles then transfer power into clubhead speed as the lower body shifts the weight to the left to pull the arms, hands, and clubhead down from the top. An open right foot at address prevents this coordination and buildup of power by encouraging a lateral movement as the shoulders turn. Squaring the right foot, however, helps prevent the body from sliding sideways—or swaying—by helping the hips turn.

The shoulder turn is automatic as a result of pushing the clubhead into and through the backswing; and the shoulders turn the hips, building power throughout the swing with the right foot square by preventing the lateral sway.

2. A slightly closed right foot helps maintain the swing center by keeping the head steady. Keeping the head steady, in the same relative position, is an important pivotal position that keeps the arc of the swing intact and enables the coiling mechanism of the body and the hitting action of the hands to coordinate at impact. A bobbing or moving head, however, is not the cause of problems but merely an indication that the entire body is moving back and forth or up and down and pulling the head off-line.

When the head moves laterally, your weight moves laterally across the right foot. Should your weight *stay* on the right on the downswing, your hands will release too soon, pulling your shoulders, arms, and hands up through the hitting zone, which causes you to look up by pulling your head up too. Swaying back through the ball—should the weight shift left—pulls your head forward beyond the impact area, and your hands release too late to deliver the hitting power.

Fundamentals position your head behind the ball at address with your chin up; and squaring your right foot helps turn your body rotationally by turning against the foot. Your head then remains steady as the pivotal point in the swing and prevents power from being released somewhere other than through the hitting zone.

3. A slightly closed right foot allows a transfer of weight to the right on the backswing and provides a solid position to push against to shift your weight back to the left on the downswing. Bracing your right foot against the movement of the backswing catches and holds the backswing movement as your weight shifts right, storing power and releasing it with good timing as your legs spring away from the braced right foot on the downswing and shift your weight left.

4. A slightly closed right foot promotes good timing by preventing overswinging. Good timing at the top of the swing moves your lower body first—back toward the target—as the initial downswing movement. Bracing your right foot promotes good timing by promoting good footwork and lower body action, whereas an unrestricted backswing, with the right foot angled open, prevents good timing by causing swaying and overswinging.

Overswinging with your hands, arms, and clubhead as a result of having your right foot open makes it difficult for lower body action to sense the feeling needed to start the forward swing. Blocking the backswing, however, with your right foot square, results in good timing by preventing your upper body from swinging too far.

5. A slightly closed right foot promotes good rhythm with strong but supple legs. A rhythmic swing is promoted by a rhythmic swinging movement of strong, supple legs. Although strong, the legs must also be free of tension at address and through the swing.

With the exception of the tension factor, the angle of your right foot could be entirely closed. With your left foot angled open, however, and your hips square at address, tension develops in the inside thigh muscle of your right leg with the foot entirely closed. As slight as the feeling is, one of two things occurs: either the hips relieve the tension by slipping open, or the right leg feels twisted rather than comfortable. Angling the right foot just a little open, however, relieves the strain, helps keep your hips square, and makes your legs feel strong but relaxed while still providing a braced right foot for the backswing action.

The Left Foot

The angle of the left foot at address determines your ability to complete the swing and transfer your weight completely from the right to left side. Although your left foot is angled open in relation to the right, the position must not be overestablished into an exaggerated open position.

FIGURE 54

On a full follow-through the weight shifts to the left and rolls across the left foot.

Following through: Completing the swing is not always what golfers *do* but what they are *able* to do by establishing correct positions.

Muscles wind up through the backswing and unwind through the hitting zone, transmitting body torque into clubhead speed—or how fast the clubhead is moving at impact—as the weight shifts left and the hips turn through the ball. Following impact, however, the swing dissolves into a free, fluid movement, a movement that must not be restricted by a closed left foot to release the hands and clubhead and keep the clubhead accelerating on through the ball into a full follow-through.

Closing your left foot blocks the left side, which prevents your hips from turning. In turn, this prevents the swing from releasing by preventing your right arm from extending through the hitting zone. Blocking out then either causes the body to move laterally through impact or else spins the left foot toward the target by spinning around on the left heel to free the left side. Unless your left foot is angled open, or else spins open, the swing cannot be completed and the clubhead will not be accelerating through impact.

Although your left foot angles outward at address, angling the foot too far open—or spinning the foot open—encourages spinning out, wherein the hips spin back through the hitting zone too far, too soon, pulling the shoulders around with them. Rather than hitting straight through the ball, the clubhead pulls inward from the target line and, according to the angle of the clubface, either pulls or slices the ball.

Weight shift: Your weight must transfer back to the left from the right to prevent hitting from the top with upper body action or falling away from the hitting zone and to continue accelerating the clubhead through the ball. When the backswing reaches the stop position of the braced right foot, your lower body starts the forward movement of the swing by springing away from the inside of the foot. A natural transference of weight can occur only if the follow-through is unrestricted with the left foot open and receptive to a continuation of the swing.

In an unrestricted swing the weight moves *to* the inside of the braced right foot, where it is caught and held, allowing the body to coil and promote good timing in the transition of the backswing to the downswing. When the weight transfers back to the left, however, into the follow-through, it rolls *across* the left foot. (Figure 54) Rolling across the foot promotes staying down to and swinging through the ball, gaining distance by extending the arms out toward the target while turning into the follow-through.

> A natural transference of weight can occur only if the follow-through is unrestricted with the left foot open and receptive to a continuation of the swing.

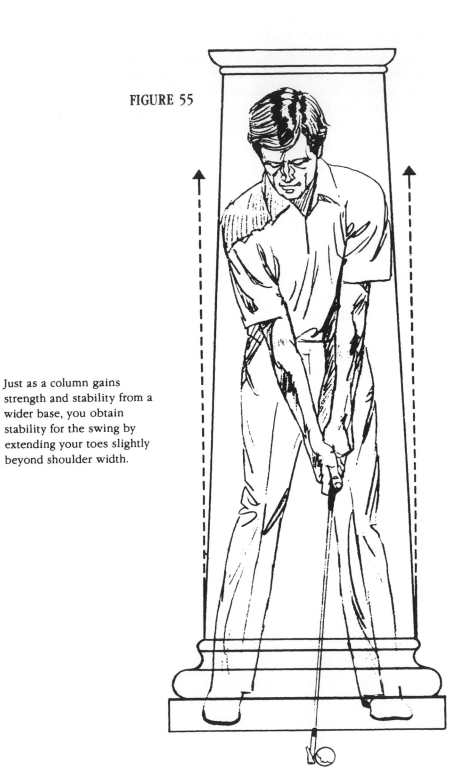

FIGURE 55

Just as a column gains
strength and stability from a
wider base, you obtain
stability for the swing by
extending your toes slightly
beyond shoulder width.

Raising up or pulling up on the ball causes topping and occurs when the hands hit up on the ball instead of through it, frequently as a result of hitting into a square left foot, which blocks swinging through the ball and keeps the weight on the right.

Positioning your feet approximately as described—with the left foot angled open in relation to the right—promotes good weight transference and coordination through the entire golf swing.

E: Determines the width of the stance.

Because the toes angle outward, the actual width of the stance in relation to the shoulders should be measured from the heels. Positioning your feet shoulder width apart then angles your toes slightly outward beyond the shoulder line—the left foot more so than the right—which provides strong stability for the swing and prevents momentum from forcing the swing off balance. Somewhat like an architectural column, strength and stability come from the foundation's being slightly wider than the top. (Figure 55)

Because the length of the shaft determines the size of the circle of the swing—the swing arc—the width of the stance should be determined by the club being used; the wider and longer the swing arc (without overswinging, of course) the more momentum, and momentum affects balance.

Woods and long irons with a big swing arc create more momentum and need a wider stance. Short irons generate less momentum because the swing arc is smaller. Since momentum is less and balance can be maintained, you can narrow your stance for more control and accuracy with short irons.

When you're using woods and long irons, too narrow a stance (inside the shoulder line) reduces the body's stability, resulting in loss of balance and generally overswinging. In an effort to maintain balance, golfers tend to hunch their shoulders to make the width of the shoulders *feel* equal to the width of the feet, which then restricts and limits the swing. Conversely, too wide a stance, while allowing you to maintain good balance and assuring a firm foundation, makes it physically difficult to make a full pivot and shoulder turn, thus shortening the backswing and generally reducing clubhead speed. Widening the stance can be helpful, however, when you need to increase stability, such as when hitting uphill or downhill, going for extra yardage off the tee, or correcting overswinging.

F: Positions the ball correctly.

The position of the ball between the feet moves left or right and forward and back with the use of different clubs.

The rules of golf, which are governed by the United States Golf Association and the Royal and Ancient Golf Club of St. Andrews, Scotland, allow each player a maximum of 14 clubs, including the putter. Although most golfers play with standard sets of woods and irons, many select clubs from various makes and models that fit their own golf game. Carrying three or four wedges or five or six woods, for instance, is not uncommon anymore.

Regardless of sets or selections, a key middle club (which would normally be the five iron) should be used in practice and for instructional purposes because the length of the club is "average" between long- and short-shafted clubs. Although the ball is positioned differently with the use of different clubs, establishing an address position with the five iron also establishes a basic position, while developing a standard procedure, for positioning the ball correctly with all golf clubs.

Although no one can say exactly where "the spot" should be to comfortably fit each individual swing, following a fundamentally exact routine at address helps each golfer consistently position the ball correctly with the use of every club. Six steps are involved:

1. Assume the left-hand grip.
2. Stand upright with your feet together.
3. Extend your left arm in a straight arm–shaft position.
4. Square the clubface to the target with the clubhead directly behind the ball.
5. Square your feet to the clubface.
6. Then *separate your feet from the clubhead rather than from the ball.*

To consistently position the ball correctly, follow the six steps listed on this page.

Following this procedure helps you keep your weight distributed equally between your feet while positioning the ball correctly.

Accurately positioned, the ball is between and away from the feet at a point where each golf club will contact the ball squarely in the center of the clubface, right at the bottom of the swing. On page 44 the five iron was placed on the ground behind the ball where the clubs intersect. Separating your feet from the vertical club to shoulder width, leaving the clubhead centered between your heels, positions the ball slightly forward of center, where the five iron will make square contact with a slightly descending blow at the bottom of the arc.

Generally speaking, from the five iron through the wedge you play the ball slightly forward from the center of the stance by centering the clubhead between your heels. As the shafts get longer, the ball is played progressively farther forward until the ball is off the left instep for the driver.

When the ball is positioned correctly, it lies within a rectangular area more or less determined by the height and build of the golfer and the length of the driver and wedge. (Figure 56) The rectangle is defined by the position of the ball off the left instep for the driver (A) and in the center of the stance for the shorter wedge (B).

Ball position is so important in golf that it can either promote or prevent other correct swing movements. Hitting a little behind or on top of the ball or a little off-center on the clubface or releasing early

FIGURE 56

The ball is positioned within a rectangular area: the driver and ball off the left instep (A) and the irons progressively back toward the center of the stance (B).

or late can often be corrected or prevented just by positioning the clubhead—which positions the ball—more carefully in relation to the feet.

The difference between a mis-hit shot and a solid connection is not measured by inches but often by only quarters of an inch. A good point to remember is that many mis-hit shots are very close to perfection, and fine-tuning the game may require only adjusting the ball position.

Positioning the ball correctly prevents a subconscious tendency either to fall away from a ball positioned too far back or to sway toward a ball positioned too far forward.

Separating your feet from the ball by not positioning the clubhead first (A) positions the clubhead too far back in the stance (B). (Figure 57) On the downswing the clubhead either hits the top of the ball by contacting the ball before reaching the bottom of the swing arc, smothers the ball with the clubface hooded, or pushes or slices to the right by hitting the ball before the clubface is square. More often, however, in a subconscious effort to adjust the swing to the ball position, rather than shifting your weight left, you fall away from the ball, either skulling or topping the ball or hitting the ground behind it.

It is important to position the clubhead directly behind the ball at address to position the ball correctly. A casual placement of the clubhead several inches behind the ball (A) positions the ball too far forward (B). (Figure 58) The clubhead either hits a "fat" golf shot by hitting the ground before hitting the ball or tops the ball by catching it on the upswing. In an effort to make square contact, the body may sway forward, pulling, pushing, or slicing the ball, depending on whether the shoulders open through impact or the hips block the follow-through.

Positioning the Driver

Although the shaft is longer and the ball is played farther forward in the stance, the procedure for positioning the driver is the same as for positioning the five iron.

The long shaft and straight face of the driver make it difficult to make square contact with the ball unless the ball is positioned forward toward the left heel; therefore the left foot barely steps forward to make an accurate alignment. Placing the left heel in line with the clubface positions the ball off the left instep. Moving the right foot to shoulder width then moves the entire body right—without changing other established positions—and automatically establishes an accurate driving stance. (Figure 59)

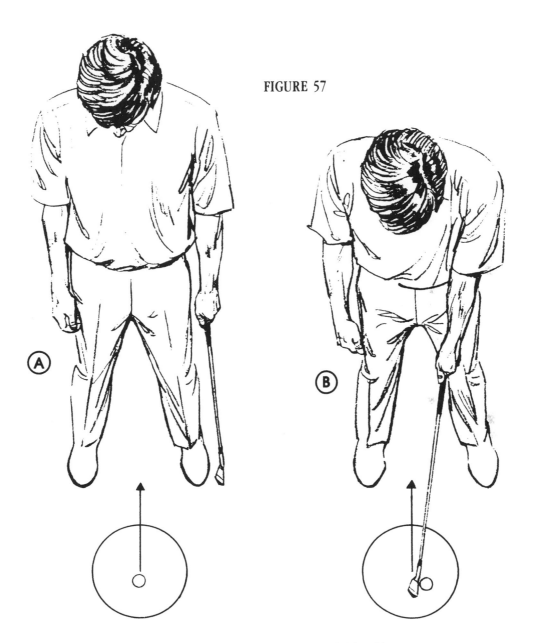

FIGURE 57

Separating your feet from the ball rather than from the clubhead by not positioning the clubhead first (A) positions the clubhead too far back in the stance (B).

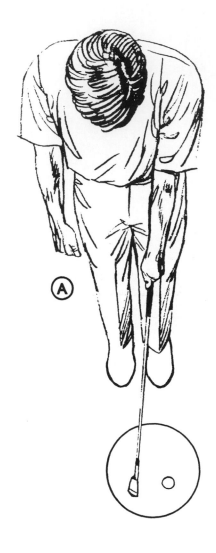

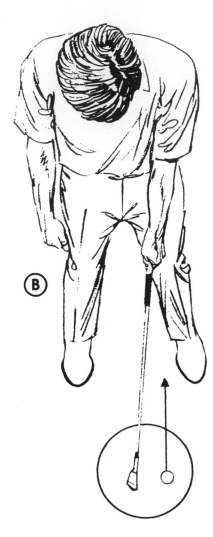

A casual placement of the
clubhead several inches
behind the ball (A) positions
the ball too far forward (B).

FIGURE 58

Positioning Long Fairway Woods and Irons

Although long fairway woods and irons are not positioned quite as far
forward as the driver, they are still positioned forward of center. Using
the same procedure for positioning the driver, just step progressively
farther forward with your left foot before positioning your right.

Positioning Medium Irons

The medium irons are the four, five, and six. The four iron is played
forward of center, whereas the six iron is positioned in the center as the
five is. Medium irons are also used around the green, where the stance
begins to narrow.

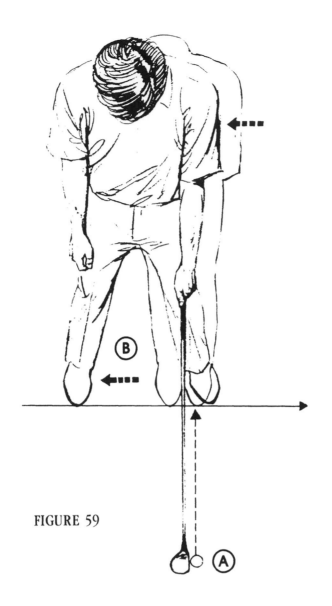

Positioning the Driver

Stepping forward only slightly and aligning the left heel to the clubface positions the ball off the left instep (A). Moving the right foot to shoulder width then moves the body to the right to establish the driving stance (B).

FIGURE 59

Positioning Lofted Woods

Lofted woods replace both long and medium irons. Because of the lofted clubface, they may be easier to use, particularly where loft and carry are as important as distance. They are generally positioned the same as the irons they replace.

G: Provides guidelines for adjustments in playing short irons.

Short irons are unique. Not only do they obtain their own maximum distance, but they are also used for an unlimited variety of short shots to and around the green. The versatility of short irons makes positioning them difficult to understand at times because below the five iron is a game within a game, where the stance is adjusted according to the shot being made. Precision and accuracy become more important than distance with the use of the same golf club.

All of the woods and irons, from the driver through medium irons, are played with a totally square stance for full golf shots and the feet at shoulder width. Although the mechanics are the same for *full* golf shots with short irons, the shorter the iron and the shorter the shot, the more the stance narrows and opens, and the weight is set left, whereupon choking down on the club and moving the hands in closer gives better arm and hand control.

Narrowing the Stance and Choking Down on the Club

When you're swinging short irons, the swing becomes more upright and the arc of the swing narrows because the shaft is shorter, whereupon you can maintain better control and balance by progressively gripping the club down lower—or choking down on the club—and narrowing the stance. The shorter the shot, the narrower the stance; consequently, the feet are initially well within the shoulder line, narrowing even more so with the use of shorter clubs when you're making short shots.

Opening the Stance and Positioning the Hands Closer

Along with narrowing the stance for short shots, opening the stance restricts a full pivot, which in effect turns a full golf swing into a smaller golf swing by shortening the length of the backswing. With the club-head in closer, choking down on the club makes the swing more upright and the swing arc smaller, whereupon better control of the clubhead is maintained with the hands in closer and a shorter back-swing.

The procedure for opening the stance and positioning your hands in closer is best understood by first choking down on the club and then following the same procedure for setting up square by positioning the club with your left hand only and establishing two parallel target lines. Rather than placing your left foot *on* the directional line, however, step short of the line according to the shot being played (A), then complete the stance with your right foot by stepping *beyond* the directional line the same distance (B). (Figure 60) Stepping closer to the ball positions the hands closer for better control of the clubhead. The shorter the shot and the narrower the stance, the more open the stance should be.

With your feet angled open to the directional line, your knees, hips, and shoulders will want to swing open too. Although your feet and hips

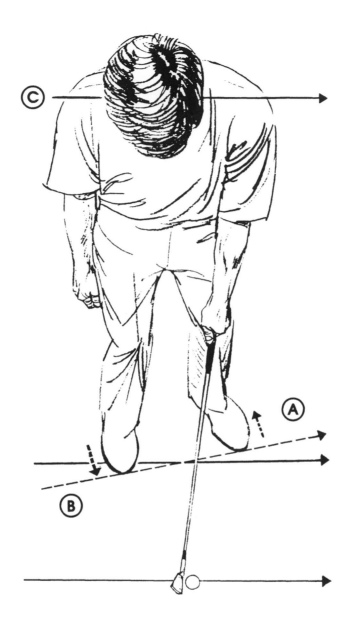

To open your stance for short shots, step short of the original directional line with your left foot (A) and then step the same distance past the line with your right foot (B) while keeping your shoulders square (C).

FIGURE 60

may be open to the target line, the original directional line is still a guideline for swinging and is now maintained by your keeping your shoulders square. Since the arms hang straight from the shoulder line, swinging the club on target, down the target line, is somewhat easier with the shoulders square. Open shoulders at address help slice or cut the ball by swinging from outside in across the target lines—a shot that should be used only by experts.

Below the five iron the stance is adjusted according to the shot being made. Golfers vary widely in how they use open positions, so determine how you'll use them not by doing what other golfers do but by experimenting on your own. First understand the purpose of opening the stance; then practice and compare both square and open positions.

The key to using an open stance is in learning how much to open the stance to regulate the length of the backswing for the shot being made, because the length of the backswing is determined by the length of the shot. The shorter the shot, the more open the stance should be to help control and shorten the backswing. Whatever the shot, however, the backswing and follow-through are the same, from the driver through the wedge, from full golf shots with all golf clubs to short shots to the green.

You will develop confidence in *hitting* short shots only by shortening the backswing so as to be able to follow through at least the same distance forward as in the backswing. "Quitting on the shot"—or stopping at the ball—is always a result of swinging back too far, which prevents being *able* to hit on through the ball and into the follow-through.

A completely open, very narrow stance is used for short chip or pitch shots, and the stance widens and moves more toward square for hitting longer shots. Whatever the distance, however, the feet are separated initially for that particular shot as determined by practicing different setups and by practicing the follow-through with a shortened backswing. Sense and feel, which are so important to this phase of the game, can be developed only through experimentation and practice.

The line of flight and directional line together form the target line. They are established parallel when you set up to the ball and are used as guidelines throughout the golf swing. When *all* positions are open—the feet, hips, and shoulders—golfers tend to start the clubhead on that line, which starts the clubhead at an angle to and outside the line of flight. Either the swing pattern changes and loops the clubhead back to the line of flight, or the clubhead returns to cut across the ball by cutting across the target lines. While used effectively and intentionally by experts who swing from outside in with an open stance and clubface to hit high cut shots, opening the shoulders along with the feet and hips can be risky and expensive for less experienced golfers. Unless practiced to perfection, cutting the ball may lead to shanking rather than to making career golf shots.

The same kind of expertise enjoyed by those who use open positions to finesse the ball does not have to be duplicated by all who play golf. Perfection is for experts. Once golfers *become* expert, however, they should give some consideration to experimenting with stance

The shorter the shot, the more open the stance should be to help control and shorten the backswing.

positions and short irons for short shots to the green, essentially because proficiency continues to develop through knowledge, experimentation, and practice.

Very small adjustments in the stance make big differences in the swing and are reflected in results. Proceeding slowly, an inch at a time, combined with experimental practice, will enable golfers to determine quickly for themselves how much control is needed in their own short game. Opening the clubface slightly, for instance, will hit the ball higher.

When practicing the golf swing or any part thereof, forcing additional distance by trying to hit too hard speeds up the swing, changes timing and rhythm, and pulls the ball left. Rather than leaning on a wedge and pressing for extra distance, obtain more control and accuracy by opening your stance a little to shorten the backswing, choking down on the club, and using the same grooved swing to hit a smooth nine iron instead.

Weight Distribution

When you're hitting full golf shots with longer-shafted clubs, your weight is distributed equally between your feet for balance. As your stance begins to narrow, however, with the use of short irons, establishing and keeping your weight progressively more toward the left promotes better hand action and clubhead control due to minimum body movement and less weight shift. Setting your weight forward helps keep your hands forward. The hands then return ahead of the ball, guiding the clubhead toward the target with stronger hand and arm action.

Summary

Just as in playing other shots, it is important to step *directly* into the correct position when playing short shots. This prevents you from having to realign your feet and make other major adjustments, which results in inaccuracy. With practice, golfers learn to quickly assess the shot, step up to the ball, accurately position their feet, make minor adjustments, and confidently play the shot. Concentrating on making the backswing and follow-through the same puts the same golf swing on the shorter shots as on the longer shots, from a full golf swing with square positions to a miniature half or "soft" three-quarter swing with short irons using an open, narrower stance.

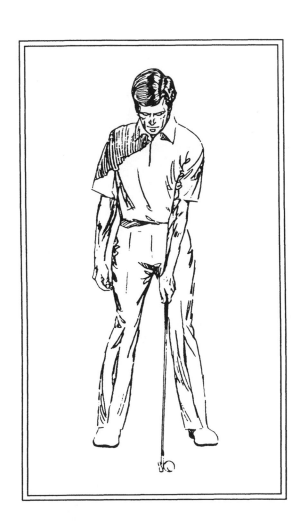

Chapter Ten

Fundamental No. 6:
Flexing the Knees Toward Each Other

Up to this point we've established a single position which is influenced in different ways as the knees flex toward each other. Because the purpose of setting that position is to change it in the sequential process of building, it is important to rebuild the position exactly as described.

Sitting down to the ball is an important step in securing the lower body at address. Meanwhile, established positions that affect alignment, posture, and balance remain unchanged.

The Procedure

Standing upright with your hips rolled under, release the hips by flexing your buttocks backward. At the same time, flex your knees inward while keeping them parallel to each other and to the line of flight. Weight will move to the inside of your feet. As your body lowers slightly, let your left hand drop comfortably down and inward from the straight arm-shaft position. All of the movements should be very slight, and *accuracy results from flexing the knees inward rather than from bending the knees forward.*

Importance of the Procedure

Flexing the knees toward each other:
A. *maintains alignment, upright posture, and good balance*
B. *positions your left hand at address*
C. *completes correct weight distribution between and on the feet*
D. *relaxes but strengthens your legs*
E. *establishes the flat lie of the clubhead*

A: Maintains alignment, upright posture, and good balance.

"Sitting down to the ball" is a golf expression for lowering the body from the knees while keeping the posture upright, maintaining balance, and protecting the square alignment—and the reasons for doing so should be self-evident from the moment the position is established. Your feet and legs instantly cock into a strong, balanced position as your entire body gets set to move powerfully and actively through the swing.

Although an important fundamental procedure that prevents addressing the ball with your hips rolled under—which is a very weak position—sitting down to the ball is also a very slight, almost imperceptible movement. But then critical movements throughout the golf swing are often very slight. The feeling is that of sitting down on the shaft of a club: first leaning over and placing the shaft under the buttocks (A), then sitting *down* on the club while straightening back *up* again (B). (Figure 62)

As your knees flex inward they also bend slightly forward; and flexing the hips back to stick the seat out a bit straightens your lower back while keeping your head and shoulders positioned for the best shoulder turn. The movement helps you maintain good posture and balance simply by counterbalancing the forward knee movement. Flexing the knees inward and keeping them parallel—to each other and to the line of flight—maintains a square alignment by keeping the hips square.

Flexing the knees just slightly prevents you from lowering your body too far, which causes swaying up and down *and* back and forth while swinging. Lowering the body too far—beyond only unlocking the knees—generally causes you to hit the ground behind the ball and/or sky the ball as your body sways and pulls up through the backswing and then lowers rather dramatically and sways back

FIGURE 62

Maintaining Posture, Balance, and Alignment

Sitting down to the ball is similar in feeling to sitting on the shaft of a club: first leaning over to position the club (A), then flexing the hips back and straightening up again *while* sitting down on the club (B).

through the ball. Topping also occurs, however, when your body pulls up through the backswing and *stays* up through the ball.

B: *Positions your left hand at address.*

Standing upright and flexing your knees inward forces your left arm to compensate by moving the left hand down and inward. Again, the movement is slight—the hand moves only an inch or two—but the repositioned left hand, moving closer to center, makes it easier for you to keep your hips square and your right shoulder back while completing the grip. Although the angle of the wrist changes slightly, the clubface remains square, and your left hand is still correctly positioned slightly ahead of the ball.

Dropping your left hand slightly downward and inward bends the left wrist, as seen from both the top and side. (Figure 63) The downward bend promotes good hand action, and the inward bend enables the hands to press forward to get a "running start" on the backswing.

C: Completes correct weight distribution between and on the feet.

Sitting down to the ball and keeping your knees parallel keeps your weight distributed between and on the feet rather than letting it shift left or right. Accurate weight distribution is then completed at address when you flex your knees inward to move your weight to the inside of your feet.

Equal distribution of weight between the feet, along with a balanced position, helps you transfer your weight while swinging. But shifting the weight to the inside of the feet turns on the power system by tensing and strengthening the inside thigh muscles, reinforcing the foundation of the swing and putting feeling in the feet. Along with the almost square angle of the right foot at address, establishing and keeping the weight inside the foot further prevents the weight from rolling across the right foot on the backswing as the weight shifts right.

Rhythm, timing, and good footwork are promoted by flexing the knees inward to set the weight inside the right foot. Swaying is prevented as a result, as the shoulders and hips turn against the strong right foot and discourage a lateral movement. From the top of the swing the weight then shifts back to the left, rather than staying on the right or shifting farther right because the weight swayed over to the outside of the foot.

The overall feeling of good weight distribution is that of a boxer's stance, coupled with a feeling of being able to spring straight upward from the address position.

Although weight distribution is equal in the basic address position, golfers do have a preference in setting it left or right. Setting the weight too far left or too far right, however, causes problems throughout the swing: the knees jut forward and dip downward, shifting the weight incorrectly, lowering and raising the body and lessening the odds, by far, of returning the clubhead accurately. Following basics helps you prevent such problems.

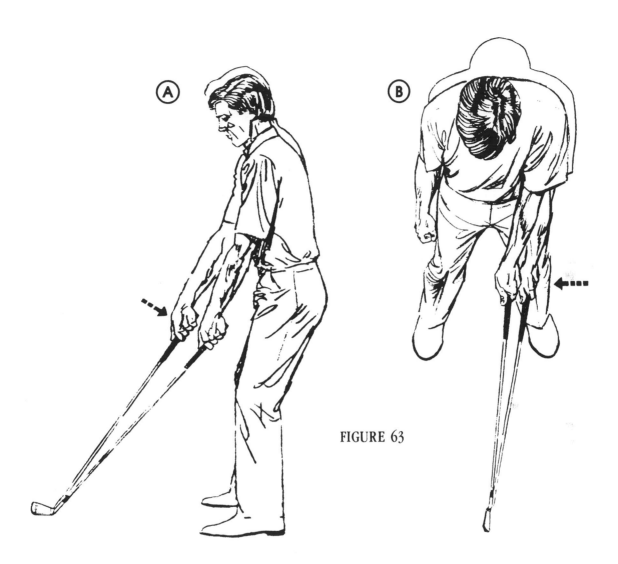

FIGURE 63

Sitting Down To the Ball

Lowering the body from the knees changes the straight arm–shaft position,
accurately repositioning the left hand by moving it down (A) and inward (B) while
keeping the hips and shoulders square.

D: Relaxes but strengthens your legs.

As your knees flex inward, the inside thigh muscles tense, strengthening your legs. Even as the muscles tense, however, they must also be relaxed and supple to promote a powerful, fluid swing. This is not a contradiction; when the knees flex inward, strength and relaxation are obtained simultaneously, because the knees cannot flex inward to strengthen the muscles without relaxing the legs by unlocking the knees.

As long as the knees are not tensed beyond a comfortable firmness, strength and power result from flexing the leg muscles. But good footwork and supple legs result from unlocking the knee joints rather than from addressing the ball stiff-legged. Lively legs can shift the weight first right and then left to coordinate with a turning, swinging movement. The difference can easily be felt simply by swinging your arms around with your knees stiff and then with your knees unlocked.

Strength and power result from flexing the leg muscles.

E: Establishes the flat lie of the clubhead.

Hitting correctly, squarely in the center of the clubface, also depends on soling the clubhead flat on the ground. Following the procedure used for sitting down to the ball drops the left hand slightly downward to sole the clubhead correctly, from the driver through the wedge.

A toe-up or heel-up position—which hits *on* the heel or toe to misdirect the shot—stems from incorrect positions that bow the wrists too high or position the hands too low. Leaning over or bending too far positions the hands too low, with the heel of the club on the ground; standing too upright or playing the ball too close keeps the wrists too high and positions the toe on the ground. (See page 54, Figure 45.)

Another factor determines whether you'll be *able* to sole the clubhead correctly: the lie of the club itself. Golf clubs must fit the player, and as long as your clubs are compatible with your own golf swing, you should have no problem playing with standard matched sets. If you're unusually tall or short, however, or have unusually long or short arms, you should be particularly careful not to establish poor positions by adapting your golf swing to clubs unsuited for your use.

Your stance preferences, height, and swing ability should determine the length of the shaft, which may vary by several inches. If you cannot comfortably position the clubhead correctly by the method described, however, the shaft may be too long or too short for you. Or it may indicate that the lie of the club itself is incorrect. At any rate, golf professionals are fully qualified to fit equipment to any golfer.

The length and lie of clubs, as well as shaft flexibility, grip size, swing weight, and overall weight of clubs, can all be determined for each individual player. And for those who are serious-minded, proper equipment is an important asset in golf.

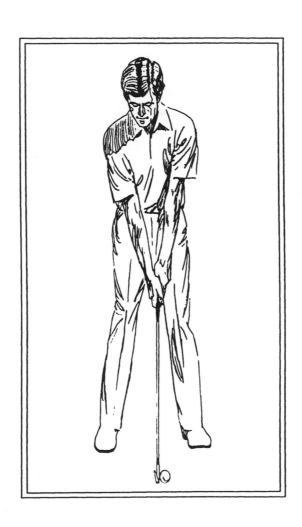

Chapter Eleven

Fundamental No. 7: Completing the Grip

So much emphasis has been placed on positioning the club with just the left hand that you probably wonder by now why virtually every golfer you've ever seen addresses the ball with the grip already completed. Aside from the fact that leaving the right hand off the club is a learning technique, there are two varieties of golfers: those who instinctively use fundamentals and those who don't—the proficient and the inexperienced.

Proficient golfers address the ball using familiarity and feel, personalizing the procedure but systematically doing so with accuracy and understanding. Although the hands are on the club together, the right hand is generally placed *loosely* until *after* positions are secured—in effect still off the club as the clubhead moves back and forth and up and down in the setup procedure. On the other hand, inexperienced golfers are apt to approach the ball with the grip firmly established; inadvertently initiating a series of positions that, although comfortable, are also incorrect.

Certainly all golfers eventually develop a stylized system for addressing the ball, but their proficiency continues to evolve through their understanding of the concepts of the basic swing. Addressing the ball with the grip firmly completed simply prevents an opportunity to comfortably attain the other important objectives of alignment, posture, and balance. While the left hand is positioning the clubhead, the right hand is off the club to prevent muscles activated by the use of the right arm and shoulder from interfering with attaining these objectives.

While you're learning the procedure for setting up to the ball, it soon becomes apparent that withholding the right hand from the club until your knees are flexed contributes to your learning how to promote accuracy throughout the golf swing. Once you've developed the procedure, you can address the ball in any comfortable manner, even by positioning the clubhead with your right hand or with the grip already completed. (See page 108, Figure 75.)

FIGURE 65

The Procedure

▸ Rebuild positions as they have been established up to this point. (Figure 65)

▸ Without disturbing other positions too much in the "sitting down" position, comfortably bend your left arm and raise the clubhead upward to complete the grip. (Figure 66)

▸ Bearing in mind that your right hand is lower than your left when you position the clubhead, note that *your right arm and shoulder should be lower than your left in the address position.* So, relax your right arm and drop your right shoulder as the firm, straight left arm extends once again to position the clubhead. Be certain to keep your hips and shoulders square and your knees parallel so the entire position is square. (Figure 67)

FIGURE 66

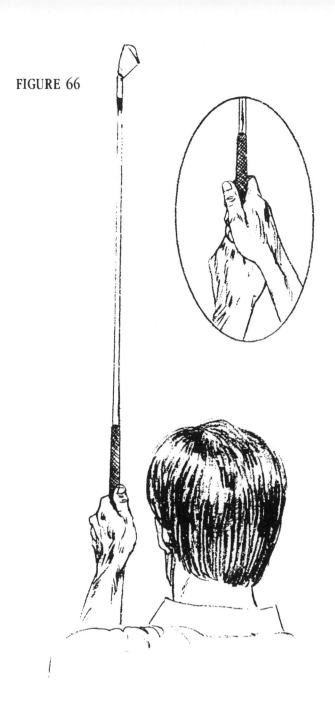

FIGURE 67

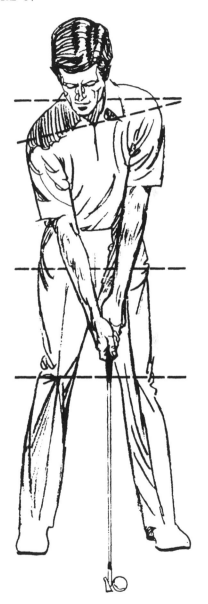

Importance of the Procedure

Completing the grip correctly:

A. *protects the square position of your hips*
B. *squares your shoulders*
C. *allows you to maintain an upright posture with good balance and weight distribution*

A: Protects the square position of your hips.

One of the more difficult positions for golfers to establish and maintain at address is the square position of the hips. If that position is not protected, your hips can easily slip open as your right arm extends downward and forward to secure the right-hand grip. In the address position, for instance, your right hand grips the club lower than your left. With your hands correctly ahead of the ball your right hand must move several inches downward and to the left, whereupon, if given the opportunity, the movement of the right arm diagonally downward easily pushes your hips open. (Figure 68)

Since open hips are generally accompanied by open shoulders, it is imperative that your hips remain square to maintain a square alignment. Waggling the clubhead off the ground while firming the right-hand grip helps keep your hips square, especially when accompanied by sitting down to the ball. Both actions help overcome the muscular influence the right arm otherwise has on the movement of the hips.

Sitting down to the ball *before* securing the right-hand grip overcomes the muscular influence the right arm has on the hips. First of all, your left hand drops down and inward, moving your left hand closer to your right and eliminating some of the muscular conflict by minimizing the distance the right hand must otherwise extend. Second, unlocking the knees relieves the muscular tension that causes the problem by relaxing the muscles somewhat. At this point your right hand is almost in position to complete the grip, and muscular movement is far less likely to push your hips open.

Although sitting down to the ball removes most of the muscular conflict, the short distance the right arm has yet to extend will still influence the hips unless you can protect the position through mental awareness and practice. Knowing how easily the hips slip open—and knowing how to prevent it—is the best defense.

FIGURE 68

Unless their position is protected, the hips easily slip open as the right arm extends downward and forward to secure the right-hand grip.

FIGURE 69

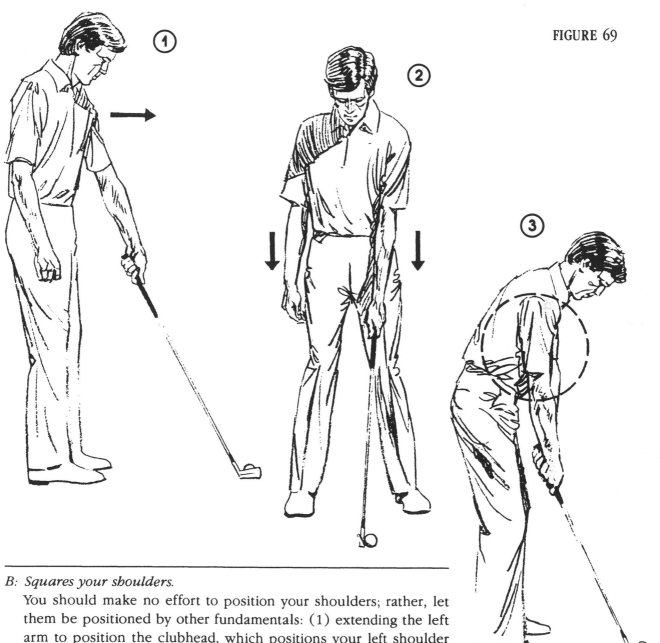

B: Squares your shoulders.

You should make no effort to position your shoulders; rather, let them be positioned by other fundamentals: (1) extending the left arm to position the clubhead, which positions your left shoulder forward; (2) sitting down to the ball before completing the grip, which allows you to maintain an upright posture and keeps your hips square; and (3) letting your right arm and shoulder drop *lower* than your left while completing the grip, which keeps your right shoulder *back*. (Figure 69)

  Once the swing radius is measured and your feet are positioned, raising the clubhead off the ground to secure the right-hand grip will not change other positions—unless you *re*positioned your feet. Therefore, extending your left arm to replace the clubhead—while

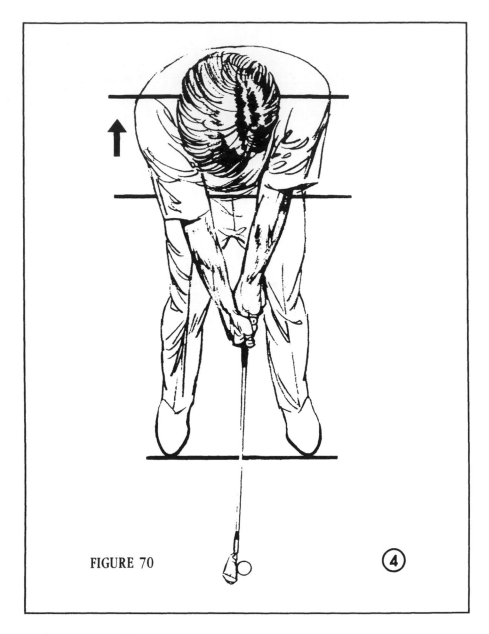

FIGURE 70

④

keeping a softer right arm with the right shoulder back—repositions
the shoulders square (4). (Figure 70)

A simple technique can be used in the address position to
quickly make certain that the hips and shoulders are square. Just
"stand up to square up": First, assume the address position; then
remove your right hand and stand up straight, whereupon any open
position will automatically return to square. Now keep positions
square while sitting down again and bring the right hand from
underneath the left to complete the grip. This keeps your right arm

lower than your left, your right shoulder back, and your shoulders square.

Your left shoulder is positioned to turn around and under the chin with the backswing movement. The right shoulder, out of the way and ready to turn, is positioned to return to square at impact and pull under the chin on into the follow-through—all natural movements in a natural golf swing.

C: Allows you to maintain an upright posture with good balance and weight distribution.

An upright posture and a balanced position at address promote a balanced, upright swing. A common practice, however, is to step up to the ball with the grip completed, lean over too far, drop the head too low, and establish open positions with the weight on the toes. From such a position it is physically difficult to swing comfortably, naturally, or correctly.

Your shoulders need to turn at right angles to your spine in golf, just as they do in the baseball swing—which is one of the reasons it is naturally easier to swing a baseball bat correctly than it is to swing a golf club: the body is standing upright, and the swing is horizontal.

The more the spine is tilted, positions are open, or your weight is on your toes, the more difficult it is to swing the arms and club correctly on the right swing plane. The same is true with standing too upright by positioning the ball too close or standing too stiff-legged. Although seldom a problem in golf, standing too upright, just as leaning over too far, is also prevented just by following good procedure. The better your posture, the better your balance; the better your balance, the easier it is for your arms to coordinate with your weight shifting back and forth and the shoulder turn.

The sequence in which fundamentals are presented establishes and protects your posture, weight distribution, and balanced position. You position the clubhead with just your left hand while standing upright; then you flex your knees and lower your body *before* extending your right arm to complete the grip. The sitting-down position allows you to maintain established positions as your upper body leans forward only enough to complete the grip.

With practice, once you develop the procedure, confidently setting up to the ball becomes a quick, comfortable, and accurate routine—even with the grip already completed.

To quickly make certain that the hips and shoulders are square, just let go with the right hand and "stand up to square up."

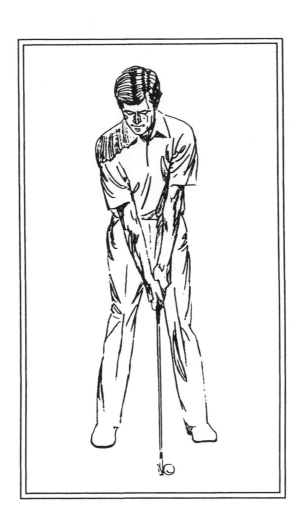

Chapter Twelve

Fundamental No. 8: Rolling the Elbows Inward

The final movement in establishing the position of address is rolling the elbows inward toward each other, firmly securing positions a fraction of a second before the backswing starts and triggering the start of the swing.

The Procedure

Rebuild the position of address; then roll your elbows toward each other to straighten and firm your left arm. As your elbows roll inward and your arms move closer together, keep your right arm relaxed, with the right elbow lower than the left and pointing toward the ground. Since relaxing the right arm has a tendency to relax the right-hand grip, however, make certain the grip stays firm.

Importance of the Procedure

Rolling your elbows inward:
A. *prevents tension at address*
B. *firmly positions your left arm*
C. *loosely positions your right arm*
D. *positions your arms to swing together throughout the golf swing*
E. *locks in a full extension of the arms*

A: Prevents tension at address.

Rolling your elbows toward each other as a final movement at address prevents tension at address and through the swing by keeping your arms relaxed while you set up to the ball. Although your left arm extends to measure the swing radius (see page 48), extending your arms rigidly while setting up to the ball creates muscular tension, making it difficult to waggle comfortably into a coordinated position.

It takes time to coordinate positions while setting up to the ball. Once they are coordinated, however, with the right-hand grip secured, rolling your elbows together just as the backswing starts strengthens muscles throughout your body with just enough tension for the swinging movement. Your left arm is firm without tension at address.

B: Firmly positions your left arm.

Beginning golfers are often given well-intentioned but sometimes useless advice about keeping the left arm straight through the backswing. Nothing will keep your left arm straight, however, unless your left arm is firm *before* the backswing starts.

A firm left arm at address and through the backswing helps you turn your shoulders and promotes accuracy at the top of the swing by completing the shoulder turn; and accuracy at the top of the swing leads to accuracy at impact.

Think of your left arm and the shaft as one long rod, hinged only in the middle by your wrist, which "breaks" through the backswing. If, by bowing your left arm outward, you allow this rod to have two hinges, at both the wrist and the elbow, your arms will swing into a floppy, loose entanglement at the top of the swing, which in turn will prevent your left side from completing the shoulder turn and obtaining a maximum swing arc. Only an inept slapping at the ball results. Your hands pick up the clubhead through the backswing and throw it down from the top of the swing either into the ground behind the ball or over the top of the ball. The resultant chopping action destroys the swing and should be reserved for felling trees or hammering nails, not playing golf.

To demonstrate the importance of rolling your elbows in, extend your left arm with the "pocket" of the elbow facing somewhat skyward and pull against your left wrist with your right hand. Your left arm is braced without tension and stays straight (A). Now loosely

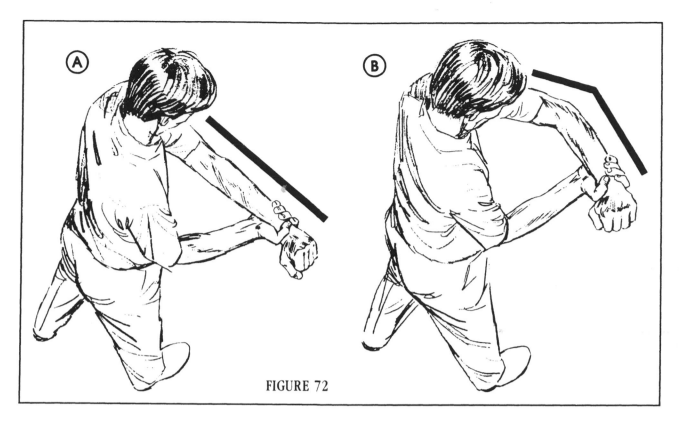

FIGURE 72

Testing Left-Arm Firmness

Rolling the elbows inward at address helps strengthen the left arm while you are
swinging (A), but bowing the left arm outward encourages the arm to bend (B).

extend the left arm without rolling the elbow in and repeat pulling
against the wrist. Unless the muscles are rigid—which creates *exces-*
sive tension—the arm easily "gives" because the elbow bends (B).
(Figure 72)

Pulling against the arm is only an indication of the force exerted
on the elbow by momentum through the backswing. It is physically
difficult to resist such force—especially with speed involved—unless the left elbow is first rolled inward and the arm firmly positioned before the backswing starts.

When you're rolling your elbows together, remember that positions must be accurate but must not be overestablished. Forcing your
elbows in *too* tight restricts a comfortable swinging movement by
creating tension in the forearms and shoulders. Figure 72 demon-
strates how far inward you should roll your elbows to maintain
firmness without locking the elbow joints or causing tension by
stretching your arms too tight.

C: Loosely positions your right arm.

Although the procedure for completing the grip, as explained in Chapter 11, helps square your shoulders and position your right arm and shoulder lower than the left, rolling your elbows together helps even more to establish a sometimes difficult position *as* the backswing starts.

Rolling your elbows together positions your arms differently while, at the same time, allowing them to attain common objectives. Firming the left arm helps strengthen it through the backswing, which is needed to turn the shoulders and complete the shoulder turn; loosely positioning the right arm lower than the left helps square the shoulders at address. This positions the right shoulder to turn out of the way as soon as the backswing starts. At the same time, rather than "flying" upward, the right arm is positioned to fold through the backswing with the elbow pointing down as well as to return close to the body from the top of the swing.

Extending your right arm the same as the left, or positioning your right arm higher, prevents a smooth backswing and causes two problems: (1) the right elbow tends to push outward rather than downward as the clubhead leaves the ball, and (2) albeit *ever* so slight, the "flying" right elbow blocks the shoulder turn and pivot. The first problem tends to loop the clubhead from the top of the swing, throwing the club off-plane and flatter when the right elbow pulls downward, which leads to either pushing or slicing. The second problem prevents completing the shoulder turn, which causes coming over the top and pulling. Since precision through the golf swing is required for both clubhead speed and accuracy, even slight discrepancies such as these cause major problems in the end results.

Along with loosely positioning the right arm as the elbows roll inward, there is a tendency to loosen the right-hand grip. Therefore, always check the firmness of the two middle fingers before the backswing starts.

D· Positions your arms to swing together throughout the golf swing.

Although your right arm folds through the backswing and your left arm folds in the follow-through, your arms do swing together, in the same relative position, throughout the golf swing.

Rolling your elbows inward positions your arms together, and keeping your arms together helps coordinate swing action for a sound, repeating swing. Retaining control of the clubhead depends

FIGURE 73

The arms extend *together* at just one point—just beyond impact where the extension of the left arm passes to the right.

on first positioning the arms together and then preventing their separation somewhere through the swing.

E: Locks in a full extension of the arms.

Fully extending your arms while swinging allows you to maintain the swing radius for a maximum swing arc. In turn, a maximum swing arc helps generate maximum clubhead speed. The arms extend *together*, however, at only one point. Just beyond impact both arms are fully extended as the extension of the left arm passes to the right. (Figure 73)

Keeping your arms relaxed helps you coordinate positions while setting up to the ball, whereupon rolling your elbows together just as the backswing starts "locks in" extension, rather than tension, and strengthens your left arm to extend through the backswing.

Although your right arm is lower and more relaxed at address, extending your *right* arm through the backswing—with the elbow pointing down—helps extend and strengthen the *left* arm at the top of the swing. The right arm will straighten only to the extent that the left arm allows. Keeping the right elbow in *too* close restricts the shoulder turn and shortens the swing arc.

Chapter Thirteen

The Waggle

Quickly and confidently addressing the ball, which is accomplished in a matter of seconds, is a matter of first understanding objectives, then establishing exact positions, and then smoothing those positions together into a coordinated relationship by learning to use the waggle.

Learning to waggle is the key to starting a sound, repeating pattern for a rhythmic, coordinated swing. It's not easy to understand the purpose of waggling, however, unless you first establish positions in sequence with a knowledgeable application of fundamentals.

In general the purpose of waggling is fourfold:

1. to develop consistency and rhythm at address and through the swing by following an exact procedure for establishing and coordinating positions with continuous, rhythmical movement
2. to replace conscious thought through the swing with concentration at address by planning ahead for an overall action or result of the swing
3. to attain objectives automatically by sense and feel so as to program good timing, rhythm, and concentration
4. to relieve tension while setting up to the ball

Addressing the ball with rhythm starts a rhythmical swing from the moment the clubface is squared to the target. As you establish positions, a continuous rhythmic movement of feet, knees, hips, hands, and arms coordinates with a rhythmical movement of the clubhead to overlap and adjust fundamental positions.

You attain overall objectives of alignment, posture, balance, weight distribution, and ball position simultaneously, along with coordinating tension-free independent positions, by applying fundamentals in sequence with continuous movement. With practice golfers instinctively become familiar with the feeling of coordination and accuracy and automatically roll their elbows in as a final waggle procedure to continue the movement of the swing.

Waggling quickly blends specific fundamental positions into one continuous movement through feel and reflex action, establishing and keeping positions waggled into place until the backswing starts of its own accord. Once you develop and comfortably "groove" the swing in practice, the backswing starts automatically. Then you can direct your thinking toward swing action *while* setting up to the ball, thereby replacing conscious thought while swinging with concentration at address.

Although defined similarly, *conscious thought* and *concentration* affect the golf swing differently. Conscious thought is mental awareness, generally directed toward one specific position or movement with deliberate thought and application. Although often present at address to establish exact positions, a sudden application of any conscious thought once the swing is under way quickly institutes some independent action, which changes timing and rhythm. On the other hand, you can replace conscious thought while swinging with concentration at address—thereby avoiding the risk—by learning how to set up automatically while, at the same time, learning how to (1) plan ahead for overall swing action or (2) plan the application of one key thought.

Planning ahead for swing action while setting up to the ball programs that action at address by emphasizing positions and movements during the waggle that accomplish the swing objective. Concentrating on one key thought, such as hitting through the ball or completing the follow-through or shifting the weight against a braced right foot while turning away from the ball, starts and maintains a smooth golf swing by excluding other thoughts, bringing to mind the old Scottish adage, "As ye waggle, so shall ye swing."

Planning ahead is part of the waggle, and the waggle is part of the swing. When golfers waggle with a plan in mind, concentration and rhythm are far more likely to remain intact throughout the swinging movement.

Just as you develop the swing itself through practice, you develop concentration by practicing concentration while setting up to the ball.

"As ye waggle, so shall ye swing."

—old Scottish adage

FIGURE 74

Combining an up-and-down waggle (A) with a back-and-forth waggle (B) settles positions into place while allowing you to rhythmically feel out a good swing plan.

The more knowledgeable and experienced you become, the less conscious thought you will need, the sooner you can apply concentration, and the less opportunity conscious thought has to affect the swinging movement. Whereas a beginner may need *all* conscious thought, an experienced golfer may not need any. Sense and feel and concentration stem from knowledge, practice, and experience and replace the need for conscious thought.

Waggling is a sense-and-feel procedure; personal instinctive responses and concentration evolve only through practice. By understanding and assuming each position independently, then speeding up the process, you develop a natural ability to address the ball both quickly and automatically.

Two types of waggle relate specifically to either positions or movements, and both are used with rhythmic application either separately or combined. A slight up-and-down movement of the body and the clubhead establishes and coordinates body positions, particularly the lower body (Figure 74A). You should use this movement initially to establish and keep positions waggled in place—particularly the square hips, which can easily slip open. As you establish positions, concentration replaces conscious thought used to establish positions with a back-and-forth movement of the clubhead behind the ball and on the line of flight to develop feeling for putting a good swing plan into effect (Figure 74B).

FIGURE 75

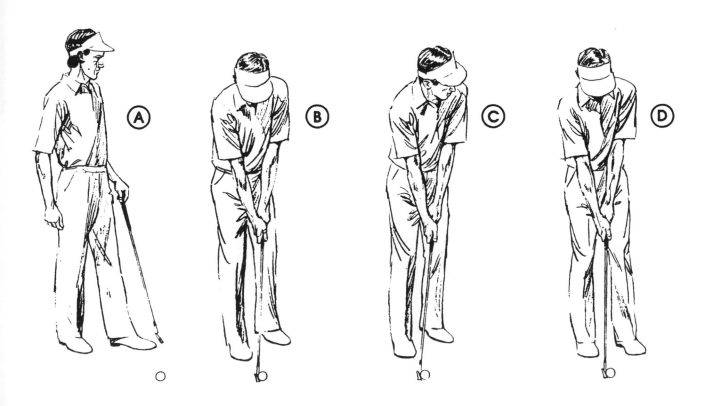

Understanding and practicing each section of the swing—in this case addressing the ball with a waggle—grooves good habits and dispels a continuing myth in golf that too much thinking causes paralysis by analysis. If you understand objectives by understanding the swing, you'll benefit from the waggle; otherwise the movement serves no purpose other than just to allow you to get comfortable.

Trusting that the fundamentals will enable you to reach specific objectives instills in you confidence in doing things instinctively, without the paralysis of indecisive thought that stems from a lack of knowledge. Once you can systematically and quickly establish the position of address, you should experiment with personalizing the movement to find a comfortable waggle of your own. To achieve consistency in swinging you have to begin with consistency at address.

As golfers gain in experience—even though they have different preferences—they often resemble each other when setting up to the ball, because they use fundamentals in the same sequence to attain the same objectives: (A) sighting the target, (B) squaring the clubface, (C) checking alignment, (D) positioning the left foot, (E) positioning the right foot and coordinating positions with up-and-down waggle, (F) "feeling out" swing action and rhythm with back-and-forth waggle, (G) checking alignment, and (H) being ready to swing.

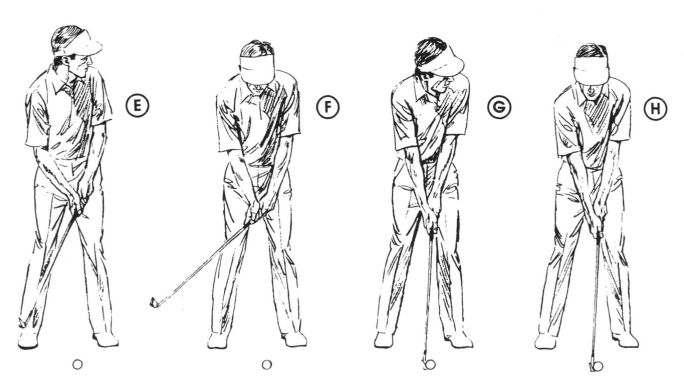

Incorporating Personal Preferences and Procedure

Through the preceding chapters you've come to understand the component parts of a sound golf swing by learning a somewhat tedious step-by-step procedure for addressing the ball. As you gain experience and confidence, you will move gradually from the stringent learning stage to a point where you can pay more attention to your own needs and preferences.

Although for the best end result you must still adhere to all of the basic objectives at address—alignment, posture, balance, ball position, weight distribution, and muscular tautness—now you can make the little changes to accommodate your style. You might change your grip a bit, widen your stance a little, stand a little taller, establish your weight a little differently, and so on. Just keep in mind that your preferences must still be based on fundamentals and should never formulate a style that will deter you from your objectives. In other words, the same principles must still apply so you can reach the same objectives.

Knowledgeable golfers who understand the golf swing soon learn how to combine personal preferences with basics to reach their goals quickly. They simply speed up the process to sight the target, square the clubface, step into an accurate position, waggle a bit, and swing. *Because* they use basics—in sequence—to attain the same objectives, their procedure is often quite similar when setting up to the ball. (See the previous page, Figure 75.)

Once you can apply the fundamentals in sequence, speeding up the waggle procedure soon allows you to blend positions and movements together automatically to attain all of the basic objectives.

PART III
The Backswing Push-Away

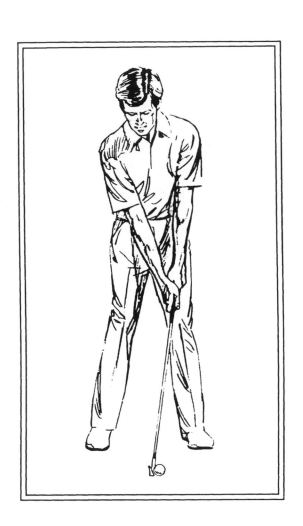

Chapter Fourteen

Fundamental No. 9: The Forward Press

The forward press is a slight forward movement of the hands and knees designed to accompany positions established up to this point. Although the movement is not intended to dictate an absolute procedure for starting the backswing—for not all golfers use a forward press—positions have been established that employ its use because the advantages of starting the backswing with a slight forward movement often outweigh the disadvantages.

It is important to develop a comfortable individual system for applying fundamentals, and you must determine for yourself whether to use this forward movement in your own golf swing. Understanding the purpose of the forward press affords you an opportunity to apply the principle involved whether you use the movement or not.

The Procedure

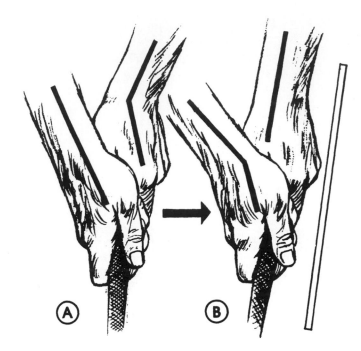

- Reestablish the address position and check your grip for accuracy. (Figure 77A)

- As you waggle positions together and roll your elbows inward, push the palm of your right hand toward the target, pushing both hands back into the original straight arm–shaft position to straighten your left wrist. (Figure 77B)

FIGURE 77

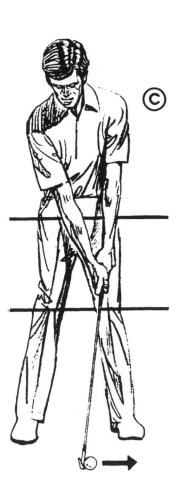

- Let your knees slide forward with the movement and be particularly careful to keep your hips and club-face square and your knees parallel. (Figure 77C)

Importance of the Procedure

Using the forward press:
A. *straightens your left wrist*
B. *protects positions already established*
C. *gives you a running start on the backswing by putting your legs into motion*
D. *helps you develop the correct weight shift and good footwork*

A: Straightens your left wrist.

The purpose of the forward press is to move your hands forward into the original straight arm–shaft position, thereby straightening your left wrist and positioning your left arm to push, rather than pull, the clubhead back with your hands. The factor that determines whether you should use a forward press is whether your left wrist still bends inward.

You may establish the push position of your left arm by either positioning, pressing, or waggling your hands forward. Regardless of method, however, the position itself is important because pushing turns the shoulders and the shoulders turn the hips. (Figure 78A)

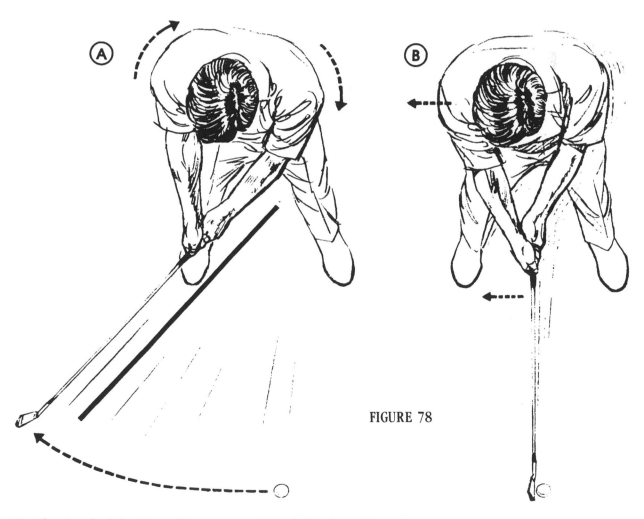

FIGURE 78

Straightening the left wrist enables you to push the clubhead into the backswing to start the shoulder turn (A), but starting the swing with the left wrist bent inward encourages swaying by positioning the hands to pull (B).

The forward movement of the hands and the backward movement of the clubhead, although quite distinct, are closely related to each other and to the waggle. Because of this relationship, you may elect either to position or to waggle your hands forward rather than use a forward press; but positioning your hands forward prevents you from starting the swing from a moving position, and waggling the hands forward may waggle positions *out* of alignment while you set up to the ball—which is more the tendency of golfers only trying to get comfortable.

Two things, especially, are in favor of using a forward press: first, you can establish positions more comfortably, as well as more accurately, with your hands toward center; second, it is easier to start the swing by using a slight forward movement. Most experienced golfers use a slight forward movement expressly for these reasons.

Taking the club back with your left wrist bent inward (Figure 78B) sets up a chain reaction that causes almost all forms of poor golf shots; the body sways laterally as opposed to turning, and the hands pull the clubhead away from the ball with quick hand action. The action whips the clubhead upward, loops the clubface open at the top of the swing, and whips the clubhead back to the ball with the face still open. *If* your weight shifts back to the left—which is not too likely—poor timing and coordination combine with late hand action to prevent you from being able to square the clubface at impact. Since preventing problems is so much easier than finding and correcting them, it really is better just to press the hands forward and push the clubhead back.

The object of the forward press is to push your hands forward only so far as to reestablish the straight arm–shaft position—and the movement is frequently so slight as to be almost imperceptible. Pressing your hands beyond that point pushes the hips and clubface open while "cocking" your hands into pushing the clubhead upward into the backswing—or "picking up the clubhead." Occasionally the action hoods a square clubface instead, which returns either to smother the ball at impact or to hit a low "punch" shot. An *intentional* punch shot, however, positions the ball farther back rather than positioning the hands farther forward. (Figure 79)

Nothing much can be said in favor of pushing the hands *beyond* a straight arm–shaft position. Still, a slight forward movement has many advantages.

The object of the forward press is to push your hands forward only so far as to reestablish the straight arm–shaft position.

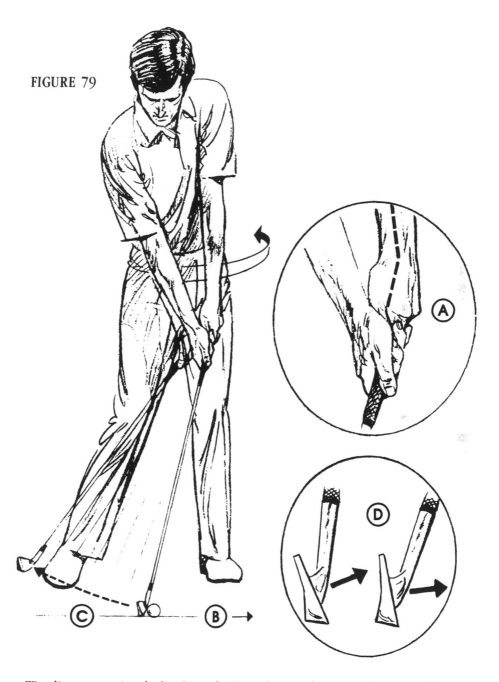

FIGURE 79

Waggling or pressing the hands too far beyond a straight arm–shaft position (A) results in problems such as pushing the hips and clubface open (B), picking up the clubhead (C), or hooding the square clubface (D).

B: Protects positions already established.

Positions that are easily changed if you either position or waggle your hands forward—as opposed to using a forward press—are the square hips and clubface, weight distribution, and position of your hands. Both the waggle and forward press protect these positions, however, by securing them *with* the waggle before you press down and forward with your right hand.

Small, seemingly insignificant things are frequently overlooked in golf. Although an apparently trivial movement, pressing the palm of the right hand toward the target—when the grip is correct—keeps the clubface square. Along with the movement, your knees and hips move slightly forward and your weight rocks gently left, then right, into the backswing movement. *Over*doing the action, however, or pulling your hands or the handle forward swings the handle outward and pushes the hips and clubface open. Preventing the clubface from swinging open also prevents your hands from being pushed away from correct positions.

Along with protecting positions at address, using a forward press ensures that your hands are again ahead of the ball, positioned to push rather than pull the clubhead as the backswing starts.

C: Gives you a running start on the backswing by putting your legs into motion.

The waggle is generally given credit for being the connecting link between establishing positions at address and getting the backswing started, which is almost true because of the smooth coordination of the waggle and forward press. The backswing starts, however, with a slight forward rocking movement, and getting a running start on the backswing gives impetus to the overall swing by having you start from a moving position. As the hands press forward, the knees and hips move too, and keeping the knees parallel—to each other and to the line of flight—helps keep your hips square. (Figure 80)

The forward press starts the movement of the backswing by helping your knees slide forward to put your legs into motion—and your knees should be encouraged to become a natural part of the forward press because the movements are closely related. Even experienced golfers who profess not to use a forward press, per se, may indicate they start the swing in motion by pressing the right knee forward. Here again, experience and feel are important and should determine preference. But inexperienced golfers who press the right knee forward are prone to incorrectly push the hips and

Even experienced golfers who profess not to use a forward press, per se, may indicate they start the swing in motion by pressing the right knee forward.

clubface open by dipping the right knee forward and then sway gracefully into the backswing by dipping the left knee back.

The sliding movement of the hands, hips, and knees is slight and very subtle and need never be exaggerated. A very slight movement starts a smooth, rhythmic backswing continuing from the waggle.

D: Helps you develop the correct weight shift and good footwork.
With your weight distributed equally at address, the forward press rocks your weight to the left, cocking your left leg toward the target and setting your weight even more strongly against the braced right foot as your lower body prepares to catch the weight shifting right.

Just as you may prefer to position or waggle your hands forward rather than use a forward press, you may also move your knees, as well as your weight, slightly forward to preset a stronger position. Again, however, any deviation from the fundamentals should be made only after you understand the basics involved and then make comparisons through practice.

Good footwork and strong, active legs are both results of first understanding and then applying and practicing basics. Neither in itself can make the golf swing work without good basics in the rest of the swing. You should consciously maneuver your feet and legs to get added thrust and power by making your feet and legs work harder only if you're an experienced golfer.

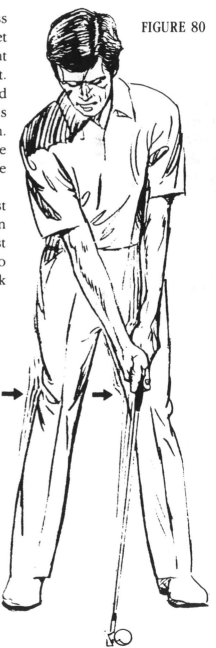

FIGURE 80

The forward press gives you a running start on the backswing by putting your legs into motion. The movement is very slight, however, and the knees remain parallel to each other and to the line of flight.

Chapter Fifteen

Fundamental No. 10: Pushing the Clubhead into a Toe-Up Position

The result of the golf swing can be determined within the first few inches of the backswing. The movement indicates very quickly whether positions established at address will promote coordination unique to the golf swing and whether positions will have time to coordinate by the speed of the swing when it starts.

Established positions at address are of critical importance to the overall swing. Good or bad—correct or incorrect—positions start to coordinate the movement the backswing starts, and positions determine the sequence of motion between the body and the clubhead that determines the rest of the swing.

For accuracy through the swing, the clubhead starts away from the ball headed toward a "toe-up" position. The position is a reliable checkpoint, indicating that the body is turning away from the ball with the clubface square and with the clubhead on the right swing plane.

Pushing into and through the toe-up position is a four-step mechanical process for learning: first by establishing accurate positions and pushing into the position, then by "breaking" the wrists and, finally, by pushing the clubhead on to the top of the swing. Once you've developed the procedure and practice, you can easily coordinate positions and movements into a smooth backswing.

The Procedure

FIGURE 82

▸ Use the waggle to reestablish positions. Roll your elbows toward each other, with the right elbow lower than the left, and firm your grip. Keep your head steady and use the forward press. (Figure 82)

FIGURE 83

▸ Almost simultaneously, deliberately *push the clubhead away from the ball by pushing your left shoulder forward and extending your firm left arm.* Let your weight shift to the right—against your right foot—but *keep your knees where they are* to prevent excessive movement. (Figure 83)

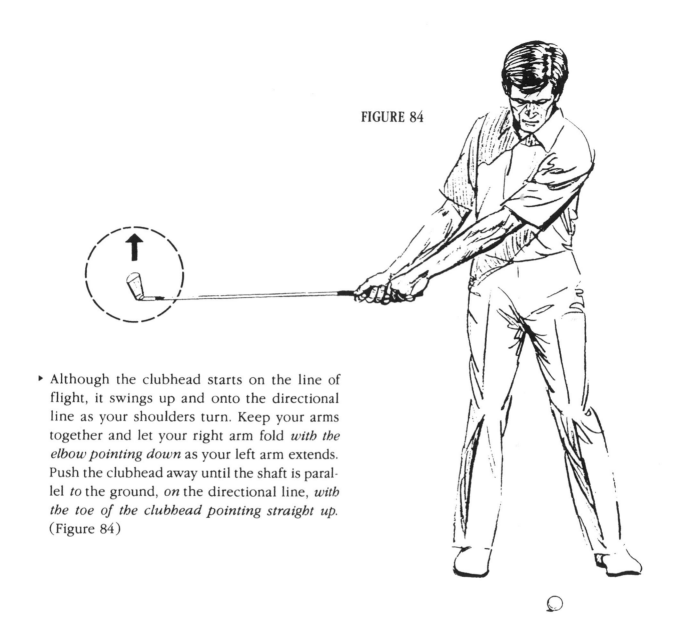

FIGURE 84

▸ Although the clubhead starts on the line of flight, it swings up and onto the directional line as your shoulders turn. Keep your arms together and let your right arm fold *with the elbow pointing down* as your left arm extends. Push the clubhead away until the shaft is parallel *to* the ground, *on* the directional line, *with the toe of the clubhead pointing straight up.* (Figure 84)

There is no doubt that the start of the backswing can be a difficult movement. You may suddenly sense a patting-the-head-while-rubbing-the-stomach feeling when you try to coordinate movements such as keeping your left knee from being too active while shifting your weight to the right and pushing your left shoulder forward while keeping your right elbow down. With practice, however, you will quickly develop feeling for coordinating these movements, and they will soon become subconscious rather than conscious effort.

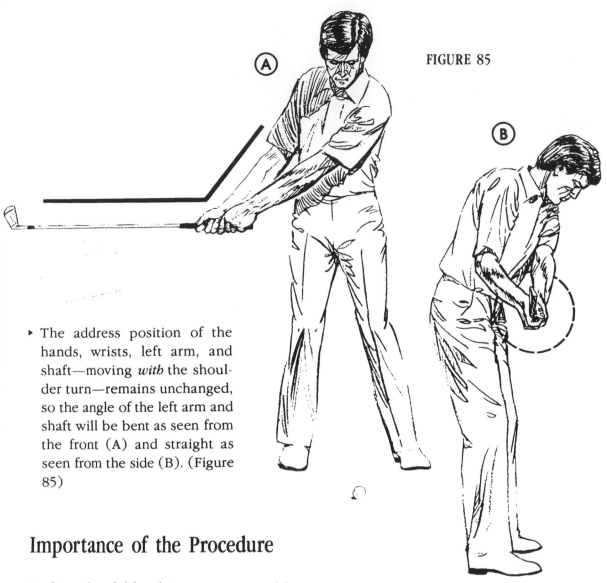

FIGURE 85

▸ The address position of the hands, wrists, left arm, and shaft—moving *with* the shoulder turn—remains unchanged, so the angle of the left arm and shaft will be bent as seen from the front (A) and straight as seen from the side (B). (Figure 85)

Importance of the Procedure

Pushing the clubhead into a toe-up position:

A. *starts the hands and clubhead on the right swing path with a maximum swing arc*

B. *maintains a pivotal position for the shoulder turn and helps prevent swaying*

C. *starts a "coil-recoil" action of the upper and lower body*

D. *keeps the clubface square*

E. *promotes natural hand and wrist action*

F. *prevents a "flying" right elbow*

G. *puts the power and swing in golf by promoting strong, active legs and good footwork*

H. *initiates good timing by preventing a fast backswing*

I. *introduces "key swing thoughts"*

A: Starts the hands and clubhead on the right swing path with a maximum swing arc.

Pushing the clubhead from the line of flight onto the directional line and into the toe-up position with a firm, fully extended left arm starts the clubhead through the backswing on the right swing plane with a maximum swing arc. Staying "on plane" is then a matter of understanding and practicing swing basics as well as understanding terms such as *swing plane*, *swing arc*, and *swing path*.

The *swing plane* is an imaginary flat surface that the hands, shaft, and clubhead should, ideally, start on and stay on throughout the golf swing (A). Although the swing is most effective when golfers swing on plane, *very* few golfers are consistently able to do so because the plane is so precise. (Figure 86)

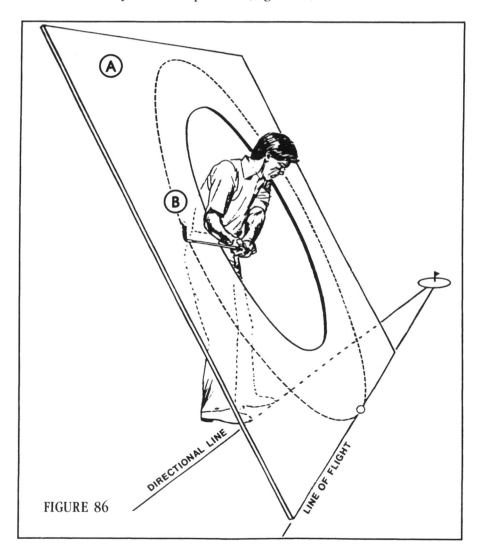

DIRECTIONAL LINE

LINE OF FLIGHT

FIGURE 86

The *swing plane* is an imaginary flat surface that the hands, shaft, and clubhead should, ideally, start on and stay on throughout the golf swing (A). The *swing arc* is the width and length of the circle on the face of the plane (B). Having the toe-up position as a guideline for the *swing path* starts each clubhead on its own correct swing plane.

The *swing arc*, which includes both the width and length of the swing, is the size of the circle on the face of the plane measured by the golf swing radius—or the length of the left arm plus the length of the club being used (B). (See page 48.)

The *swing path*, whether right or wrong, good or bad, *or* whether on plane or off-plane, is the path on which the clubhead actually travels throughout the swing. Having guidelines for the swing path, however—such as the toe-up position—helps you learn how to swing consistently closer to the plane so as to swing better.

The shorter the shaft, the smaller the swing arc and, because the clubhead is closer to your feet, the more upright the plane will be. In other words, a driver swings in a bigger circle and is prone to swing flatter (if allowed to) than a short iron or wedge. (Figure 87)

Each golf club has its own swing plane, somewhere between flat and upright, as determined by the length of the shaft—which is one of the reasons it is more difficult to swing the driver correctly than to swing a short iron correctly; the length of the driver makes it harder to swing upright. Timing also is different with a longer-shafted club, simply because it takes more time to complete a bigger swing arc. That's why extension is important.

Although the swing plane, swing arc, and timing all vary some-what with the use of different clubs, to consistently hit toward the target with the clubface square, all golf clubs must start on and stay as *close* as possible to their own swing plane. Extending your left arm and pushing any clubhead into and through the backswing toe-up position not only starts that particular golf club on its own correct swing plane but also initiates good timing and builds clubhead speed by providing a maximum swing arc.

Having the toe-up position as a backswing guideline for the swing path prevents you from starting the clubhead too far outside or too much inside the target lines. Starting the clubhead sharply "in-side" flattens the swing plane, and swinging the clubhead too far outside prevents the shoulder turn.

Swinging the clubhead sharply inside and flattening the plane swings the hands behind, rather than up and over, the right shoulder at the top of the swing, from where they cannot pull—or *be* pulled—downward. (Figure 88A and B) Although hooking or pushing will occur should the swing return the same way—which very rarely happens—starting the clubhead sharply inside generally returns the *upper* body first from the top of the swing because the hands swing around from the top rather than pulling downward. This loops and

FIGURE 87

The shorter the shaft, the more naturally upright the plane—which is why it is easier to swing upright, as opposed to flat, with the short irons (A) than it is with the woods (B).

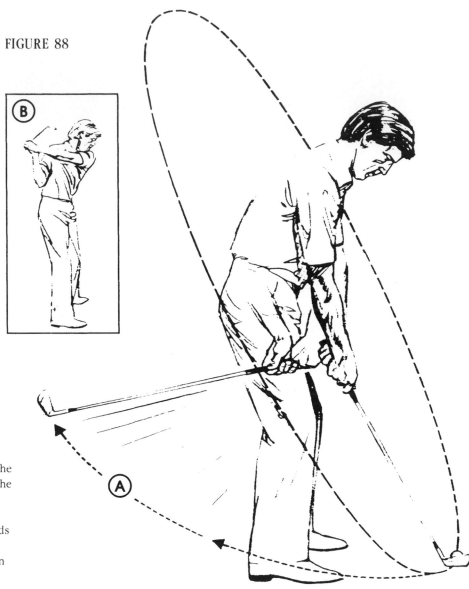

FIGURE 88

Starting the clubhead back sharply inside (A) flattens the swing plane and positions the hands behind the right shoulder (B). Rather than pulling downward, the hands loop the clubhead from the top to swing from outside in (C).

throws the clubhead from the top to outside the line of flight to slice or pull the ball or even shank it to the right. (Figure 88C)

Pushing the left shoulder forward rather than downward when pushing into the toe-up position maintains a vertical axis, which helps keep the swing center intact. In turn, this pushes the hands, shaft, and clubhead upward into the right swing plane as the shoulders turn around the head at right angles to the spine. As long as the swing *center* remains intact, the swing arc can be as wide as the length of the club allows. To attain these objectives, however, it is

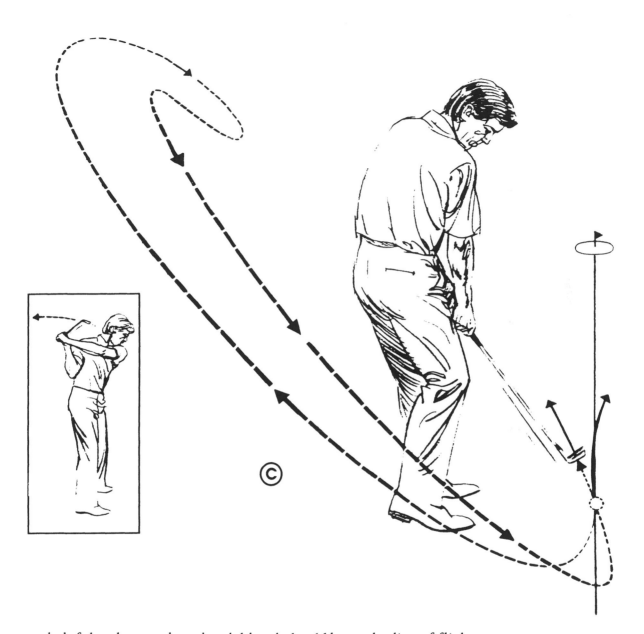

helpful to know when the clubhead *should* leave the line of flight and swing onto the directional line.

Occasionally golfers are instructed to "take" the clubhead back "on the ground, straight back on the line of flight." A golfer who follows this advice too literally, however, is pulled sideways, which keeps the clubhead *and* the golfer on the line of flight too long. Forcing the clubhead to stay on the line of flight beyond where it should swing up and inward prevents a shoulder turn, pulls the head off-line, and causes swaying across the right foot with the clubface closed. Conversely, pulling the clubhead sharply inward—rather than pushing toward the toe-up position—may swing the clubface open and prevent swinging upright by flattening the swing plane.

Regardless of ball position or club selection, a good rule of thumb in golf is to let the clubhead leave the ground and line of flight, moving toward the toe-up position—which is on the directional line—as the clubhead passes your right foot. (Figure 89) Placing a tee at that point forms a right angle from the ball to your foot, and knocking the tee down in practice will help you visualize this checkpoint when playing.

Playing woods and long irons positions the ball forward, automatically keeping the clubhead on the ground and on the line of flight longer than when you play short irons, which are positioned farther back. If you have difficulty making a big extension into the backswing while, at the same time, preventing a lateral sway and related problems, you will have less difficulty if you make a timely exit *off* the line of flight and onto the directional line. Keeping accuracy in mind, remember that the directional line is the other half of the target line—and both are used as guidelines for swinging the club on plane while obtaining a maximum swing arc.

B: *Maintains a pivotal position for the shoulder turn and helps prevent swaying.*

Keeping your chin up and your head steady while pushing the clubhead away from the ball keeps your chin out of the way for the shoulder turn and keeps the vertical axis fixed throughout the golf swing. Maintaining this vertical axis and swing center while pushing your left shoulder forward and keeping your knees in place is a key to important objectives.

Keeping your knees forward and pushing your left shoulder forward as the club starts back prevents your hips from moving laterally as soon as the backswing starts. The shoulders then turn at right angles to the spine, turning the shoulders against the hips to start a natural shoulder turn and pivot. Dipping the left shoulder downward, however, or dipping the knees down and inward, tends to push the hips laterally and prevent the shoulder turn.

The importance of pushing the clubhead away with your left arm and shoulder, as opposed to pulling with your hands, can quickly be seen: pushing the clubhead away while shifting your weight, keeping your right elbow down, and pushing against your right foot promotes the shoulder turn (Figure 90A), but pulling—or

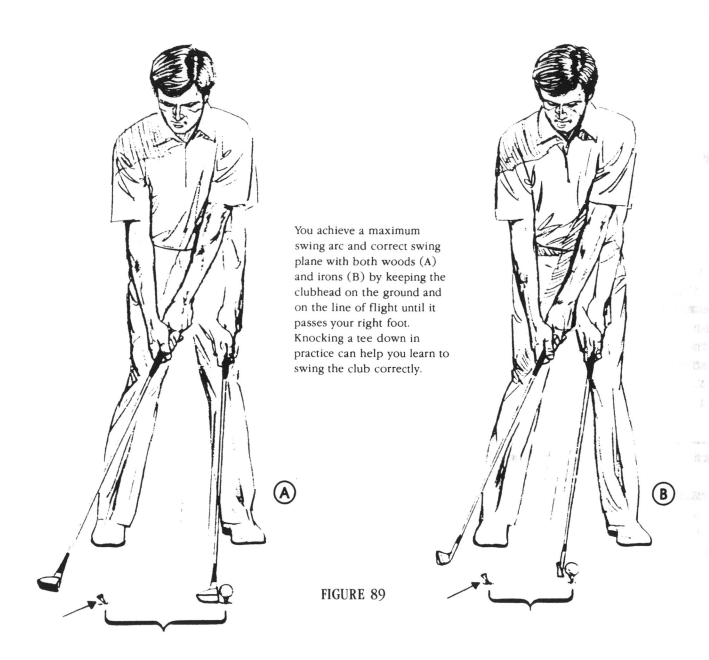

You achieve a maximum swing arc and correct swing plane with both woods (A) and irons (B) by keeping the clubhead on the ground and on the line of flight until it passes your right foot. Knocking a tee down in practice can help you learn to swing the club correctly.

FIGURE 89

taking—the club back with your right arm or hands prevents a shoulder turn and promotes a lateral sway (Figure 90B). Swaying sideways—where your right hip moves sideways rather than turning away from the ball—is the opposite of pivoting rotationally, and unless your shoulders turn and your hips stay put as the club starts back, either your body sways laterally or your hips and shoulders turn together as the backswing starts, which prevents building torque.

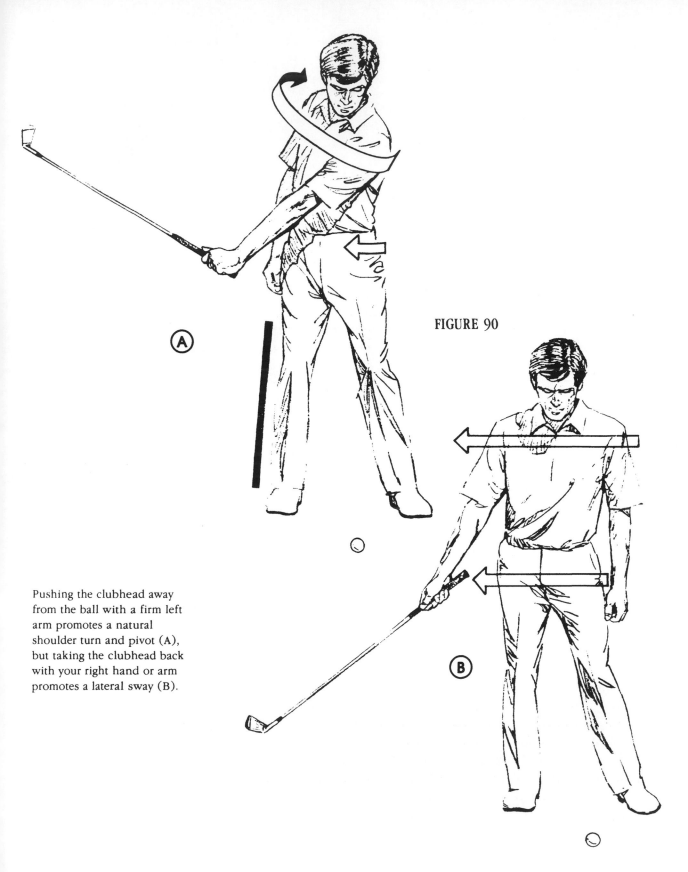

FIGURE 90

Pushing the clubhead away
from the ball with a firm left
arm promotes a natural
shoulder turn and pivot (A),
but taking the clubhead back
with your right hand or arm
promotes a lateral sway (B).

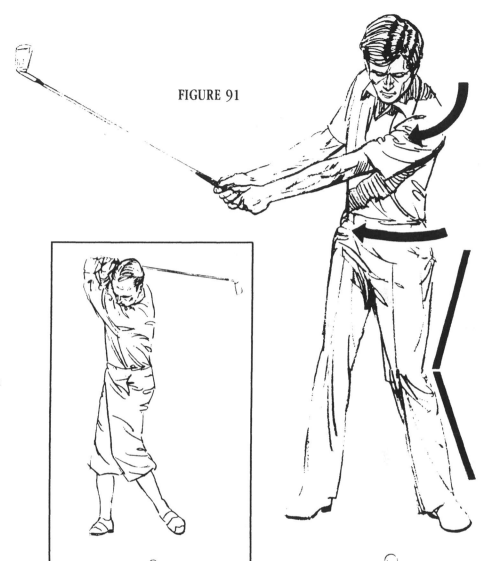

FIGURE 91

The "Classic" Swing

The hips and shoulders turn together—as in the Bobby Jones era—when you swing your left knee inward at the *start* of the swing.

C: Starts a "coil-recoil" action of the upper and lower body.
   Square positions at address encourage your body to turn as soon as the clubhead leaves the ball. Since the natural reaction of the hips is to turn freely with the arms and shoulders, however, many golfers mistakenly believe that accentuating this coordination will promote a big, powerful swing. Such is not always the case. A "modern power swing" has evolved that briefly restricts hip movement so as to turn the shoulders against the hips—and *letting* the shoulders turn the hips, by preventing a fast pivot, is one of the keys to developing power and distance. (Figures 91, 92, and 93)

Turning the shoulders against the hips by briefly restricting left *knee* action winds the muscles of the upper body against the resistance of the lower body. Although the upper body coils against the lower body, the *lower* body *re*coils first from the top of the swing, pulling the arms, hands, and clubhead down from the top and back through the hitting zone with strong leg action.

Although a modern power swing is prevalent on both the men's and women's tours, it is not necessarily an appropriate goal for everyone. "Different strokes for different folks" is certainly true in golf. Many golfers prefer to let the hips turn freely, and others who sway should definitely learn to turn the hips whether sooner *or* later.

FIGURE 92

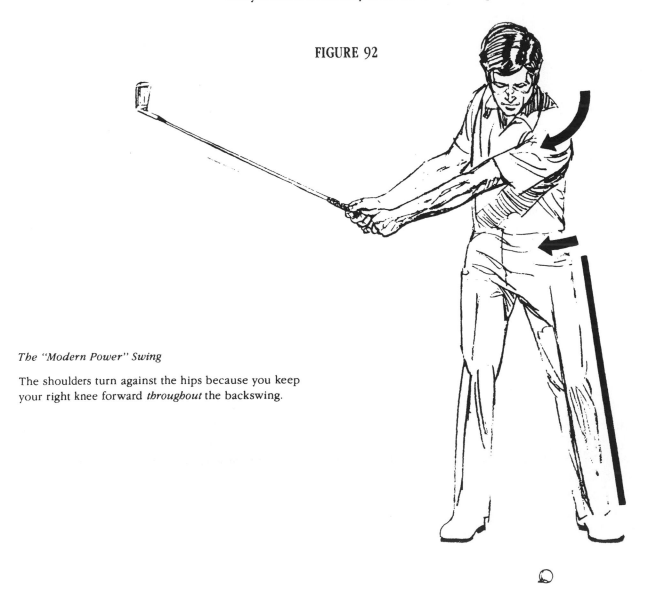

The "Modern Power" Swing

The shoulders turn against the hips because you keep your right knee forward *throughout* the backswing.

Whatever the choice, however, the hips must turn rotationally rather than laterally to help prevent swaying. And, in order for the middle of the body to turn *around* in the swing, the right hip needs to turn away from the ball on the backswing.

Pushing the clubhead into the backswing starts a slight pivot, but delaying left knee action delays the pivot. Moving against this slight resistance as the backswing continues on to the top, the left leg then pulls inward, pulling the left heel off the ground, in the "coil-recoil" action. But timing influences coordination. If the hips and shoulders turn together, or the hips are free to turn too soon (because you dip or bend the left knee the *moment* the backswing

FIGURE 93

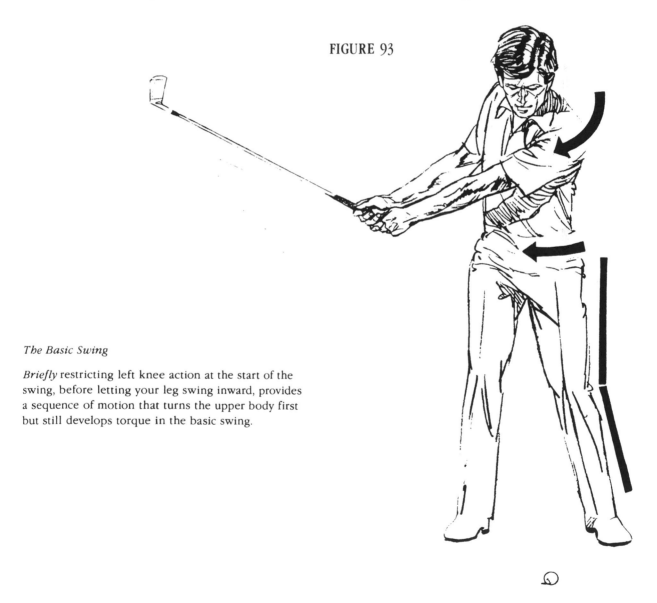

The Basic Swing

Briefly restricting left knee action at the start of the swing, before letting your leg swing inward, provides a sequence of motion that turns the upper body first but still develops torque in the basic swing.

starts), the hips turn beyond a point where the coiling mechanism takes place naturally. Overdoing the action usually bends the left arm, an action somewhat similar to wringing out a washcloth by turning both hands in the same direction. Either torque must then be created on the downswing with well-timed *lower* body action moving back toward the ball, or the clubhead will swing too far at the top of the swing, which results in loss of control over the clubhead and no power at all.

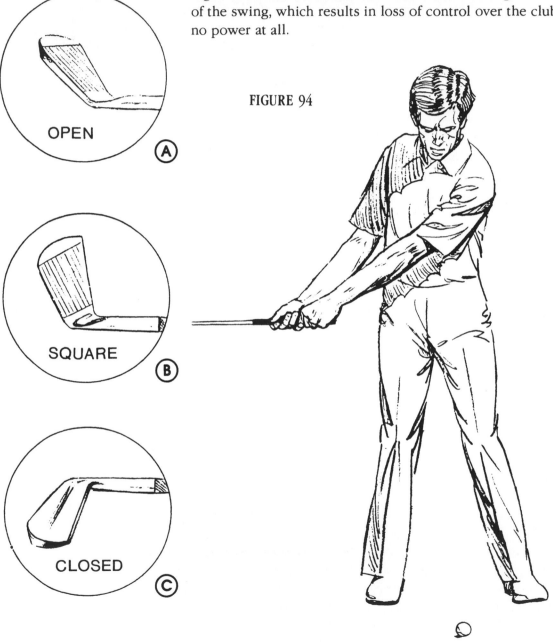

FIGURE 94

OPEN Ⓐ

SQUARE Ⓑ

CLOSED Ⓒ

Clubface angles through the toe-up position.

Whether you're striving for more power or not, preventing the left knee from dipping down or bending forward as soon as the backswing starts is of fundamental importance in the basic golf swing. This, in itself, creates a certain amount of coil. Trying to wind the backswing *too* tight, however, by keeping the left knee forward too long in the swing, may result in too much restriction, thereby adding an unnecessary complication to an otherwise far less complex backswing movement. Just as you have a choice in using a forward press, however, and depending on your proficiency, you also have a choice in determining how much restrictive left leg action is comfortable, or even necessary, to add additional power to any golf swing. Understanding the backswing on through to the top of the swing, along with practice, should help you make that decision.

D: *Keeps the clubface square.*

For the clubface to return square at impact, it must be square at address, square through the backswing, and square at the top of the swing. Through the backswing the clubface is square at the point where the shaft is parallel to the ground, on line with the toes, and the toe of the clubhead is pointing straight up. The wrist break then cocks the hands upward from this position to establish the square clubface at the top of the swing.

The clubface angle at the top of the swing generally returns the same way at impact. A square clubface returns to square and hits the ball straight, but an open or closed clubface returns to slice or hook as well as pull or push. Unless slicing or hooking is intentional, such shots represent swing problems; consequently you should occasionally check the clubface angle at the top of the swing to detect other discrepancies.

Although it is physically difficult to swing into and hold a position at the top of the swing to check the clubface angle, accuracy through the toe-up position corresponds with accuracy at the top. Therefore the toe-up position becomes a good checkpoint—particularly in practice—for the clubface angle. "Toe up" represents square. (Figure 94B) If the toe points backward, with the clubface facing skyward, the clubface is open. (Figure 94A) If the toe points forward, with the clubface facing downward, the clubface is closed. (Figure 94C) If the clubface is either open or closed, you need to make a swing correction. "Flying" the right elbow and/or swaying, for instance, causes a closed clubface; turning or rolling the hands into the backswing swings the clubface open.

Accuracy through the toe-up position is essential for accuracy through the rest of the swing—and it is one of the easiest checkpoints in golf.

E: Promotes natural hand and wrist action.

Although swinging the club and hitting the ball go hand in hand, from the time the clubhead leaves the ball until it returns to the hitting zone, you should make no effort to swing the club with your hands. Well positioned at address, your hands are then controlled by the shoulder turn, left arm extension, right elbow action, the weight shift, and wrist break. As your wrists break through the backswing, your hands are moved through and into other correct positions—and they are pulled back down by lower body action moving back through the ball. If you're unaccustomed to using your hands to hit the ball without also swinging the *golf club*, you should consider checking the other basics.

The thumbs are a key to checking natural hand action. They are positioned on top of the shaft at address and are on top of the shaft in the toe-up position. In this position your hands are placed the same as if they were drawn back independently in a hitting action—which employs the natural use of the hands throughout the golf swing. The pushing action and shoulder turn "fan" the clubhead into the toe-up position, on the right swing plane, with the thumbs on top and the clubface square. (Figure 95)

Cocking the left hand downward at address not only establishes an upright posture but also enables the hands to cock upward through the wrist break. (Figure 96) To prevent unnecessary problems created by a quick "pickup," however, the cocked-down angle remains the same from address to the toe-up position.

F: Prevents a "flying" right elbow.

Power and momentum originate from many different sources, but they arrive simultaneously at impact for distance off the tee. Your body supplies the power through your shifting your weight and turning, but the clubhead builds momentum by combining arm and hand action with the shoulder turn. A flying right elbow, lifting upward through the backswing, separates power from momentum by separating firm arm action from the shoulder turn.

Although the right arm folds as the backswing starts, the right elbow has a strong tendency to fly or float upward rather than

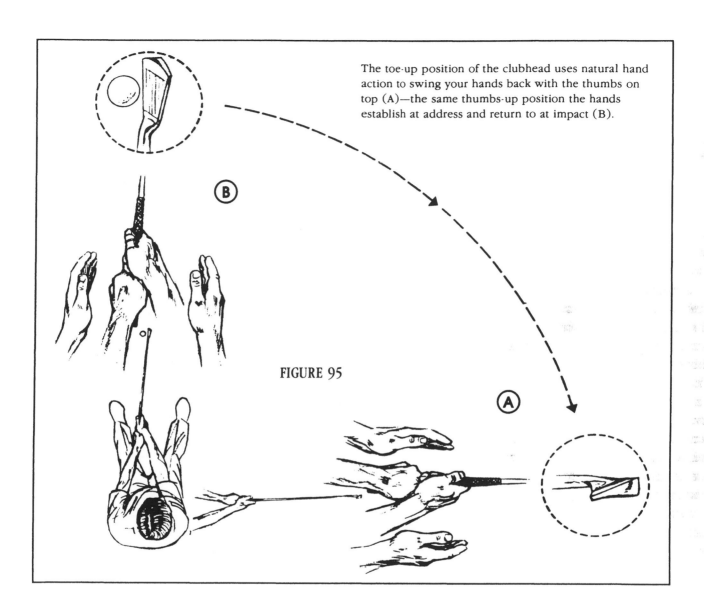

The toe-up position of the clubhead uses natural hand action to swing your hands back with the thumbs on top (A)—the same thumbs-up position the hands establish at address and return to at impact (B).

FIGURE 95

point down toward the ground. Keeping the elbow pointing down, however, welds the body and arms together as a cohesive unit to prevent their working independently—and it is absolutely essential to a sound, repeating swing.

Flying refers only to the elbow lifting upward, not to how far it moves outward and away from the side. Your elbow must move outward. Keeping the elbow in too tight to prevent its flying restricts a full golf swing and is generally a result of misunderstanding the expression "keep your elbow down." The word *extension* in the phrase *extension through the swing* refers to *both* the left and right arms throughout the swing. Through the backswing, extension of the right arm—even though the right arm folds—helps strengthen the left arm. And the right arm will extend only as far as the left arm will allow.

The position of the right elbow is a good place to look for trouble when shots are simply erratic for no apparent reason. When the elbow flies upward, there is little or no clubhead control because the hands and arms swing free from the body to produce a loose, erratic swing. You must then rely on accidental coordination rather than on firm control to get good results.

Any poor shot results from flying the right elbow since it is exceedingly difficult to turn the shoulders and wedge the clubface square through the toe-up position. The most common result is swaying into the backswing with a closed clubface, which causes pulling the ball at impact. The clubface stays closed through the backswing, prevents a shoulder turn and pivot, and compounds the problem at impact by causing swaying back and forth. (Figure 97)

Swaying laterally back through the ball with the clubface closed

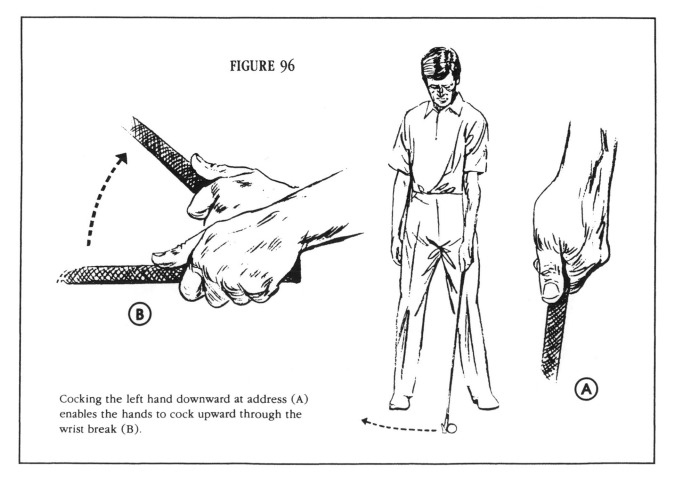

FIGURE 96

Cocking the left hand downward at address (A) enables the hands to cock upward through the wrist break (B).

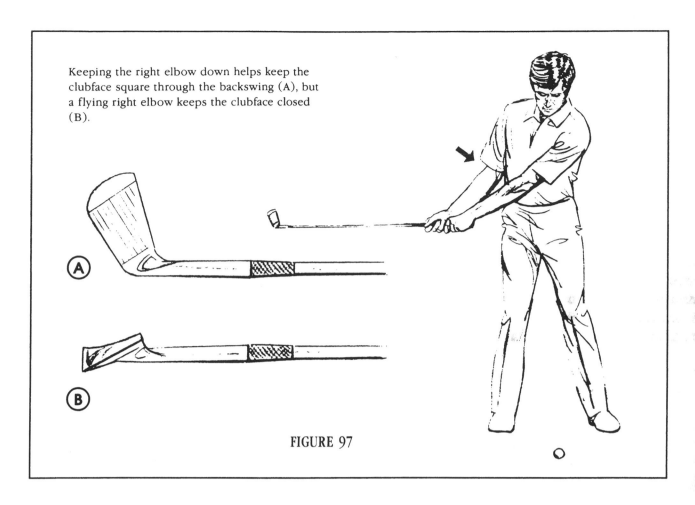

Keeping the right elbow down helps keep the clubface square through the backswing (A), but a flying right elbow keeps the clubface closed (B).

Ⓐ

Ⓑ

FIGURE 97

also hoods the clubface and removes the loft of the club. Combined with a fast backswing, it results in a smothered pull or hook which rarely leaves the ground. Although these various problems are all common results, suddenly pointing a flying elbow downward at the top of the swing causes any variety of erratic shots by looping the club off-plane and the clubface open at the top of the swing.

The difference between a right and wrong elbow position is frequently so slight as to be undetected even by experienced golfers. It generally takes a very alert and knowledgeable golfer to spot this particular deficiency in an otherwise flawless swing. A flying elbow should be suspected, however, when both arms extend at address with the right arm positioned higher than the left. Keeping the elbow down helps you wedge the clubhead upward into a controlled groove that can be repeated for consistency in a sound golf swing. (Figure 98)

*Origin of the
Controlled Groove*

Keeping the arms together
and the right elbow pointing
down wedges the clubhead
upward into a controlled
groove that can be repeated
time after time (A). A flying
right elbow lifting *upward*
through the backswing
separates power and
momentum by separating the
arms from the body turn (B).

FIGURE 98

G: Puts the power and swing in golf by promoting strong, active legs and good footwork.

A well-timed, rhythmic swing depends on strong, active legs and good footwork to promote a swinging movement. The word *swing* and the fact that they hold a tool in their hands, however, make many golfers restrict the swing to their hands and arms, leaving their feet and legs inactive. If you have difficulty *using* your feet and legs, it might be helpful to remember that the swinging movement of the legs, combined with good footwork and the weight shift, helps push and pull the arms and club and puts the swing in golf.

You have established key positions that promote a swinging movement. Your body is balanced in a sitting position with your knees unlocked and your posture upright, and your feet have feeling as a result of good weight distribution. The forward press then slides your knees forward, putting your legs into motion and starting a rhythmical swing. As your left arm and shoulder push the clubhead away from the ball, your legs flow with the movement to continue a smooth and rhythmic "one-piece" swing. Oddly enough, however, this smooth, comfortably coordinated *feeling* can prevent a powerful swing.

Golfers are prone to just go along with a comfortable feeling by trying to help the arms and club swing upward with excessive knee movement, dipping the left knee down and inward or bending the left knee too far forward as well as swaying the right knee sideways. Few things, however, affect the swing more adversely than overly active knees as soon as the backswing starts.

Letting the left knee bend straight forward as soon as the backswing starts keeps the weight on the left instead of shifting it right and instantly lowers the body. The body also lowers when the weight shifts correctly if the left knee dips down and inward.

With your weight shifting *left* to the top of the swing and your body moving downward, the downswing can start only by pushing off the left foot, thereby shoving the body away from the ball as the weight shifts right. This rather dramatic "firing and falling back" routine, coupled with swaying up and down, throws the clubhead upward from the top of the swing, back over the top of the ball. Looking up and topping result as the head is pushed up and the body pushed backward with the reverse weight shift.

Dipping or bending your left knee the moment the backswing starts tends to lower the body considerably. The left leg then straightens on the downswing, forcing the body to suddenly spring upward and pull away from the ball. Although topping or hitting

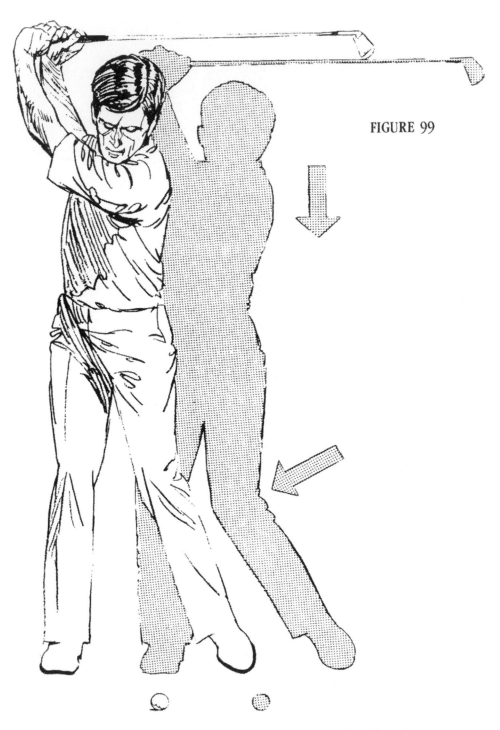

FIGURE 99

Keeping the left leg cocked slightly toward the target as the weight shifts right prevents a reverse weight shift and swaying up and down by preventing the left knee from dipping down or bending too far forward. The action keeps a small amount of pressure against the inside ball of the left foot.

behind the ball results from dipping or bending the left knee slightly, the more the body lowers and rises, the farther the body is shoved up and away from the hitting zone with the weight on the right, whereupon "whiffing" the ball completely is a not uncommon occurrence.

Anchoring the base of the body turn, by briefly restricting left knee action, fortifies the left side with strong driving power as the downswing starts. This essential driving power is lost, however, if the unrestrained left knee dips or bends excessively from the start of the swing. Although women, in general, are apt to be more "rhythmic" players than men and therefore more prone to dip or bend the knee, this maneuver frequently affects men as well.

To incorporate strong, active legs and good footwork into a swinging movement, you often must make conscious effort—in the learning and practice stages—to keep the left leg cocked just slightly toward the target. This prevents your knee from dipping down or bending forward at the start of the swing and is actually the beginning of good footwork and a strong leg drive. As you complete the backswing, the action will be smoothed into a naturally coordinated swinging movement as pressure builds against your left foot and your left leg pulls inward to the top of the swing. For the moment, however, just keeping your left knee where it is as your weight shifts right helps prevent an action that is almost too comfortable and prevents a powerful swing. (Figure 99)

> Timing and balance, not speed or strength, are the essence of good coordination.

H: Initiates good timing by preventing a fast backswing.

The speed of the swing is regulated and set the moment the backswing starts, and the clubhead must never be muscled into the backswing with such speed that positions do not have time to coordinate. Timing and balance, not speed or strength, are the essence of good coordination. Good timing is simply the smooth transition of the backswing, which starts with upper body action, to the downswing, which starts with lower body action. And good timing in a sound, repeating golf swing occurs only with good coordination.

A fast backswing is the bane of the game, usually preventing the very things a golfer strives for, such as control, consistency, accuracy, and distance, by not giving positions time to coordinate. The old hustler's slogan "Give me a man with a fast backswing and a fat wallet" is not to be taken lightly. *Many* a wager has been based on the speed of a fellow golfer's practice swings during the wait to tee off.

Although stored-up power through the backswing and downswing is released at impact, neither brute strength nor speed is needed to produce this power, either by winding the muscles tighter or by swinging the golf club faster. Combining basic positions with good swing mechanics and deliberately pushing the clubhead away from the ball allow you time to negotiate the otherwise complex movements of the golf swing—particularly such things as keeping the left knee forward at the start of the swing while turning and catching the weight shift. It is difficult to attain objectives with precise movements when the hands, for instance, are actively engaged in yanking the clubhead around with a fast backswing.

The word *swing* is an interesting term in golf in that it can elicit two different responses to swinging the clubhead back. Swinging can start by either pushing or pulling, just as starting a child's swing. Given a choice, golfers often prefer to pull the club with their hands, inadvertently creating a fast backswing by whipping the clubhead back. Pushing, however, prevents the whipping action but still starts a swinging movement by putting the legs into motion.

Thinking of pushing as very deliberate and almost in slow motion, just as pushing a child's swing, helps immeasurably in starting a smooth and well-timed swing.

I: Introduces "key swing thoughts."

Up to this point, we've been building the swing by presenting only a foundation for the swing itself; conscious thought has been needed to establish accurate positions. Now that the swing is underway, however, fundamentals already applied must be trusted to do their jobs so as to free the mind to concentrate on a good swing plan. As mentioned earlier, concentration is an important asset in golf and should not be wasted on something that can be relegated to fundamentals.

Trusting already established positions enables golfers to develop what are called *key swing thoughts*—deliberate concentration applied to anything specific that either helps the golf swing work when actually playing golf or helps you develop the swing in practice. Until the swing is sound and positions are correct, you should use key swing thoughts in practice as guidelines and checkpoints for developing a well-grooved swing.

At this stage of the swing you can use four swing thoughts—one at a time in practice—as guidelines to check and groove the backswing:

1. Start a deliberately slow backswing.
2. When the shaft is parallel, check to see that the left knee is not dipping down or bending forward.
3. Check to see that the right elbow points toward the ground.
4. Check to make certain the toe of the club points upward.

Conscious thought in practice applied to positions or movements eliminates conscious thought when playing by building your confidence in doing things instinctively. When you're playing golf, your concentration can then be focused on a key swing plan directed at results.

Key swing thoughts are invaluable in eliminating conscious thought when you're playing; they help you program and concentrate on a good swing plan, such as swinging into and holding the follow-through position. It is generally agreed, however, that until your swing is sound and grooved in practice, having more than one swing thought or changing thoughts while swinging only confuses your timing. The more knowledgeable and experienced you are, though, the more thoughts you can apply—which, in essence, is called concentration. Those who understand the swing often combine swing thoughts into key swing movements or images to practice just a portion of the overall swing.

Until you're experienced, never lose sight of the fact that the purpose of golf is to swing the club and hit the ball; this way you'll avoid getting lost in a maze of thoughtful, mechanical confusion by just trying to make something work. *The highest level of proficiency occurs when the least amount of thought is given to the mechanics of the swing.* To avoid unnecessary mental entanglements, use key swing thoughts—just as fundamentals—in practice to help you develop a swing that can be trusted when you're actually playing golf.

Many factors will always affect and change your swing, and part of the unique challenge of golf is to find and correct problems when trouble does occur. Such is the value of being able to be analytical. You should never, however, analyze or correct your golf swing as a result of only an occasional poor shot. The occasional mis-hit ball, which even the experts encounter, should always be recognized and accepted as a direct result of being only human—that is, less than perfect.

Chapter Sixteen

Fundamental No. 11: The Wrist Break

Golf instructors are generally reluctant to classify the wrist break as a fundamental. Because hand and wrist actions are combined and natural, they prefer to view the movement as just a natural result of good hand action. It does not, however, necessarily follow that the wrists will break *correctly*, and a correct wrist break is frequently overlooked as an underlying factor in good hand action.

You need to understand the wrist break just to continue understanding the overall swing. The wrist break should be natural, but it is still a connecting movement between the body and the hands. Since hand action determines clubhead action, it is important to know how the wrists break correctly as well as naturally, where the wrists should break, and how positions affect the movement.

Because the wrist break is considered natural, its importance as a fundamental movement is usually obscured by the fact that it occurs somewhere within the larger movement of the entire backswing. But the backswing, which includes many coordinated movements, often becomes even more complex when you try to connect address positions with the top of the swing without understanding the wrist break.

Studying the wrist break as an independent movement stops the camera, so to speak, making the backswing less complex by allowing you to see how and where the wrists should break for good hand action through the backswing.

The Procedure

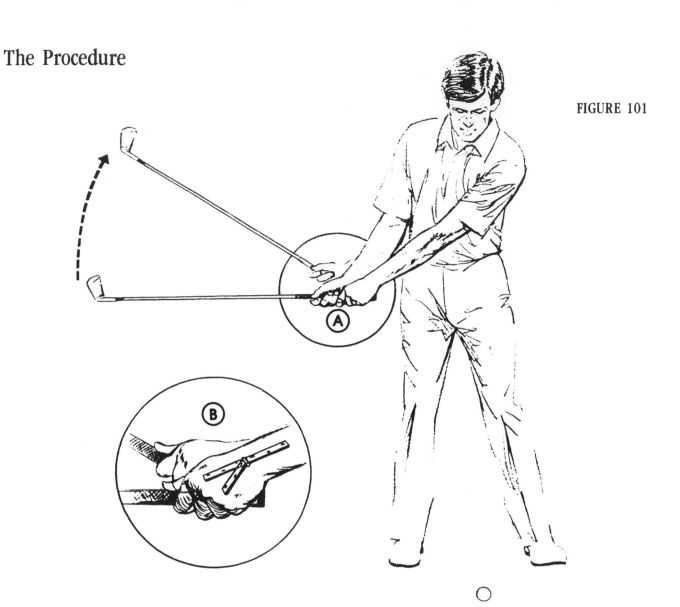

FIGURE 101

- ▸ Waggle positions into place, use the forward press to straighten your left wrist, and push into the toe-up position. (Figure 101A)

- ▸ Keeping your left arm and the shaft in line with each other and the shaft parallel to the directional line, simply hinge your left hand straight upward from the base of the thumb. (Figure 101B) The clubhead will move two or three feet or more, although exactly how far is unimportant as long as the hands are fully cocked upward, *the left wrist is straight* (as opposed to kinking inward or bowing outward), and the toe of the club continues to point straight upward *on* the directional line. (Figure 101C)

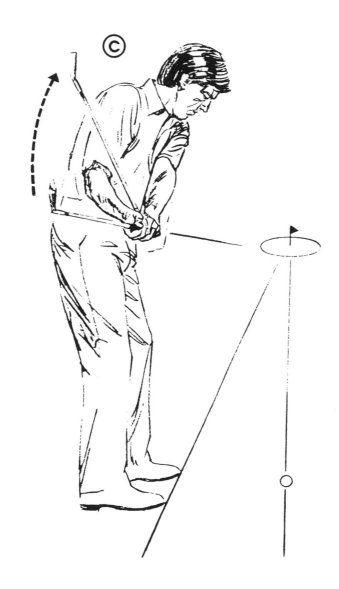

Importance of the Procedure

Breaking your wrist correctly:

A. *keeps your left wrist straight and keeps the clubhead on the right swing plane*

B. *promotes good hand action*

C. *develops clubhead speed by coordinating the wrist break with the shoulder turn*

D. *controls the starting or stopping of swing action*

A: Keeps your left wrist straight and keeps the clubhead on the right swing plane.

The toe-up position of the clubhead in the backswing is a guideline for swinging through the backswing correctly as a result of a correct wrist break. And swinging through the wrist break correctly keeps the club on plane, with the clubface square throughout the backswing.

The left-hand grip and position of the left hand at address are important factors in hand action, not only through the wrist break but throughout the swing as well. To demonstrate how positions at address help swing the club correctly, the left hand only can be used to simulate hand action.

FIGURE 102

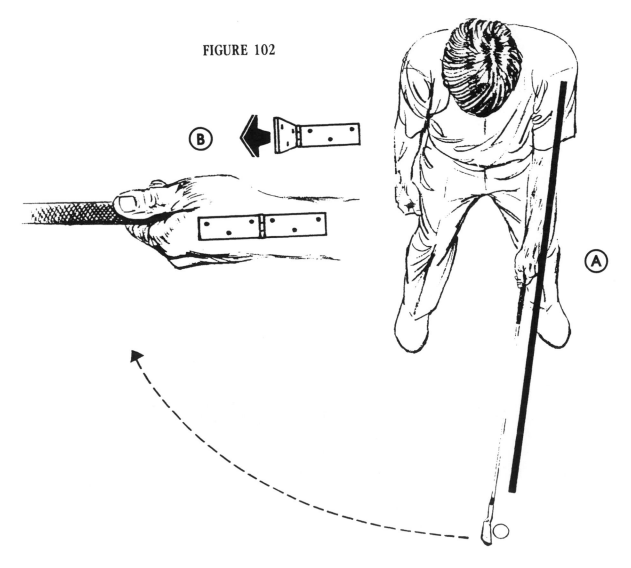

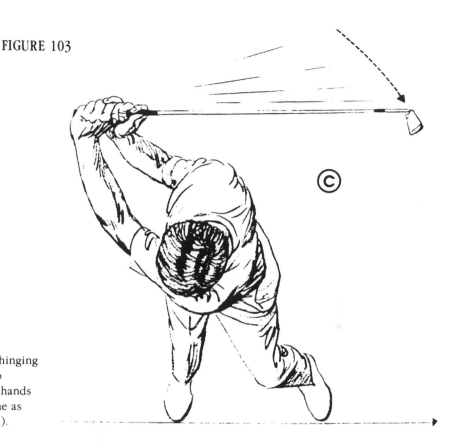

FIGURE 103

A straight left wrist (Figure 102A) hinging straight upward through the toe-up position (Figure 102B) swings the hands and club behind the directional line as the shoulders turn (Figure 103) (C).

The straight arm–shaft position at address, either established by the waggle or reestablished by the forward press, straightens the left wrist in line with the back of the hand, the arm, and the shaft. (Figure 102A) Hinging the wrist straight upward from the base of the thumb, on the directional line, cocks the hand straight upward to maintain the straight wrist through the wrist break. (Figure 102B) Although mechanically doing so cocks the hands straight upward on the directional line, when you're actually swinging through the backswing, the rotational movement of the body turning away from the ball directs the path of the clubhead from the ball, through the toe-up checkpoint, then on behind the directional line to the top of the swing. (Figure 103) As your shoulders turn and your weight shifts right, good hand action then very naturally swings the clubhead up and around on the right swing plane.

Since your hands and arms move into and through the backswing by and with the shoulder turn, your wrists break naturally, without active hand action, by momentum through the swing. Swinging on plane then becomes the result of previously established positions and beginning swing movements combined with practicing to coordinate the action.

Although the path of the clubhead and hand action must be smooth and constant from address to the top of the swing, there is no set action or swing plane that is right for everyone. Nor should flat or upright swings be considered good or bad for all golfers. You'll develop your own golf swing, and the quality of the golf you play, as well as swing results, should determine what's right for you. For good results, however, the clubhead should never go *too* far afield from what is both fundamentally correct and physically possible for you—in this case trying to connect the bottom of the swing with the top of the swing with some kind of wrist break that contributes to good performance.

B: Promotes good hand action.

No effective golf swing can be developed without good hand action, essential parts of which are a correct grip and an accurate wrist break. Neither hand action nor the wrist break should be forced to contribute, however, because both actions are—or should be developed as—natural.

Your hands are pushed into the backswing and on through the wrist break by other swing movements. And all fundamentals, particularly those that affect the weight shift and shoulder turn, affect hand action. The hands swing through the wrist break *correctly*, however, only when they are well positioned, whereupon the wrist break and good hand action become natural.

Because swing movements such as the wrist break rely on the accuracy of positions, the golf swing should always be based on fundamentals to establish these positions carefully. Although using fundamentals ensures that the hands are well positioned before they are pushed into and through the backswing, not everyone establishes *exactly* the same setup, even when using the same fundamentals. Physical build and comfort (as well as personal preference as you become more knowledgeable) also affect positions.

Although both hand action and the wrist break correspond with each individual's setup, for the hands to cock upward through the backswing they must be cocked downward at address; but they shouldn't be cocked too far downward or too far upward as a result of poor positions.

Although *how* the wrists break is determined by the angle of the left wrist at address—which should either be positioned straight or straightened by the forward press—a determining factor in *where* the wrists break is the preset up-and-down angle of the wrists at address,

FIGURE 104

(A)

(B)

Setting the hands too low by leaning over too far (A)
promotes an early wrist break below hip level (B).

which positions the hands to cock early or late through the back-swing. This preset up-and-down angle is determined by how far you are sitting down to the ball, how far your body is leaning over or standing upright, and how far your arms extend to position the (See page 54, Figure 45.)

Leaning over too far or positioning your hands too low precocks the hands to a degree where they are almost fully cocked upward at address. (Figure 104A) This causes less hand action through the

Setting the hands too high by standing too upright (A) promotes a late wrist break above hip level (B).

backswing and a sharper shoulder turn. The parallel shaft position occurs very low and early, below the hips, resulting in a shorter, more compact swing. (Figure 104B) Conversely, cocking the hands completely *downward*, by standing too upright or raising the wrists too high (Figure 105A), establishes a parallel shaft position farther into the backswing, above hip level (Figure 105B), as a result of a bigger swing arc and a later wrist break. The swing is usually more fluid, sweeping more with the arms.

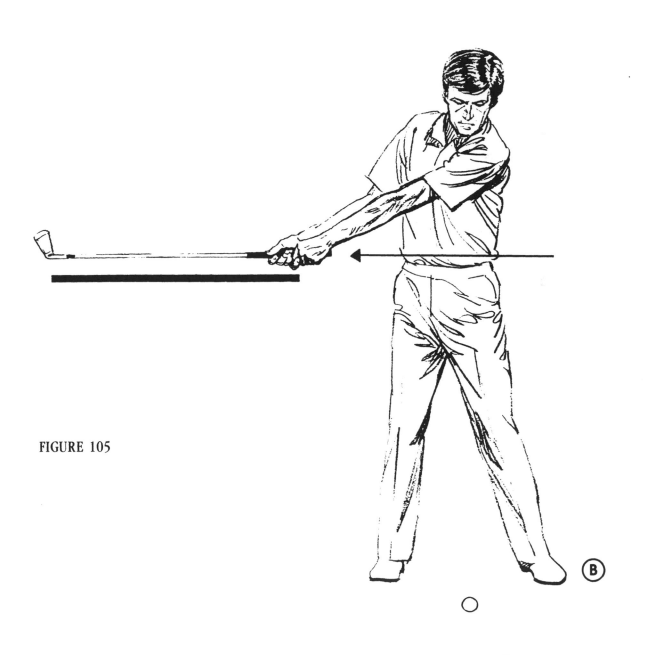

FIGURE 105

Although an early or late wrist break may not be incorrect, fundamentals that prevent leaning over too far or standing too upright (A) promote a wrist break from hip level (B).

Individual setups that deviate from basic positions may not necessarily be inaccurate or even incorrect. They do, however, cause an early or late wrist break, either below or above hip level, as opposed to a more basic position and conventional action (Figure 106A) where the hands and shaft swing onto the parallel line and the wrists break from hip level. (Figure 106B) In general you should try to avoid establishing extreme positions that preset the angle of the wrists too high or too low, which tend to cock the hands upward either early or late. *Exactly* where each golfer reaches the backswing parallel shaft position, however, is really incidental to a good golf

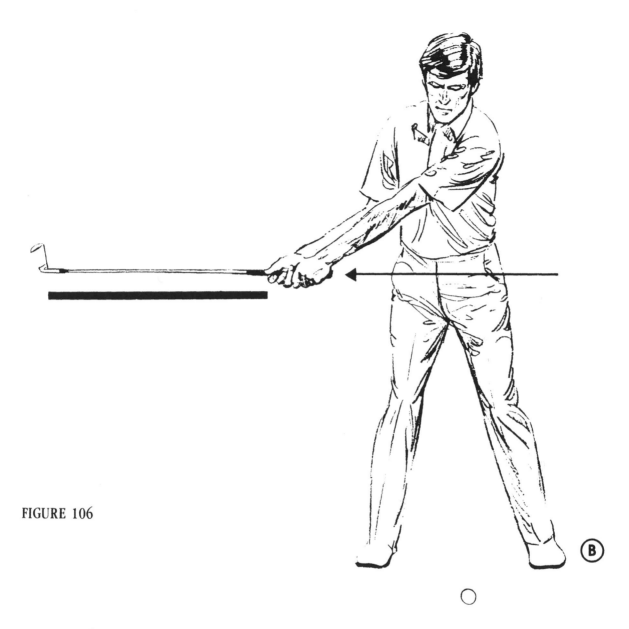

FIGURE 106

swing—as long as positions are not extreme and the hands can still cock upward from the point where the left arm is fully extended and the shaft of the club is parallel to the ground.

The position of the hands in the basic golf swing encourages your wrists to break very gradually from the start of the swing, which in effect they do. Because of a strong hitting instinct, however, your hands also encourage your wrists to break very quickly, especially with a fast backswing. But allowing your hands to control the clubhead, by cocking your hands sharply upward before reaching the parallel shaft position, causes you to pick up the clubhead and

FIGURE 107

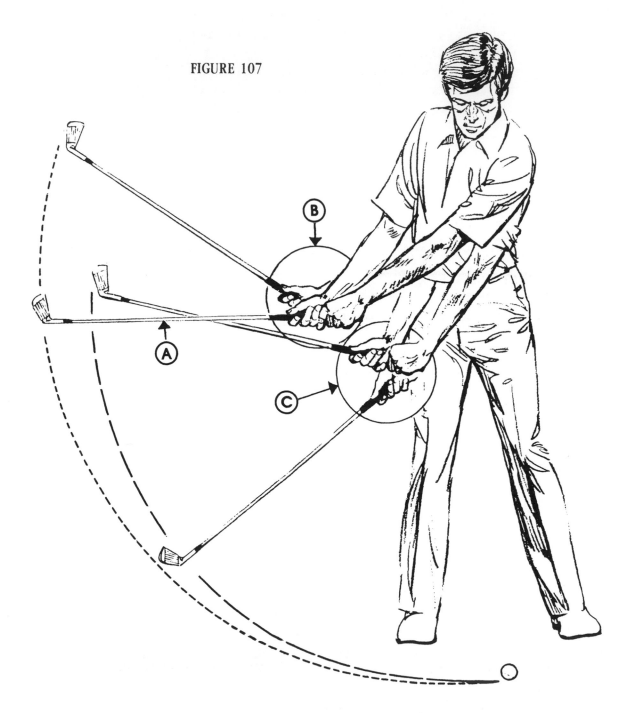

Extending the left arm into a parallel shaft position (A) before the hands cock upward (B) prevents you from picking up the clubhead and narrowing the swing arc due to breaking the wrists too soon (C).

narrow the swing arc (Figure 107); and picking up the clubhead increases momentum at the top of the swing, invariably bending your left elbow due to additional stress.

Very few golfers are able to incorporate a very quick wrist break into the backswing without such problems as bending the left arm, throwing the clubhead from the top, and falling away from the ball. Rather than the hands and clubhead being released through the hitting zone, the hands are released too early, which results in either throwing the clubhead into the ground behind the ball, hitting on top of the ball, or even topping the ball on the upswing as the weight shifts *right* through impact instead of shifting left. When combined with swaying through the ball, "chopping" back down with the driver is the most common cause of skying as the clubhead hits under the ball at impact.

Experienced golfers who deviate from basics, such as those who cock their hands quickly and set the angle early, still use fundamentals. Using personal preference as well, however, they simply adapt the fundamentals to intentionally establish the parallel shaft position low and early to compact the swing, giving themselves more leverage, more body control, and a later release of the hands through impact. As long as the left arm extends through the backswing and the hands can still cock upward from where the shaft is parallel to the ground, setting the angle early may narrow and shorten the swing arc, but the action is not as severe or destructive as picking up the clubhead as the clubhead leaves the ball.

Although experienced golfers may benefit from adjusting or even changing swing mechanics, most of those who deviate too far from basics just continue to encounter problems by establishing poor positions that cause incorrect swing movements. For most golfers, strictly adhering to fundamentals will produce the best results.

Knowing how and when the hands *should* cock upward prevents any mental leeway that allows the wrists to break too soon—or occasionally too late. This concentrates hand action through the toe-up position of the clubhead at hip level. With this in mind, here is a good four-step procedure:

1. Establish a correct setup.
2. Push the left shoulder forward for a good shoulder turn.
3. Keep your arms together and sweep the clubhead toward the toe-up position with a firm, straight left arm.

4. Finally, from the toe-up position, *let* the weight of the clubhead cock your hands upward for natural hand action—bringing to mind an old Scottish adage: "Leave yer axe at home, Laddie, and bring yer broom."

C: Develops clubhead speed by coordinating the wrist break with the shoulder turn.

As mentioned earlier, by not teaching how and where the wrists should break, golf instructors frequently leave the wrist break in an elusive place "somewhere through the backswing." Not quite certain where this action should take place, golfers have a tendency to allow the wrists to break too soon, or occasionally too late, to promote good timing and coordination.

Power in golf is generated by the body and transferred to the clubhead through the hands. Although the wrists break naturally, learning to let the hands cock upward from the point where the shaft of the club is parallel to the ground and on the directional line coordinates the wrist break with the shoulder turn and pivot to develop additional hitting power. The wrist break simply stores this power through the backswing for delivery at impact in the form of clubhead speed.

D: Controls the starting or stopping of swing action.

Although the wrist break is part of overall swing action, it is also part of the setup in that hand, wrist, and swing action can all be "felt out" during the waggle in a little bottom-of-the-swing maneuver behind the ball. Just as the forward press gives you a running start on swing movement by putting your legs into motion, the waggle gives you a running start on swing accuracy by breaking the wrists back and forth while edging the clubhead toward the toe-up position and returning the clubface square. Keeping your left wrist straight and cocking the hands straight upward by using the waggle procedure programs your hands to start the clubhead on the right swing path.

Waggling the hands and clubhead provides a final opportunity for you to get set for the shot. This sense-and-feel procedure helps train your mind and muscles to start the swing automatically; with practice you'll find the backswing starting of its own accord on one of the waggle movements. (Figure 108) At this point positions must be established flawlessly and movements coordinated, because

FIGURE 108

Waggling the clubhead back and forth with hand and wrist action (A) gives you a running start on swing action until the backswing starts of its own accord with a firm left arm and shoulder turn (B).

beyond the wrist break through the backswing, momentum of the clubhead combines with the shoulder turn and weight shift for reflex action on the downswing—making it increasingly difficult to stop the swing for "overs" to correct a faulty beginning.

Stubbing the clubhead on the backswing makes it doubly difficult to stop the swing to start again. As the clubhead releases from being stuck for a moment, it quickly snaps on through the wrist break and into reflexive movements. Stubbing is caused by either planting the clubhead too firmly behind the ball—particularly against the grain of the grass—or positioning the hands behind the ball where the hands pull downward.

Using an up-and-down or back-and-forth waggle helps prevent stubbing problems by lifting and setting the clubhead softly behind the ball with the hands slightly ahead. When stubbing does occur, a deliberately slow move away from the ball makes it possible to stop the swing and start again by minimizing the force of the backswing movement.

Chapter Seventeen

Fundamental No. 12: Completing the Backswing

To complete the backswing, you simply continue pushing the clubhead on through the toe-up position with a firm left arm. Consequently, this part of the swing depends on the accuracy of previously established positions.

Preestablished positions have in effect built one whole position through the wrist break. If this position is accurate, the fundamental movement that completes the shoulder turn also completes the backswing, accurately establishing positions at the top of the swing that help complete the rest of the swing with power and ease.

The Procedure

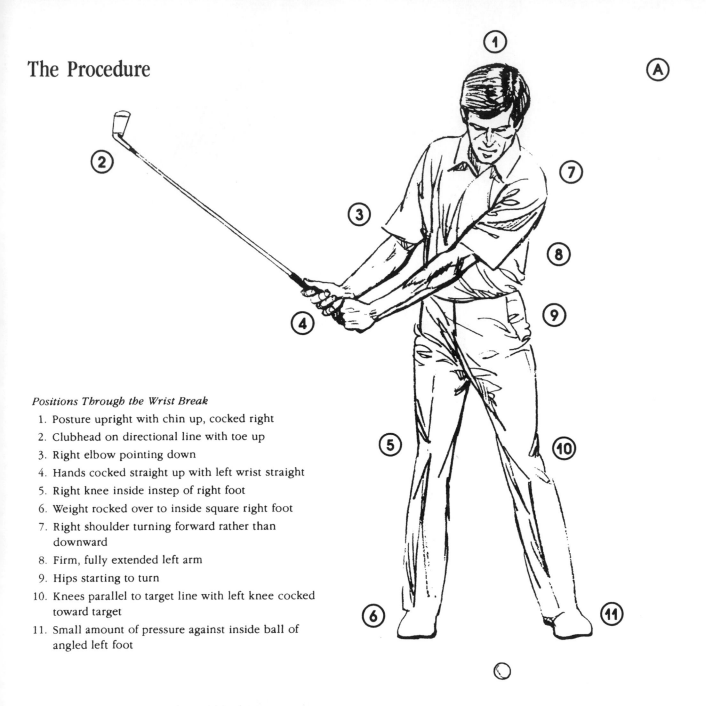

Positions Through the Wrist Break

1. Posture upright with chin up, cocked right
2. Clubhead on directional line with toe up
3. Right elbow pointing down
4. Hands cocked straight up with left wrist straight
5. Right knee inside instep of right foot
6. Weight rocked over to inside square right foot
7. Right shoulder turning forward rather than downward
8. Firm, fully extended left arm
9. Hips starting to turn
10. Knees parallel to target line with left knee cocked toward target
11. Small amount of pressure against inside ball of angled left foot

▶ Rebuild the swing by waggling positions into place. Use the forward press and, being particularly careful to prevent the left knee from being too active, push the clubhead into the toe-up position. Break your wrists mechanically; then check to see that all positions defined in the illustration are as accurate as possible. (Figure 110A)

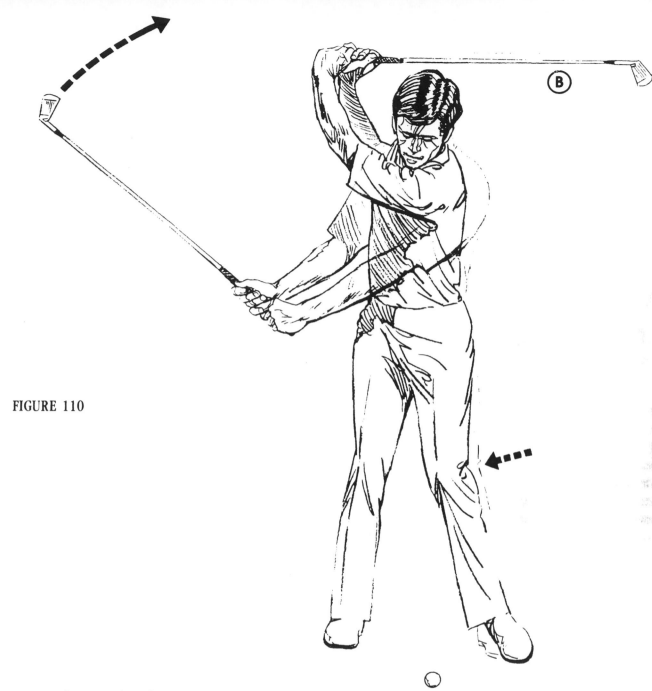

FIGURE 110

From the wrist break position, to complete the backswing, push the clubhead upward with a firm left arm and simply turn away from the ball and around the strong right leg to complete the weight shift and shoulder turn. Let your shoulders turn your hips and let the left leg *swing* inward. Keep your left knee aimed ahead, however, by maintaining pressure against the inside ball of the left foot. This pulls the left heel inward and lifts it off the ground. The clubhead swings behind the directional line at the top of the swing, and the hands swing upward either toward or over the right shoulder. (Figure 110B)

Importance of the Procedure

Completing the backswing:

A. *completes the weight shift and shoulder turn*

B. *promotes natural left heel action and maintains the swing center with good footwork*

C. *swings the left leg inward and promotes good timing*

D. *completes the coil-recoil action by completing the shoulder turn*

E. *establishes correct positions at the top of the swing*

A: Completes the weight shift and shoulder turn.

Flexing your right knee inward and setting your weight inside the square right foot strengthens the right side for the weight shift, whereupon pushing against the right foot while turning away from the ball and pushing the clubhead through the toe-up position to the top of the swing completes the weight shift and shoulder turn.

Although no single position or movement should ever be given precedence over others when applying fundamentals, very few movements make a good swing feel better—or work better—than just keeping the right elbow down and turning around the well-positioned right leg while shifting the weight correctly through the backswing.

B: Promotes natural left heel action and maintains the swing center with good footwork.

Although most of the weight shifts to the right through the backswing, a small amount remains on the left to maintain the swing center and help prevent swaying; consequently a small amount of pressure continues to build against the inside ball of the left foot as your heel lifts slightly and your leg pulls inward. The action not only helps you stay steady over the ball but also establishes a very important "ready" position of the left foot for when the weight shifts back to the left. Your left knee now juts forward, but without dipping downward, as your heel lifts off the ground and pulls inward with left leg action. How far your knee juts forward is related to how far your heel lifts naturally. The important thing, essentially, is that you develop natural footwork through practice as your weight shifts back and forth.

Never make a conscious effort to keep your left heel down or lift it through the backswing. Good footwork develops naturally as a result of left leg action coordinating with the shoulder turn and pivot as your weight shifts right. Although your left heel *generally* lifts off the ground and pulls inward with the backswing movement, the action of the left *knee* controls the movement of the leg, which in turn determines the action of the heel.

Keeping the left heel on the ground throughout the backswing is a very natural part of the golf swing for many great players—Ben Hogan and Seve Ballesteros, for instance—but keeping the heel down is a *result*, not a *cause*, of developing more torque and more control by preventing quick left leg action. Although this action may add power for more experienced golfers, swinging flat-footed to the top of the swing is a major cause of the reverse weight shift for most golfers because it prevents the leg from swinging inward and keeps the weight on the left. And when you consciously lift your left heel, you generally lift the heel straight up to get the same adverse results. You can develop a better swing by practicing the natural action of the left heel in a swinging leg movement that culminates in good foot-work.

To sense the feeling of good timing in coordinating swinging legs and good footwork with a hitting action, turn a short iron upside down and grasp the shaft below the clubhead as if you were holding a stick. Keep the head in place and just whack the grass with the stick—first with the right hand, then with the left—while turning your body and shifting your weight back and forth. Study the natural actions carefully, for the swinging-hitting action of the feet and legs is the same as for hitting a golf ball.

C: *Swings the left leg inward and promotes good timing.*

Keeping your knees parallel by preventing your left knee from dipping down and in or from jutting too far forward and preventing a quick pivot by briefly restricting left knee action, are movements unique to the golf swing and meant to develop a coil-recoil action between the upper and lower body. Once you understand that, however, you should make every effort to practice and groove the swinging action into a natural movement. Your left leg must swing inward to put the swing in golf. Swinging legs, good footwork, and the shoulder turn and pivot are all part of the whole. One cannot be independent of the others.

The left knee, in particular, continues to be a key to good leg action. Keeping a little pressure against the inside ball of the left foot throughout the backswing helps you keep your knee forward while, at the same time, letting the leg swing inward as your body turns away from the ball (Figure 111). You should practice keeping the knee forward only as the backswing starts. Remember that the point of learning any swing movement is not to encourage conscious action while playing, in this case either restricting or promoting leg movement, but to help you understand the overall swing so you can groove the swing in practice.

The small movement away from the ball is a critical moment in golf because it directly influences timing—and timing affects coordination. A deliberately slow move, if only for the first few inches, allows you time to coordinate essential positions and movements the moment the backswing starts. It takes time to catch your weight inside your right foot as your weight shifts right *and* keep pressure against the ball of your left foot as your leg swings inward. Good legwork and footwork then more than compensate for lack of speed and muscle through the backswing by preventing such things as swaying back and forth or up and down, overswinging, or a reverse weight shift while, at the same time, adding driving power to the legs.

It takes work and practice to coordinate the movement of the knees, legs, and feet to groove good legwork and footwork. Trying to maintain or establish positions with conscious thought while swinging, rather than grooving them into subconscious, reflexive movements through practice, exaggerates actions and changes rhythm through the swing. In this case it keeps the left knee anchored too long in the swing, keeps the left heel on the ground, and prevents the leg from swinging inward. Pushing the clubhead into a completion of the swing pulls the left leg into a swinging movement as the shoulders turn the hips. Aiming the left knee forward, as opposed to keeping the knee forward, will not prevent the swinging movement. Experimentation and practice, along with checking and waggling positions, soon promote natural leg action and important footwork.

FIGURE 111

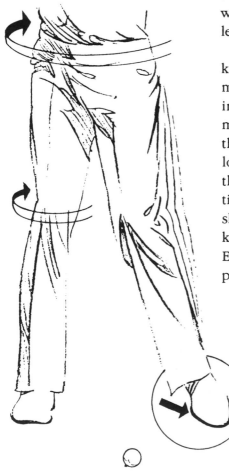

As the body turns away from the ball (around the right leg) and the weight shifts right on the backswing, a small amount of pressure builds against the inside ball of the left foot as the left leg swings inward with the heel off the ground.

D: Completes the coil-recoil action by completing the shoulder turn.

Whether the golf swing is natural or unnatural does not necessarily depend on your inherent ability. Certainly some people have more natural coordination than others, but particularly in golf, you develop coordination using fundamentals to coordinate positions and movements. Nowhere is this more pronounced than at the exact junction of the swing where the arms swing upright together as the body turns rotationally.

Although you shouldn't expect to swing outside your physical ability, all golfers—even senior golfers—fulfill their own potential by completing the shoulder turn. Those who are not physically adept, however, should not expect to swing as far as others, because forcing the shoulders to turn beyond what is natural ruins the timing of a good golf swing.

A parallel shaft at the top of the swing is commonly used to indicate a completed shoulder turn. A more accurate indication, however, is not how far the shaft swings but whether the lower body starts the downswing and the hands pull downward as a result of reflex action created by the shoulder turn.

Reflex action occurs when the upper body coils against the resistance of the lower body and the lower body recoils to start the downswing. Coil-recoil translates into torque and release. *Torque* is defined as "a force causing rotation," and *release* is defined as "to let go" or "let loose." Although commonly referring to the hands and clubhead through impact, release is the releasing of any action anywhere in the swing at just the right moment to get the best results—which includes the lower body. Unless the lower body releases *first* from the top, however, to pull the hands and clubhead down, the hands and clubhead release too soon from the top of the swing.

Good swing mechanics encourage reflexive actions from the start of the swing—and *all* positions and movements contribute something to the cause and effect.

Anchoring the base of the body turn just as the backswing starts, by keeping your left knee forward, is an important key to coiling the upper body and torquing the big back muscles between the shoulders and the hips. Very little restraint is needed, however, to make the system work; only enough to prevent the hips from turning too soon or from turning too far along with the shoulder turn. Keeping a small amount of pressure against the inside ball of the left foot while completing the backswing will help you develop the reflex action.

Coil-recoil translates into torque and release.

In the study of fundamentals you've learned that the shoulders turn the hips. In the application of fundamentals, however, since the backswing happens so quickly, a good swing thought in practice is to make certain that the hips turn rotationally, rather than laterally, by turning just the right hip away from the ball after the backswing starts. A key swing thought, remember, is deliberate concentration applied to anything specific that either helps you develop the swing in practice or helps the swing work better when playing. In this case grooving the swing in practice is extremely important to coordinate footwork and leg action with the shoulder turn and pivot.

Square hips at address enable your hips to turn as far right as left from the center of their rotational ability. Restricting your hips somewhat develops more power as your hips make a one-quarter turn through the backswing and a three-quarter turn back through the ball. (Figure 112) Completing the shoulder turn by pushing the clubhead on up to the top of the swing causes a release of the hips from the top in the recoil action. Momentum of the clubhead as it approaches the top of the swing helps hold the shoulder position *at* the top that fraction of a second necessary for lower body action to start back first.

Golfers who establish accurate positions and push through the toe-up position—by pushing the left shoulder forward with a firmly extended left arm—generally have no problem completing the shoulder turn. Extending the right arm with the elbow down wedges the clubhead upward; and the simultaneous action of both arms in the swing contributes to good action.

The shoulder turn should not be maneuvered or controlled. Manipulating the shoulders—either around the head, under the chin, or up and down—not only overemphasizes the action but also complicates timing and rhythm and prevents the hands and clubhead from staying on plane. Positions at address coordinate with swing movements, and like other swing movements, completing the shoulder turn should ideally be only the result of all fundamentals being used correctly.

E: *Establishes correct positions at the top of the swing.*
The exact position at the top of the swing that returns the clubhead squarely and powerfully through the ball is so dependent on so many things that less-than-perfect golfers are seldom able to assume this basic position with any degree of consistent accuracy.

FIGURE 112

Coil-Recoil

Keeping the left knee forward just as the backswing starts produces more power as the hips make a one-quarter turn through the backswing and a three-quarter release back through the ball.

Although the average golfer should not expect to play perfect golf by always swinging into this top-of-the-swing perfection, every dedicated golfer should strive for near perfection to compensate for things that do go wrong. The more fundamentals that coordinate with a full shoulder turn, the more likely you are to reach your own level of proficiency by consistently swinging as *close* as possible to this top-of-the-swing position; and consistency is a more realistic goal than perfection for most golfers.

The golf swing is demanding, but not to the point of being inflexible. Although the accompanying illustration depicts the perfect position at the top of the swing, that is because it depicts the perfect golfer—a nonexistent entity. Remember that you need not obtain these *exact* results to play creditable golf.

Pushing the clubhead on through to the top of the swing with a firm, fully extended left arm completes the shoulder turn and automatically establishes the following positions. Studying these checkpoints will help you understand what can be flexible in your own golf swing. (Figure 113)

1. The left-hand grip is firmly in the fingers with the left thumb directly under the shaft. This position is not flexible. The last three fingers of the left hand must be very firm to prevent you from dropping the club or letting go at the top. The left thumb reinforces this strong grip, and the two together prevent you from overswinging or dropping the club below parallel. The left thumb helps hold positions at the top of the swing during the transition of the backswing to the downswing—and it is a good position to learn to feel at the top.

2. The left arm is firm but may flex somewhat. The old adage that admonishes golfers to keep the left arm stiff is outmoded and incorrect in describing how the left arm should react. The action is really a matter of semantics: the arm must be straight, as opposed to bent; it can be flexed, as opposed to rigid; and the summation of the two is that it *must* be firm. How much flex develops depends on several things: the position of the arm and elbow at address; individual strength to withstand momentum of the clubhead through the swing; and, most of all, timing and tempo determined by the speed of the backswing.

A deliberately smooth backswing with a full shoulder turn helps keep the left arm firm at the top of the swing by pushing the clubhead to the top *with* the shoulder turn rather than flinging it up there with the hands.

FIGURE 113

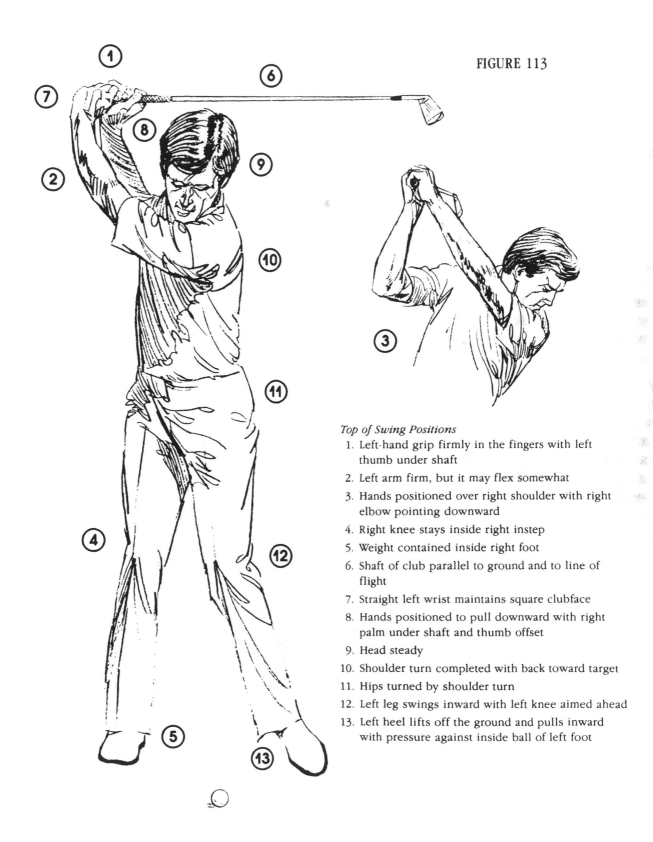

Top of Swing Positions

1. Left-hand grip firmly in the fingers with left thumb under shaft
2. Left arm firm, but it may flex somewhat
3. Hands positioned over right shoulder with right elbow pointing downward
4. Right knee stays inside right instep
5. Weight contained inside right foot
6. Shaft of club parallel to ground and to line of flight
7. Straight left wrist maintains square clubface
8. Hands positioned to pull downward with right palm under shaft and thumb offset
9. Head steady
10. Shoulder turn completed with back toward target
11. Hips turned by shoulder turn
12. Left leg swings inward with left knee aimed ahead
13. Left heel lifts off the ground and pulls inward with pressure against inside ball of left foot

3. The hands are positioned toward or over the right shoulder as the right elbow moves away from the side, pointing downward. Swinging your hands up and back toward the right shoulder prevents the swing from being too flat or too steep beyond the toe-up position—and how far from the side the right elbow moves is determined by the length of the shot, which determines the length of the backswing. Short shots with a short shaft require a shorter backswing, which keeps the elbow in close, but the right elbow *must* move away from the side for a full golf shot to prevent both narrowing the swing arc and restricting the shoulder turn. There is a vast difference, however, between the elbow pointing down and moving away or moving away by flying upward. Combining a full shoulder turn with flying the elbow, for instance, swings the club beyond parallel and across the line at the top of the swing. In a well-controlled swing the right elbow points down toward the ground at address and through the backswing, which positions the elbow at the top to pull the hands and clubhead down.

4. The right knee stays inside the right instep. There is no leeway in this position. Once your knee goes beyond your right instep, your weight is rolling across your right foot and pulling your body laterally. A good checkpoint in practice is the relationship of the knee to the instep to make certain the body is turning and not swaying off the ball.

5. The weight is shifted to the inside of the right foot. This position and movement cannot be flexible. The weight must shift to the right to

FIGURE 114

Swinging parallel (A);
swinging behind parallel (B);
swinging beyond parallel, or
"crossing the line" (C).

shift back to the left in the coil-recoil action of the upper and lower body. The upper body coils against the lower body by turning the shoulders and shifting the weight against the strong right foot. The recoil action of the lower body then springs away from the right foot, shifting the weight back to the left to start the downswing action.

Flexing the right knee inward and setting the weight inside the square right foot strengthens the right side for the weight shift, whereupon pushing the clubhead through the toe-up position and turning away from the ball—by turning around the strong right leg—prevents rolling across the right foot through the backswing while coordinating the rest of the backswing movements.

6. The shaft of the club is parallel to the ground and to the target line. Although most golfers rarely swing exactly parallel, you can use this checkpoint when swinging woods and long irons (Figure 114A) as a measure of accuracy at address and good clubhead control through the backswing. Since it is not easy to see positions at the top, however, and since golfers are apt to be concerned more with getting the club to the top than with where the shaft is when it arrives, it is a good position to have checked occasionally for discrepancies in the swing.

Swinging behind parallel by swinging flat or "laying off" (Figure 114B), or swinging across the line by swinging beyond parallel (Figure 114C), indicates that you're swinging off-plane by either swinging the club around your body or allowing your hips to turn too far with the

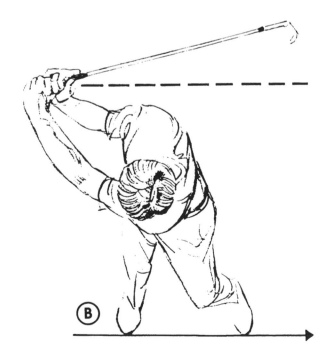

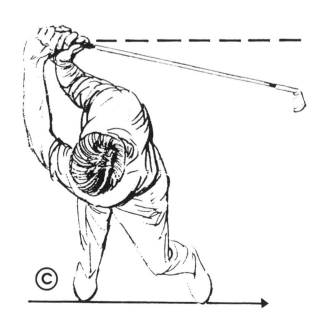

FIGURE 115

Swinging short of parallel (A);
swinging below parallel due
to overswinging (B).

shoulder turn from the start of the swing. Swinging short of parallel with woods or long irons (Figure 115A) may indicate an incomplete or restricted shoulder turn, too wide a stance, swinging flat-footed, or an incorrect wrist break and flat swing pattern. And overswinging—or swinging below parallel (Figure 115B)—is caused by any number of things: letting go with the left hand, bending the left arm, swinging too fast, collapsing the left wrist, angling the right foot open, or, just as in *crossing* the line, overturning the hips and shoulders.

Overswinging is a much more common and a more serious problem than a shorter, restricted swing, because your hands swing too far beyond a point where good lower body action moving back to the left can pull the hands downward. When your hands swing too far beyond the top of the swing, it is difficult to shift your weight left because the clubhead is thrown outward and upward from the top of the swing and momentum from the clubhead action prevents the weight from shifting left by keeping it on the right.

Overswinging is seldom the result of just one thing, making it difficult to correct at times. If not too excessive, however, overswinging may be corrected by one of several methods: lengthening the left thumb to a long thumb position, firming the left arm and grip at address, starting a more deliberate movement away from the ball, checking the wrist break for a square left wrist, and correcting positions and movements that promote a shoulder turn while preventing excessive turning of the hips along with the shoulders.

If overswinging remains a problem, regardless of corrections, practicing a three-quarter backswing while working on the *follow-through* will help you develop a shorter backswing to position your hands correctly. It simply takes more practice to correct overswinging by changing some of the swing thoughts.

Although many golfers swing off-parallel or off-plane and still return to a good position at impact, it takes almost perfect timing and control to swing too far from parallel or too far off-plane and still coordinate good lower body action with good hand action to pull the hands and clubhead down from the top and hit squarely through the ball—at least with any degree of consistency.

All positions and movements affect swinging parallel to both the ground and target lines, and physical build and ability as well as individual style are also determining factors. Young, flexible golfers, for instance, or those with somewhat fluid swings, frequently swing below parallel; senior golfers with less muscular flexibility very seldom swing so far; and very strong golfers with short, compact swings are often very short of parallel and still get excellent results.

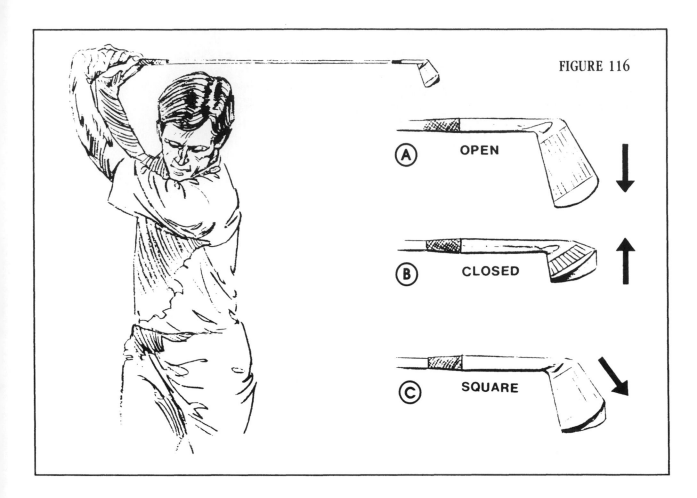

FIGURE 116

(A) OPEN

(B) CLOSED

(C) SQUARE

Clubface Angles at the
Top of the Swing

An open clubface (A) points
the toe toward the ground. A
closed clubface (B) aims the
face toward the sky. A square
clubface (C) is halfway in
between.

Every factor has some bearing on swinging parallel (and swinging
short of or beyond is not all bad if not too excessive), but an angled
alignment of the shaft to the ground or to the target line is most likely
caused by swing defects. Most golfers who consistently fail to reach or
swing beyond parallel with woods or long irons are just losing power
with a faulty golf swing.

7. *The straight left wrist maintains a square clubface.* A square
clubface at the top of the swing is more apt to return to square at impact
than one that is open or closed. To square the clubface at the top, you
must establish a straight left wrist at address and maintain it through the
backswing. A firm left arm and full shoulder turn then push the shaft on
up to parallel, where a straight left wrist becomes the key to a square
clubface.

Clubface angles at the top are indicated by where the toe of the
clubhead points: an open clubface points the toe of the clubhead
straight toward the ground (A); a closed clubface turns the clubface

FIGURE 117

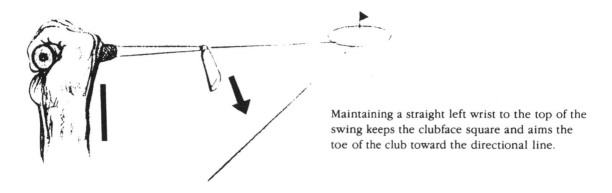

Maintaining a straight left wrist to the top of the swing keeps the clubface square and aims the toe of the club toward the directional line.

FIGURE 118

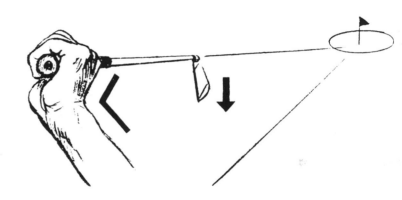

Kinking the left wrist at the top of the swing opens the clubface and points the toe of the club straight down.

FIGURE 119

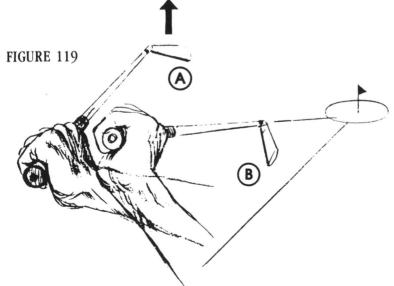

Collapsing the left wrist through the backswing also flattens the swing plane. Although the angle of the clubface may appear to be closed (A), the clubface is open at the top of the swing—the same as with an upright swing and the same wrist action (B).

skyward (B); and halfway in between the two is the correct square position (C). (Figure 116)

When the shaft of the club is parallel, a straight left wrist and square clubface aim the toe of the club directly toward the directional line (Figure 117), whereupon the clubface returns to square at impact with the left wrist still straight, the arm and shaft straight in line with each other, and the left hand in the strongest backhand hitting position.

Keeping the left wrist entirely straight at the top of the swing is difficult. As your body turns away from the ball and the clubhead continues upward, a slight concave kink may start to develop as your left wrist gives through the backswing to compensate for the two opposing directions. Although it is more comfortable to let the wrist kink inward—and you should not be overly concerned if you're unable to maintain a completely square position—a bending left wrist through the backswing progressively opens the clubface, pointing the toe of the clubhead toward the ground. (Figure 118) The swing plane flattens, and the more the left wrist kinks as it approaches the top of the swing, the more difficult it becomes to return the clubface squarely toward the target at impact.

The position to be avoided at the top of the swing is a completely open or closed clubface. Along with the tendency of the left wrist to kink, there is a tendency toward total collapse and dropping the club-head at the top—*unless* your wrist is straight as your hands cock upward through the toe-up position.

When your hands cock through the backswing with your left wrist bent inward, your hands swing upward incorrectly, with the left palm under the shaft rather than the right. As momentum increases the bend, either the swing flattens as the wrist collapses (A), which opens the clubface completely (although it may appear to be closed with the flat swing pattern), or, if an upright swing can be maintained, the same open clubface is established at the top (B). (Figure 119) Either position at the top of the swing generally returns the clubface open to slice the ball because the clubface is too far out of alignment to square the face at impact. Slicing also occurs with the left wrist straight if the swing pattern is flat because the clubface cuts across the ball at impact.

An otherwise perfect downswing with the weight shifting left and the arms pulling downward may even accentuate the collapsing of a weak left wrist, not only hurting the kinked-in wrist at impact but either toeing the ball off to the right or else smothering the ball off to the left as the right hand overpowers the left.

Although inaccuracy at the top of the swing causes poor golf shots, you should not become unduly concerned with an open or closed clubface at the top because neither is a *direct* cause of poor results at impact. Incorrect top-of-the-swing positions are, in themselves, incorrect positions as the result of some address or swing defect. Unless you're intentionally slicing or hooking, or "drawing" the ball left or "fading" it right, when the clubface is anything other than square it really makes little difference whether it is open or closed at the top.

Just as incorrect positions throughout the swing must be prevented or corrected, so must errors with the clubface be avoided. And knowing what *prevents* inaccuracy is the essence of understanding clubface angles.

8. The hands are positioned to pull downward with the right palm under the shaft and the thumb offset. Positioning your hands to work effectively from the top of the swing is very difficult without the other basics that position the hands correctly. It is important to know where the hands should be at the top, however, so you can work on other basics that help position the hands correctly. Overswinging, for instance, swings your hands too far back, leaving them unable to pull downward, and an incomplete shoulder turn rarely swings them far enough.

In addition to a straight left wrist, a corresponding position that strongly reinforces the hands at the top of the swing is the right palm under the shaft with the thumb offset. The position is a good checkpoint, indicating not only strong, accurate hand positions but also a completed shoulder turn with the right elbow down. Positions and movements that *enable* the right palm to swing under the shaft, such as swinging your hands high toward the right shoulder, a good grip, and weight shift, help correct a chronic slice.

Along with the palm under the shaft, the offset right thumb prevents the right hand from stopping the swing too soon, enabling the shaft to continue on to parallel at the top by completing the shoulder turn.

9. Your head remains steady. Maintaining a steady head is a key pivotal position that keeps the swing center intact, thereby enabling your shoulders to turn around your head and at a right angle to your spine because of the fixed position. Although keeping your head steady may occasionally be a good swing thought, this deliberate action by itself seldom compensates for missing fundamentals. A steady head should be only an indication that your body is not swaying off the ball on the backswing, moving through the ball at impact, or moving up or down. A steady head is more apt to occur as a result of establishing positions that prevent swaying, such as squaring the right foot and

FIGURE 120

Shadow test for moving head.

keeping the chin up. Thus keeping your head steady by keeping an eye on the ball becomes a useful swing thought.

A simple check for head movement is to face away from the sun and align your head's shadow to some point on the ground while practice-swinging. If your shadow moves off that point, you must correct the swing itself to prevent the back-and-forth or up-and-down movement. (Figure 120)

10. The shoulder turn is completed with your back toward the target. A full shoulder turn normally turns your back to the target as your shoulders turn 90 degrees from the address position. (See page 176, Figure 114A.) Although many may not be able to turn this far, all golfers must complete the shoulder turn within their ability to promote reflexive lower-body action from the top of the swing; otherwise either the hands and clubhead start back first or the right shoulder starts forward, rather than pulling downward, from the top of the swing—and much too soon. Although slicing results most commonly from throwing the clubhead from the top, other inaccuracies such as pulling, smothering, and hitting behind the ball also result from simply not completing the shoulder turn.

11. The hips are turned by the shoulder turn. A full pivot on the backswing is the natural result of a full shoulder turn because the shoulders turn the hips.

12. The left leg swings inward with the left knee aimed ahead. Although good leg action is essential to a good golf swing, many variations in natural leg action, as well as footwork, can be found in golf. But natural is not necessarily the best unless it produces good results. Although there can, and should, be some leeway in how the feet and legs respond in golf (and *every* effort should be made to develop natural movements), understanding how the left leg should swing inward is important in practice to help you develop the best coordination.

13. The left heel lifts off the ground and pulls inward with a small amount of pressure against the inside ball of the foot. Keeping a small amount of pressure against the inside ball of the left foot as your weight shifts right helps you keep your head in place and stay steady over the ball. Combined with shifting your weight and turning, this lifts your left heel naturally and bends your left knee forward as your left leg swings inward. Although leg action and footwork are still individual preferences and take practice, working toward improvement in these two areas is especially helpful to more experienced golfers who want to improve in golf.

Chapter Eighteen

Practicing the Backswing

Now that you have the necessary tools, building a sound, repeating golf swing is a matter of learning to use those tools with confidence and proficiency. You can't build or repair anything by keeping the tools inside the box. You must take them out and use them.

If you've been reading this book just as a reference, flipping through in search of things you think may help your golf swing, you may have missed the importance of the step-by-step procedure for developing your swing. It is not enough to presume that positions and movements you thought were correct—and therefore remain unchecked—are in fact contributing to a sound golf swing. Misapplication of even one fundamental may adversely affect your whole swing. If you have not been using this manual as a textbook for learning, now is the time to review fundamentals up to this point.

In a step-by-step learning process you will generally find at least one fundamental that needs correction. Like comfortable old shoes, these imperfections become so ingrained that they may be difficult to part with. New fundamentals, however, just like new shoes, soon become comfortable with use.

Applying just one new fundamental that seems foreign to your swing will make the entire swing feel different. You can develop confidence in making changes, however, by becoming familiar with how a new position or movement feels at the exact place where it is incorporated into the swing. That is, conscientiously apply the fundamental involved, practice the correction, then gradually adapt it to its immediate surroundings.

The success of the downswing and follow-through is determined largely by cause and effect, in that the downswing reflects established positions at address followed by a good backswing. Although it may be difficult to refrain from hitting balls or playing golf, practicing just swing mechanics in the areas needed to correct or improve the swing will pay dividends later on.

Units of the swing that have been introduced and can be practiced separately are the grip, position of address, waggle, forward press, toe-up position of the clubhead, wrist break, and top-of-the-swing position. Starting with the grip, repeatedly practice each unit that uses a new fundamental until that part of the swing is comfortably correct. Only then should you connect that unit and those that precede it with the next.

Connect units in the swing slowly and gradually, as well as deliberately and precisely. It is important to feel, as well as know, how corrected fundamentals fit and affect each other. When all of the units are accurate and can be connected deliberately, a sound setup and a reliable backswing are simply a matter of smoothing out the process into a continuous, well-timed movement, from first stepping up to the ball to reaching the top of the backswing.

Because we've been building the swing in bits and pieces, it's quite possible that you see one or two fundamentals as more important than the others. No matter how exciting it may seem to have discovered "the secret" to a better swing, you must keep this one element in proper perspective. The golf swing is a combination of many things, and no fundamental, no matter how important it seems, should ever be given precedence over others as *the* solution to the swing. The only workable "secret" in golf is the rhythmic application of *all* of the fundamentals.

Rhythm is not to be confused with tempo in the swing. Tempo is the speed with which each individual swings naturally, and tempo varies between very fast and very slow. Rhythm, however, is the smooth acceleration of the arms and clubhead within the tempo of the swing that builds up power and clubhead speed with good coordination and creates good timing. Although tempo varies among individuals—and even among shots by an individual player at times—rhythm must not vary within the tempo of the swing.

Within each golf swing where all of this takes place, there can be only one fast *place*—or one single fastest moment—because the body cannot coordinate within a swinging movement to swing fast twice. To

> The only workable "secret" in golf is the rhythmic application of *all* of the fundamentals.

generate clubhead speed and release the power through the ball, this accelerated movement cannot be made away from the ball but must be reserved for the arms and hands accelerating down from the top for the one fastest moment to occur at impact.

When your swing is sound, practicing the backswing to combine rhythm and tempo is just as important as establishing and practicing basics, because results through the rest of the swing depend almost totally on timing. Maintaining rhythm, however, depends on first developing and then protecting a vulnerable part of the swing—concentration. Concentration is not easily obtained to begin with and is hard to regain if lost.

Tempo, rhythm, and concentration—which all add up to good timing—are initially determined by your natural temperament and disposition, which affect your attitude. This in turn is reflected in the pace and rhythm of walking in golf as well as in swinging a golf club. The fragile nature of concentration is such, however, that it is easily shattered by any of many factors that affect disposition and change attitude: sudden outside distractions, a change in weather, temporary imperfection, even the pace and attitude of other golfers. Any of these factors can quickly change your timing by changing your tempo and rhythm. This too may be reflected in a change of pace in walking as well as in the swing—either of which is quickly affected by a loss of concentration triggered by a change in attitude.

Developing concentration is a talent in itself. Once you've developed it, you must remain consciously alert to the fact that a loss of concentration results in—and is affected by—a sudden change in timing in the swing itself. Aside from learning to be more patient and becoming more tolerant, staying away from distractions, such as idle conversation, and accepting limitations are two of the easier ways to retain concentration.

You can sometimes restore rhythm and timing when your concentration has been disturbed just by changing your walking pace and restoring rhythm to the waggle by smoothing the rhythm of walking down the fairway and stepping up to the ball and using the same smooth rhythm in the waggle when setting up to the ball. Concentrating on the rhythmic movements of walking and waggling synchronizes rhythm with tempo and improves overall timing; you walk and waggle more slowly to slow down a fast backswing or move a little faster to become a little more aggressive.

Playing golf does not have to be a frustrating, club-throwing event, although many golfers make it so by not preparing themselves to meet the personal challenge of the game through practice. Frequent practice not only instills confidence and a rhythmic, well-timed swing—by forcing you to use fundamentals and practice rhythm and timing—but also strengthens your hands, coordinates positions, grooves the swing, and develops muscle memory. More than that, however, the more you practice *off* the golf course, the more reliable your swing will be *on* the course. When you arrive at the first tee with a sound golf swing and lots of confidence, you'll need less concentration for setting up to the ball and swinging, which means you can apply more concentration to enjoying the game at hand. And practice makes the difference.

PART IV
The Short Swing

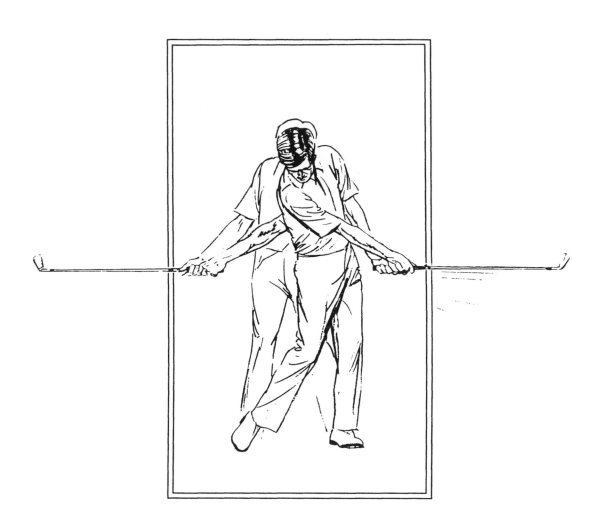

Chapter Nineteen

The Purpose of the Short Swing

When your arms remain extended through the full golf swing, your hands make close to a full circle from the top of the backswing to the completion of the follow-through. The short swing is practiced in the bottom half to three-quarters of this circle, where the hands swing below shoulder level on both the backswing and follow-through. (Figure 121)

The short swing introduces two new fundamentals: the toe-up position of the clubhead in the follow-through and hitting with the right hand. With the exception of positions at the top of the swing, this short section uses all of the fundamentals, thereby producing a miniature, or short, complete golf swing. It is an excellent place to develop the swing in practice as well as to check the swing for accuracy.

The downswing and follow-through mostly reflect what happens preceding the action, but starting the downswing without guidelines is like starting across country without a road map. It is simply easier to negotiate the full golf swing by knowing where the swing is going before the downswing starts.

Guidelines through the short swing help you start the club on the right swing path and keep the swing on plane with a square clubface, whereby you swing the clubhead back and through along the target lines. Without guidelines the clubhead easily swings off-plane somewhere, which changes the club direction through impact. Rather than

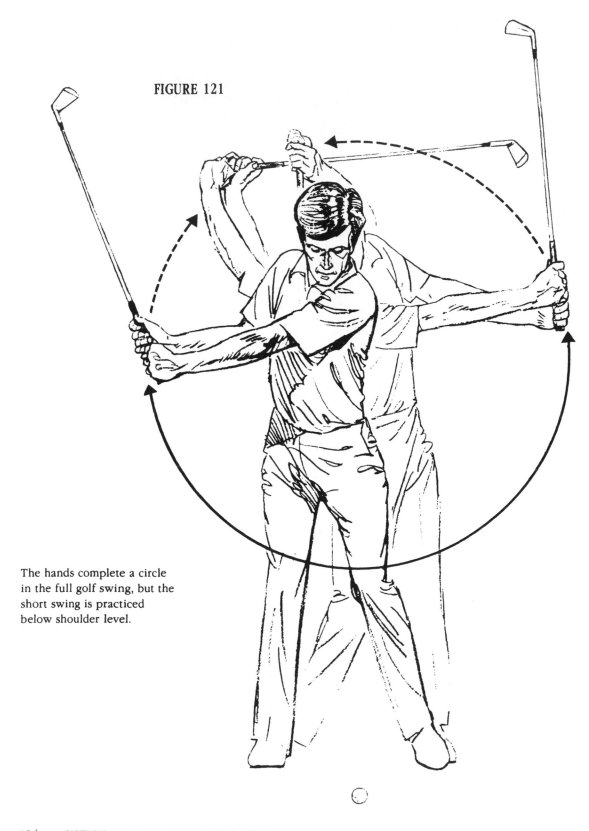

FIGURE 121

The hands complete a circle
in the full golf swing, but the
short swing is practiced
below shoulder level.

194   HOW TO MASTER A GREAT GOLF SWING

swinging down the target line with a square clubface, you swing the clubhead either from outside in to slice or pull the ball or from inside out to hook or push the ball.

As a practice area, the short swing eliminates any tendency you might have to apply force and power while focusing attention on the importance of coordination, timing, and rhythm as keynotes in the swing. Power comes later as a result of practicing good hand action and correct swing movements to swing the club and hit the ball more effectively.

Chapter Twenty

Fundamental No. 13:
The Toe-Up Position of the
Clubhead in the Follow-Through

The toe-up position of the clubhead in the follow-through corresponds with and is opposite the toe-up position in the backswing. (Figure 123) Studying the position will help you understand how the clubhead continues on through the ball on target while, at the same time, teaching you how to swing into and through the position as a result of other positions and movements.

The Procedure

▸ Reestablish the toe-up position of the clubhead in the backswing as shown in Chapter 15. From this position, swing into the opposite toe-up position as follows.

▸ Keep your head in place and your arms together and move your right knee straight toward the target to shift your lower body left. Encourage your right leg to pull inward by pushing against your right foot and let your right heel lift off the ground.

▸ As your weight shifts left, pull your right elbow down close to the body, pull your left arm strongly through the ball, and extend and straighten your right arm into the opposite toe-up position on the directional line. Just as in the backswing toe-up position, your thumbs will be on top. (See page 139, Figure 95.)

▶ Once the position in the preceding steps feels comfortable—which, in itself, takes practice—include the following important action:

Shoulder turn and pivot—clear the left side by turning your stomach toward the target, *but keep your right shoulder back and coming down rather than moving forward and around.* Since your head remains steady, in *exactly* the same "chin up, looking down" position, your right shoulder pulls back to square at impact and then moves down and under your chin as your right arm extends.

FIGURE 123

The toe-up position of the clubhead in the follow-through corresponds with and is opposite the toe-up position in the backswing.

Importance of the Procedure

Swinging the clubhead into the toe-up position in the follow-through:

A. *shifts the weight, accelerates the arms, and starts the downswing with the lower body*

B. *"sweeps" the clubhead through the hitting zone on the right swing path*

C. *maintains maximum swing arc while anchoring the swing center*

D. *promotes accuracy through the ball by releasing the hands and clubhead squarely toward the target on the target line*

E. *continues to promote good footwork*

A: Shifts the weight, accelerates the arms, and starts the downswing with the lower body.

Allowing your weight to remain on a stuck right side is a real swing wrecker, forcing your hands, arms, and shoulders—rather than your feet, legs, and hips—to initiate the downswing. But fundamentals continually direct natural body movements toward a natural golf swing, and you've been introduced to many fundamentals that will shift your weight naturally and move your lower body first—back toward the target—from the top of the swing.

Practice-swinging into the follow-through toe-up position encourages a weight shift left to accelerate your arms and clubhead through the ball. This prevents problems such as hitting from the top, hitting behind the ball, coming over the top, and falling away from the ball. Although the downswing *starts* with lower body action to prevent such problems, starting the downswing with lower body action is not exactly the same because it changes timing and rhythm. Working with timing and rhythm, however, while working with basics, helps the downswing evolve as a reflex action in a coil-recoil action of the upper and lower body.

Although any number of swing thoughts can be developed—and should be used in practice—to trigger a good downswing, just placing the clubhead in the backswing and moving the lower body and upper body mechanically between the toe-up positions will help you develop a feeling for reflexive coordination. With practice the combined action of pushing against the right foot, kicking the right knee back toward the target, and letting the right heel come off the ground as your lower body turns translates into good footwork and strong leg action through your learning to use the feet, legs, and hips. Strong legs and good lower body action depend on your using good

FIGURE 124

footwork to pull your feet inward and lift your heels slightly to prevent you from hitting aggressively with only the hands, arms, and shoulders.

Although any action of the feet, legs, and hips helps move the lower body first back toward the target, completing the shoulder turn turns the shoulders against the hips on the backswing to start the forward movement naturally. Developing this reflexive recoil action between the toe-up positions in practice will, in time, enable you to start pulling the hands, arms, and clubhead down from the top—and learning how this action feels is important.

Lower body action and release, which result from using the feet and extending the right arm, are almost identical to throwing underhand from the position of address: your head remains steady, your right arm draws back, and as your lower body turns and your right leg swings inward, your right hand releases as the right arm extends. (Figure 124) Your left arm, however, accelerates and pulls backhand toward the target to help your weight move forward—and all can be developed through practice to release and accelerate the clubhead

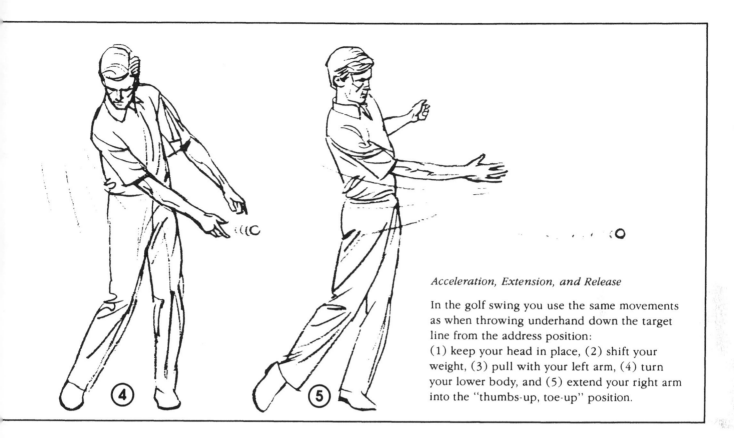

Acceleration, Extension, and Release

In the golf swing you use the same movements as when throwing underhand down the target line from the address position:
(1) keep your head in place, (2) shift your weight, (3) pull with your left arm, (4) turn your lower body, and (5) extend your right arm into the "thumbs-up, toe-up" position.

through the hitting zone instead of releasing from the top.

Trying to hit through the ball with right-arm extension *without* accelerating with the left arm results in poor timing, which results in poor coordination. The weight is prevented from shifting left because momentum comes from the right; whereupon trying to extend the right arm with the weight *on* the right causes releasing from the top, which results in hitting the ground behind the ball and taking large divots.

If you have difficulty timing the weight shift with releasing, practice the timing of the baseball swing: standing with your feet together and then drawing your arms and hands back to swing while stepping into the ball quickly stresses the feeling for what causes the pause at the top of the swing as your weight shifts left. Your arms and hands are pulled back from the top, back through the hitting zone where the right arm extends. The feeling—or pause at the top—is not of the clubhead stopping but merely a transition of the backswing to the forward swing as the upper and lower body shift gears in the coil-recoil action.

FIGURE 125

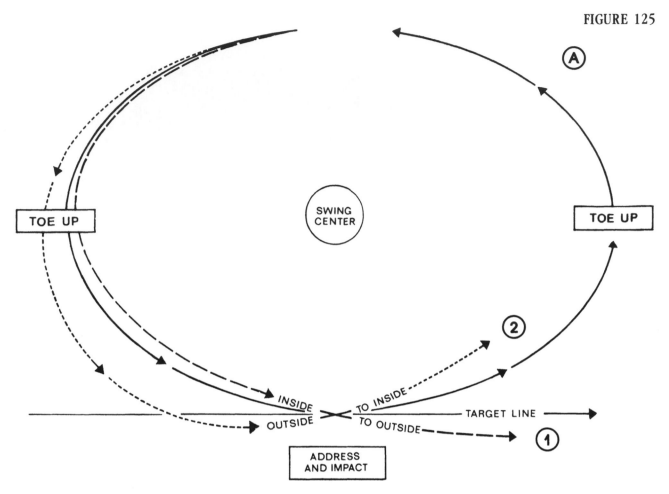

Rather than swinging *only* from inside out, which tends to push or hook the ball (1) or swinging incorrectly from outside in, which tends to slice or pull (2) (125A), swinging on plane through the hitting zone swings the club from inside to square to inside with regard to the target line (125B).

B: "Sweeps" the clubhead through the hitting zone on the right swing path.

The swing path through the hitting zone is often referred to as being either correctly from inside out or incorrectly from outside in with reference to the line of flight. (Figure 125A) More descriptively, however, when swinging correctly, the path is from inside to square to inside. (Figure 125B)

Because the clubhead swings between the toe-up positions, the swing path swings away from the ball through the backswing toe-up position, toward or into parallel at the top, back to square through

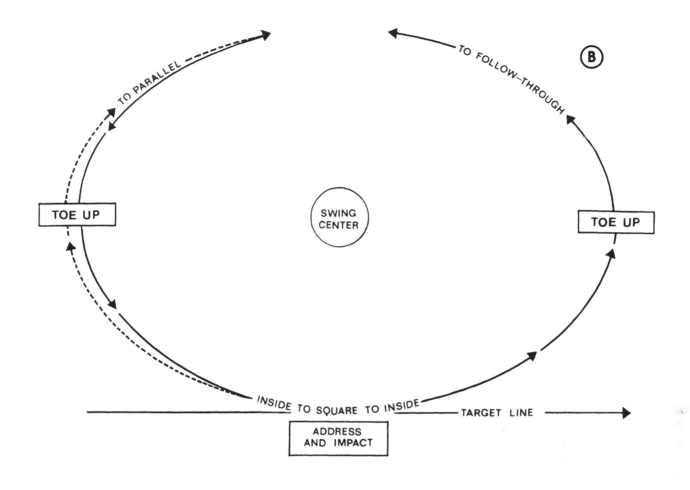

impact, down the target line through the toe-up position, and on into the follow-through. And the swing path between the toe-up positions keeps the club on plane through the hitting zone.

Shifting your weight and swinging your arms correctly starts your hands and clubhead pulling down from the top, which in turn starts the clubhead down from inside out. Swinging the clubhead *only* from inside out, however, or from outside in, either cuts across the ball to curve it left or right or, depending on the clubface angle, hits the ball straight but far off-line.

Along with an ever-present tendency of the hands to hit from the top in golf, the shoulders tend to come over the top and throw the clubhead outside. (Figure 126A) A diving right shoulder starting forward from the top of the swing prevents you from being able to swing from inside to square to inside. Keeping your right shoulder back from the top, however, enables your arms to swing correctly by returning the shoulders back to square at impact. (Figure 126B) The

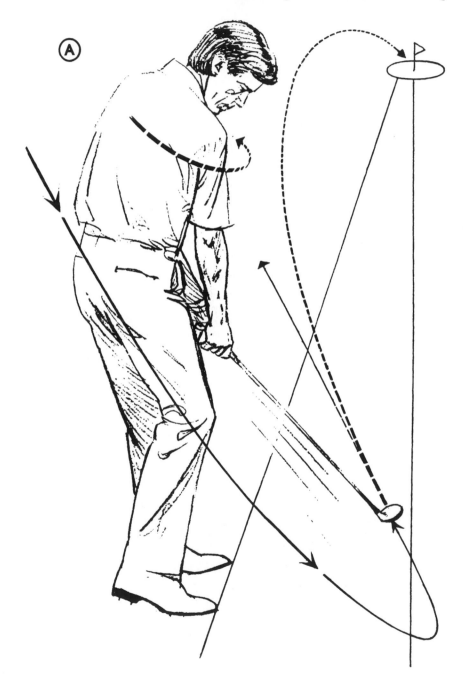

FIGURE 126

Coming Over the Top

A diving right shoulder from the top of the swing causes problems at impact by swinging the clubhead *into* the hitting zone from outside in.

shoulders then turn under the chin beyond impact as the right arm extends to swing the clubhead down the target line and through the toe-up position. Keeping your arms together and your right elbow coming down close to your body helps keep your shoulder back— and *keeping* the right shoulder back prevents you from pushing your head up, which causes looking up.

Swinging Down the Target Line

Square shoulders at impact promote swinging from inside to square to inside and down the target line.

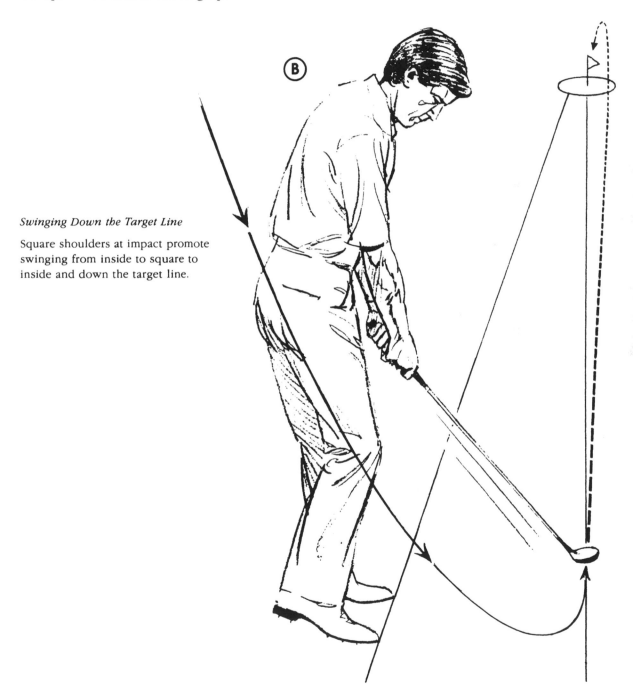

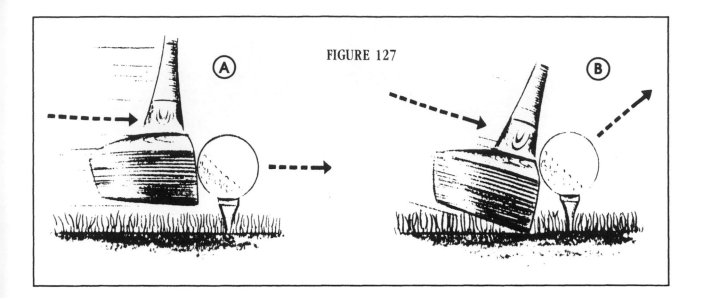

FIGURE 127

Sweeping the clubhead low
through the ball by pulling
your left arm through the
downswing (A) helps
prevent a steep angle of
attack that causes skying
the ball at impact (B).

As well as keeping the clubhead on the right swing path, pulling with the left arm and extending the right arm through the ball "sweeps" the clubhead low through the hitting zone. This prevents the clubhead from arriving in a steep angle of attack, which—with the driver in particular—causes skying the ball at impact. (Figure 127)

Practice sweeping the clubhead low and swinging down the target line by placing your hands in the backswing, keeping your right shoulder back, and practicing the feeling of backhanding the ball by pulling with your left arm while practicing the sidearm-underhand baseball throw. (See pages 200–201.)

C: Maintains maximum swing arc while anchoring the swing center.
Fundamentals position your head behind the ball at address, with your chin up. Your shoulders can then turn around your head and under your chin without excessive head movement. Although positioning your head correctly is an important address position essential for good swing action, your head also establishes and maintains the swing center throughout the golf swing.

The center of the swing can be likened to the hub of a wheel: just as the hub is the center of the wheel, your head is the center of the swing (A); as the spoke measures the radius of the wheel (B), the length of your left arm, plus the length of the shaft, measures the radius of the swing (C). (Figure 128)

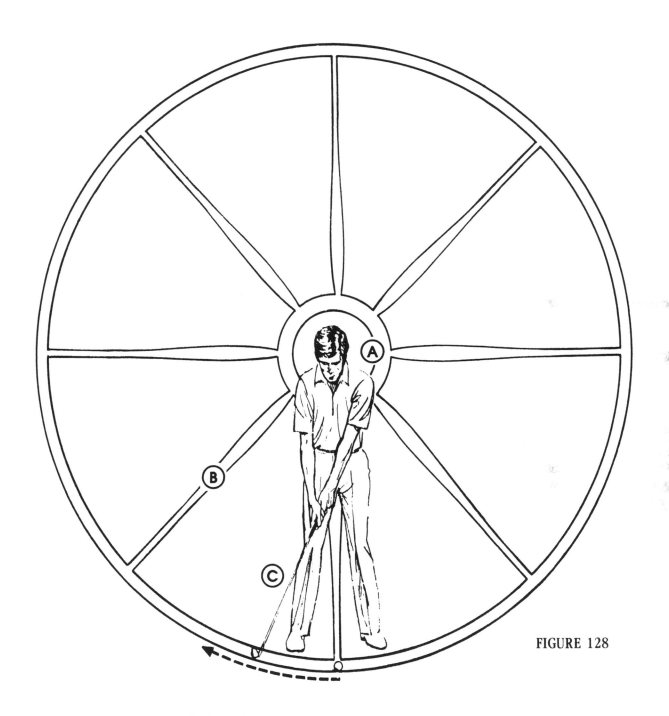

FIGURE 128

Maintaining the Swing Center

Just as the hub is the center of a wheel, your head is the center of the swing (A); as the spoke measures the radius of the wheel (B), your left arm and the shaft measure the radius of the swing (C); therefore, to return the clubhead correctly, your head remains steady to maintain the swing center.

The radius of the swing determines the width of the swing—or size of the circle—called the *swing arc.* You maintain both the swing arc and the swing center throughout the swing by extending your arms and swinging around the fixed center. *Moving* the swing center moves the swing arc, and the more the swing arc changes, either back and forth or up and down, the harder it becomes to either swing the club effectively or hit the ball well.

Many problems in golf such as swaying, looking up, falling away from the ball, and swinging off balance can be prevented or corrected simply by practicing swinging into the toe-up position while keeping your chin up and swinging around an anchored swing center.

Since excessive head movement is generally known to affect the swing adversely, golfers are frequently advised to keep the head down, which positions the chin too low, or to keep an eye on the ball, which restricts freedom of movement. However, lifting the chin and cocking it to the right is more apt to correct swing problems. This positions the head at address where it is at the top of the swing and helps prevent head movement through the backswing. (Figure 129)

Because of the many factors that make up the golf swing, no single head position is best for everyone, mostly because not everyone visualizes the ball and target in exactly the same way. For instance, not all golfers who wear bifocals have problems; but for many, having to position the chin too low to see over the bifocal portion causes visual alignment as well as shoulder turn problems. At any rate, whatever the situation, experimentation and practice between the toe-up positions can help you overcome most problems, not only by keeping the swing center intact but also by locating and practicing the best head position to promote the best golf swing possible for you.

D: Promotes accuracy through the ball by releasing the hands and clubhead squarely toward the target on the target line.

Just past the hitting zone a tucked-in right elbow and swinging legs combine to straighten and extend the right arm. Since the directional line is part of the target line, extending the right arm through the ball into the toe-up position *on* the directional line keeps your arms together on the right swing path and helps you hit directly toward the target by releasing your hands and the clubhead on the target

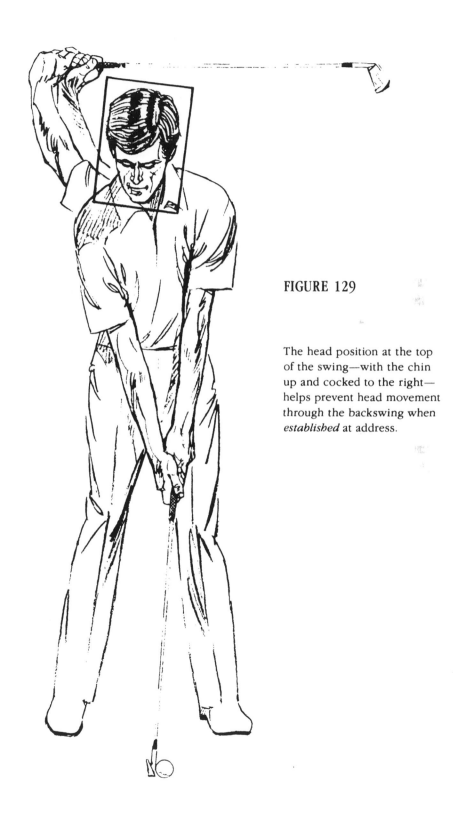

FIGURE 129

The head position at the top of the swing—with the chin up and cocked to the right—helps prevent head movement through the backswing when *established* at address.

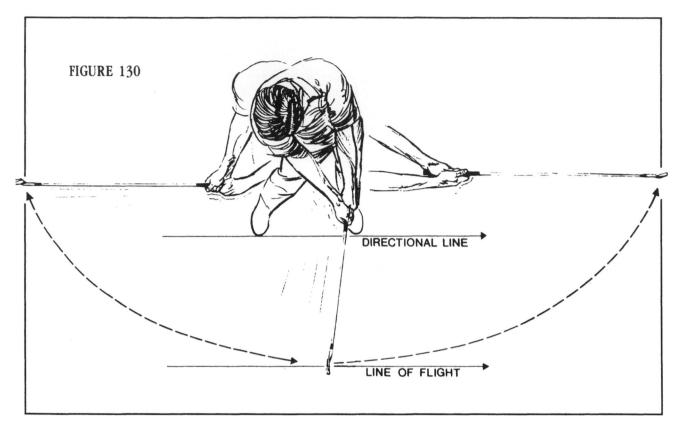

FIGURE 130

DIRECTIONAL LINE

LINE OF FLIGHT

Practice between the toe-up positions helps you keep your right arm in close and release your hands and the clubhead down the target line by extending your right arm into the toe-up position on the directional line.

line. As your lower body turns—turning the stomach toward the target to clear the left side—pulling with the left arm combines with good footwork and strong legs to pull the arms and hands on through the thumbs-up, toe-up position and into the follow-through. Practicing these actions between the toe-up positions helps you develop feeling for hitting through the ball correctly with the club-face square. (Figure 130)

Releasing your hands and the clubhead through impact with right-arm extension results in both power and accuracy. Clubhead speed, however, with the left arm firm in line with the shaft, the hands ahead of the ball, and the left wrist straight, is a result of every position and movement from the start of the swing. (Figure 131)

FIGURE 131

Accuracy and power at impact are the result of every position and movement from the start of the swing: (1) head steady behind ball, (2) shoulders square with right shoulder back, (3) right arm extending, (4) hips turning toward target, (5) right heel lifting, (6) left arm pulling, (7) straight arm–shaft position with left wrist straight, and (8) weight shifted left.

Along with keeping your head steady, encouraging your knees to slide back toward the target while turning your lower body and letting your right heel come off the ground prevents swaying laterally and blocking the follow-through. Blocking out tends to bend the left wrist inward coming into the ball, which releases the hands too early; and releasing too early causes scooping over the top of the ball by cupping the right hand under the left through impact. (Figure 132) Pulling with the left arm, however, while turning the lower body, helps keep the left wrist straight to backhand the ball through impact by preventing the wrist from bending inward.

The combination of keeping the arms together and returning the right elbow in close to the body with the right shoulder back prevents "spinning out" or whirling back into the follow-through as the lower body turns through the ball. Letting your arms separate by lifting your right elbow, or letting your right shoulder move forward from the top of the swing, however, causes coming over the top. Coming over the top with the shoulders—especially when combined

Releasing too early causes scooping over the top of the ball by cupping the right hand under the left through impact.

FIGURE 132

with good lower body action—results in spinning out by letting the lower and upper body turn together from the top of the swing.

Depending on the clubface angle at impact, both coming over the top and spinning out cause slicing, pulling, toeing, or smothering the ball (which hits a grounder to the left) because you throw the clubhead out beyond the target line, then back inside across the target lines. Good swing mechanics, however, contribute to hitting the ball straight.

Throwing the hands and clubhead down the target line—just as throwing sidearm-underhand in baseball—is a matter of coordinating the weight shift, shoulder turn, pivot, and release through practice in the short swing.

E: Continues to promote good footwork.

Letting the right heel lift off the ground and pull inward when hitting through the ball helps clear the left side by letting the hips turn; whereupon, keeping the right shoulder back and the right elbow down releases the clubhead straight toward the target as the arms extend. Keeping the right heel flat on the ground through impact, however, promotes spinning out by stiffening the right leg, keeping the weight on the right, and spinning the hips around too soon.

Correspondingly, as your weight shifts left, your left heel—which lifts off the ground and pulls inward through the backswing—returns to the ground on the downswing as the right heel lifts, the result of which is good footwork essential to shifting your weight and pulling the clubhead strongly through the ball.

Chapter Twenty-One

Fundamental No. 14:
Hitting with the Right Hand

The purpose of golf, essentially, is to swing the club and hit the ball. But golfers occasionally become so involved in the mechanics of the swing that actually hitting the ball becomes only an ineffectual net result rather than a powerful addition to the swing. When the grip is correct and the swing is sound, the act of hitting is frequently the most singularly active thing a golfer can do to trigger a straight and powerful golf shot.

The phrase *hitting with the right hand* probably conjures up a picture of the right hand taking over the golf swing, overpowering the left, and directing the ball far left of the target line. Rather than misdirecting the ball, however, the *act* of hitting is simply a fundamental action that is a necessary part of the golf swing as a whole.

Golf swing analysts often categorize players as either swingers or hitters, giving the impression that they must be one or the other. It seems reasonable, however, that better golfers who have learned what to swing and what to hit with, are undoubtedly some of both.

Although swinging the club and hitting the ball go hand in hand, just hitting the ball with what seems natural—the upper body, or the hands, arms, and shoulders—before learning to swing the club with lower body action (the feet, legs, and hips) prevents coordination by promoting swinging too fast, overcontrolling the clubhead, and hitting too soon from the top. Because of this, even experienced golfers with

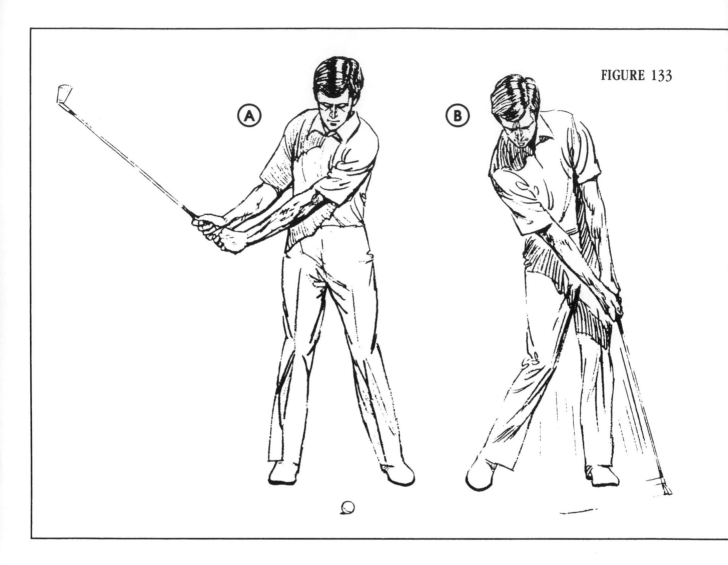

FIGURE 133

sound golf swings may be reluctant to use a hitting action as effectively as they should. There is a vast difference, however, between using the hands to control the clubhead—by initiating the backswing or downswing—and creating a hitting, or fundamental, action within the golf swing. Understanding the difference is important to being able to hit the ball with any degree of confidence.

The Procedure

▸ First develop a mentally affirmative attitude with regard to hitting the ball; then start the backswing from just beyond the wrist break position with the left heel off the ground. (Figure 133A)

▸ Follow the same procedure for swinging between the toe-up positions as described on page 197. Start, however, by repositioning your left heel on the ground as your right heel lifts. Keeping your arms together, accelerate arm action by pulling toward the target with the straight left arm and start incorporating a little right-hand hitting action against the firmness of the straight left wrist. Prevent the left wrist from bending inward by turning your hips to clear the left side. (Figure 133B)

▸ Keep your head in place (looking down, not up) and hit on into the toe-up position by extending the right arm along with the left. (Figure 133C)

Importance of the Procedure

Hitting with the right hand:

A. *establishes a hitting position within the swinging movement*
B. *coordinates hitting and swinging with good footwork*
C. *combines the natural use of both hands through the hitting zone to square the clubface at impact*
D. *helps coordinate the actions of staying behind, swinging through, and releasing through the hitting zone*
E. *stresses the importance of grip and positions in hitting straight shots*

A: Establishes a hitting position within the swinging movement.

You hit with the right hand not to hit the ball better by swinging faster or hitting harder but to establish a hitting position of the hands and arms by cocking the right elbow down at the top of the swing. Although the swing is a continuous movement from the start of the swing, you can't achieve a really effective swing without first starting a hitting action to establish this hitting position within the swinging movement.

Understanding fundamentals will help you eliminate conscious thought by knowing that certain positions that are not fundamental, per se, are automatically assumed by fundamental actions, such as cocking the right elbow down at the top of the swing. In this case just mentally setting out to hit the ball is fundamentally, as well as physically, a right-handed action that results in the hitting position of the right hand and arm.

In a hitting action, as opposed to a swinging movement, when the right hand draws back to hit, the elbow—rather than the hand and arm—starts the movement back to the left and throws the right hand into a palm-up hitting position at the top of the backswing. For example, swing your right arm to the right and swing it back to the left. Your arm and hand swing back and forth without the elbow bending. (Figure 134A) Now draw your right hand back to hit. As your arm and hand start back to the left, the elbow cocks down at the top of the swing and cocks the right hand into the hitting position. (Figure 134B)

Although the right elbow is positioned at address to point downward through the backswing, you don't cock the elbow down at the top of the swing only by preventing the elbow from flying. Setting out to hit the ball creates a different action that strongly reinforces the action of returning the clubhead with the elbow down.

FIGURE 134

Swinging the right arm back and forth keeps the right arm straight (A); but drawing the right arm back to *hit* cocks the elbow down at the top of the swing to establish a hitting position within the swinging movement (B).

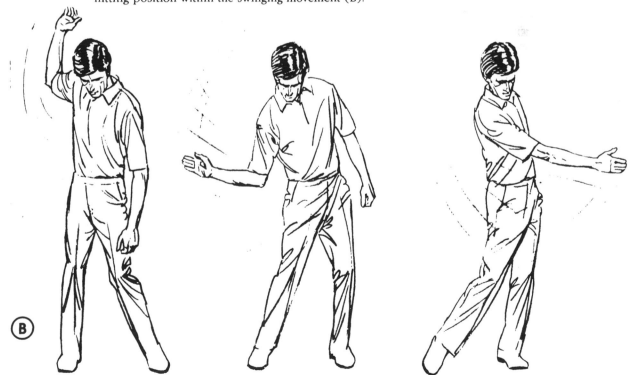

FIGURE 135

The movement of the right arm in golf is a combination sidearm-underhand, throwing-hitting action more simply defined as sort of a whipping action caused by the throwing action. Overhand or sidearm *throwing* sports, such as baseball, basketball, tennis, fly casting, etc., all employ a natural hitting action: When the right arm pulls back either to throw or to hit, it reaches a somewhat blocked position at the top of the swing. In turn this blocked position not only cocks the elbow down but also helps move the hips and shift the weight to pull the elbow downward. The elbow and the hips then pull the right arm down and forward in the throwing-hitting action. In contrast, underhand *swinging* movements, such as pitching softball, pennies, or horseshoes, keep the elbow straight.

Although the action of the right arm in golf may appear to be an underhand swinging movement, it is basically the same as any side-

Throwing underhand helps you develop good right-side action by using a hitting action to keep the right elbow down.

arm throwing-hitting action that cocks the elbow down through the backswing and then releases the hand and clubhead by extending the right arm through the hitting zone. To produce this natural action, you need only have an intent, before the backswing starts, to just *hit* the ball, which may account for the golfer who just encountered disaster hitting the ball incredibly far off the next tee.

An excellent exercise to practice that helps coordinate swinging (which is lower body action) with hitting (which is upper body action) is to establish the address position and practice throwing balls—either real or imaginary—by throwing underhand down the target line. Keep your head in place, swing your legs, and use the hitting action to throw both long and short. The act of throwing in this manner helps you develop good timing while developing a feeling for hitting with rhythmic body movements. (Figure 135)

B: Coordinates hitting and swinging with good footwork.

Golfers who misinterpret a hitting action and set out to "kill" the ball with aggressive determination and a fast backswing always encounter difficulty. Such murderous intent prevents rhythm and coordination, rushes the shot at the top of the swing, and kills the shot instead.

Although "killing" the ball appears to be an incurable affliction for most of us, remember that neither speed nor force is recommended when swinging the club or hitting the ball. Both lead to hitting primarily with the hands, which prevents good timing. Curb the killer instinct while practicing better basics to improve coordination.

Swinging *and* hitting, as demonstrated on page 219, can be negotiated even in slow motion, clearly indicating the hitting *position* at the top of the swing to be a natural physical reaction to just having the thought in mind.

Pushing the clubhead away from the ball with a strong, fully extended, straight left arm and slow beginning, combined only with this predetermined intent to hit back through the ball, cocks the right elbow down at the top of the swing. As the downswing starts, however, hitting combines with swinging, but not because you're swinging your arms and hitting with your hands. Rather you accomplish this by keeping your arms together, applying good legwork and footwork that help shift your weight left, and accelerating arm action toward the target by pulling with the strong left arm and extending the right. This helps you develop more power and better coordination by timing the weight shift with releasing the hands and clubhead through the hitting zone.

Accelerating the left arm through the hitting zone creates good timing when combined with other swing mechanics—all of which work toward preventing an early release. The shaft and clubhead then trail behind the hands from the top, enabling the clubhead to accelerate through the ball with maximum clubhead speed.

Being lazy with arm action, particularly when you're hitting only with your hands or trying to crunch it on the backswing, bends the left arm at the top of the swing. Not only do you lose power, by losing leverage, but you throw the descent of the clubhead—or angle of attack—steeply downward, which throws the right shoulder forward. Usually accompanied by swaying back through the ball, divots are taken in front of the ball and the ball hit right on top.

Pounding straight down on the ball, as well as pulling, slicing,

> Accelerating the left arm from the top of the swing creates good timing when combined with other swing mechanics.

and hitting grounders to the left, may be attributed to just failing to hit correctly—not with the hands through the backswing but by keeping the swing center intact, turning the lower body, applying good footwork, and accelerating and extending your arms through the hitting zone.

A basic physical, as well as mental, difference between most men and women is the more aggressive "killer instinct" of men to use a hitting action compared with the natural tendency of women to use a more gentle swinging movement. Since swinging and hitting together in golf require keen coordination of the upper and lower body, women often need to learn how to use their hands and arms to become stronger hitters, and men often need to learn how to use their feet and legs to become less aggressive swingers.

C: Combines the natural use of both hands through the hitting zone to square the clubface at impact.

Using natural hand action through the hitting zone is a matter of first understanding how the hands hit naturally outside the swing and then developing this hitting action within the golf swing between the toe-up positions.

When you're standing sideways and throwing or hitting toward a target with either the back of the left hand or the palm of the right—as in golf—either hand naturally assumes the exact opposite position in the follow-through from any position in the backswing as it draws back to throw or hit. Consider the action of the right hand, for instance: From shoulder level down to waist level the hand swings back and through on a flat swing plane into the same opposite position. (Figure 136A) Below hip level the hand swings upward into the backswing on a tilted swing plane and also swings upward into the opposite position in the follow-through. (Figure 136B) In each instance, however—when you're hitting correctly as well as naturally—the hand is always on the directional line of the feet when the arm is parallel, and *the thumbs are always on top*.

Unlike the action from above hip level—where the right hand stays straight and hits square on a flat plane—throwing or hitting on a tilted plane from below hip level turns the hand into the backswing, squares the hand at impact, and rolls the hand over into the follow-through. And so it is in golf. To hit effectively between the toe-up positions with the swing on plane and the clubface square, the hands must impart the same thumbs-up rolling-over action used in hitting naturally. And an incorrect grip, where the hands are not

FIGURE 136

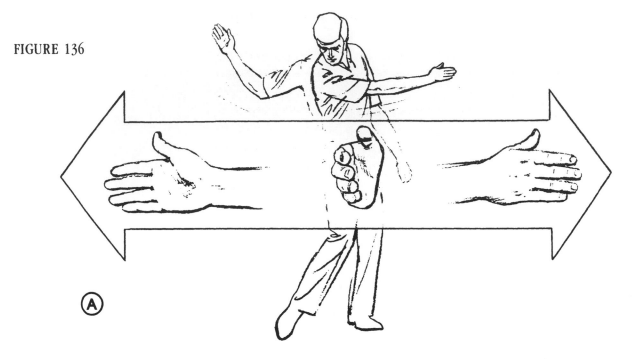

Natural Hand Action

When you're drawing back to hit squarely through a target, either hand assumes the exact opposite position in the follow-through; therefore, when you're hitting underhand in golf, the right hand rolls over through impact.

positioned square to the clubface with the thumbs on top, results in incorrect shots.

When the grip is correct, "fanning" the hands back correctly with the thumbs on top and the right elbow pointing downward contributes to a good shoulder turn. Swinging the hands back incorrectly, with the back of the left hand and the palm of the right hand facing downward, flies the right elbow and causes many problems in golf because the clubface is kept closed through the backswing and returned closed at impact. Swaying away from the ball is almost certain since turning is difficult, and poor hand action causes scooping or skulling over the top of the ball because the right hand is cupped under the left and the left wrist bent inward. (Figure 137)

Up to this point the right hand has more or less been just a steadying influence throughout the backswing. But the hand is now cocked in a hitting position, ready to deliver a blow at impact. With the right hand poised to hit the ball, a key to power and accuracy is returning the straight left wrist and straight arm–shaft address position back to the hitting zone. This strong position uses the backhanded-batting strength of the left hand to power through the hitting zone along with right-hand action. But any hitting action must be accompanied by the shoulder turn and pivot as the weight shifts

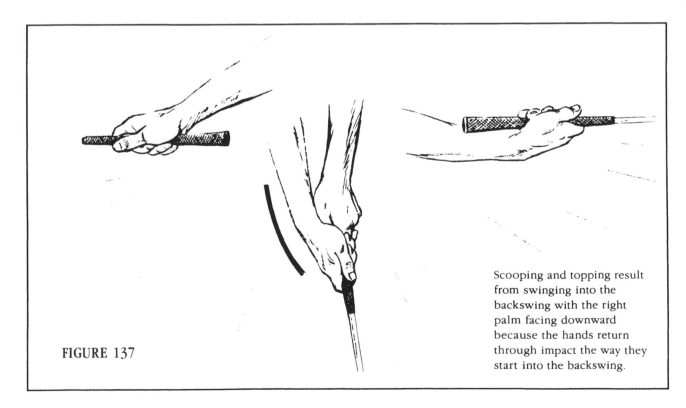

FIGURE 137

Scooping and topping result from swinging into the backswing with the right palm facing downward because the hands return through impact the way they start into the backswing.

right and then back to the left—just as throwing underhand down the target line or swinging the clubhead between the toe-up positions.

When your mind is conditioned to the fact that the golf swing is a swinging movement combined with a hitting action, your arms and hands push into the backswing closely coordinated and together in the one-piece swing. As the hands approach the hitting zone with the wrists still cocked, however, the back of the left hand, the palm of the right, and the clubface still aim forward, as in the backswing toe-up position. Although the left hand has more or less completed its hitting responsibility—simply by being pulled into a firm-wrist, backhand-batting position—the action of the hands combines to square the clubface only when the right hand actively hits through the ball into the toe-up, thumbs-up position.

Pulling with the left hand and leaving the right hand out of the hitting action commonly causes slicing, pushing, or shanking by leaving the clubface open at impact. Swinging from outside in causes slicing or shanking, and swinging from in to out causes pushing. An otherwise perfect golf shot with no right hand, although often causing shanking, may also resemble a bona fide shank by hitting on the toe of the club straight to the right, whereupon fear of shanking again compounds the problem as golfers swing a little faster, with more tension and a reluctance to hit the ball at all.

Two kinds of swings influence hand action: (1) a strong "body swing," which keeps the hands inactive by shifting the weight and turning the body so as to swing the arms and hands; and (2) a strong "hands and arms swing," which uses a stronger hitting action with less body movement. Although swinging *or* hitting (and preferably a combination of both) will deliver the blow at impact, hitting can be effective only when the overall swing is sound.

Expertise in shotmaking requires adjusting the stance, grip, or setup and often manipulating the hands when swinging so as to manipulate the ball. To hit the ball straight, however, you must hit it square, which takes sound basics and good timing throughout the golf swing.

Tommy Armour once said, "The gap between mediocrity and proficiency is a matter of timing," and one of the keys to good timing is learning to turn and move your body correctly so your hands can work naturally through impact to hit the ball straight—and the right hand will *not* overpower the left when the swing itself is sound. Centrifugal force and good timing uncock the wrists and release the hands and clubhead with more power and accuracy than trying to force the hitting action by hitting only with the hands.

"The gap between mediocrity and proficiency is a matter of timing."
—Tommy Armour

D: Helps coordinate the actions of staying behind, swinging through, and releasing through the hitting zone.

Three terms used in golf refer to actions that occur together through impact and, when coordinated, result in distance and accuracy: *staying behind the ball, swinging through the ball*, and *releasing*. Although these actions should occur naturally as a result of other swing movements, coordination is easier once you understand the terms.

Every position and movement from the start of the swing is directed toward the critical moment of impact where all of the foregoing actions occur together to hit the ball far and straight. Part of the difficulty in accomplishing this, however, lies in misunderstanding how this all takes place—thinking that all of this happens *at* impact, *from* the top, rather than from the beginning of the swing. From the top of the swing to impact, however, takes from a third to half a second—far too little time for so many actions to coordinate from the top into an effective impact position. The impact position evolves more slowly from everything that starts from the beginning of the swing.

Planning ahead for impact while setting up to the ball—in the waggle procedure—is a matter of first understanding all of the actions needed to release the hands and clubhead through the hitting zone by staying behind and swinging through the ball correctly—and the "secret" lies in developing and practicing these actions between the toe-up positions.

Staying behind the ball refers only to upper body action—keeping the head behind the ball as the shoulders return to square at impact and turning the right shoulder under the chin as the right arm extends.

Swinging through the ball refers to lower body action. Good footwork and strong legs combine to shift the weight from right to left, turn the hips through the ball, and pull the arms, hands, and clubhead down from the top.

Releasing swings the arms, hands, and clubhead down the target line as a result of keeping the arms together, pulling with the left arm, keeping the right shoulder back, and extending the right arm through the ball—all of which coordinates with the weight shift and results in accuracy and clubhead speed through the hitting zone. (See page 205, Figure 126B.)

Just setting out to hit the ball, along with maintaining the swing center and completing the shoulder turn, helps coordinate swing actions that release the hands correctly. Without the many actions that keep the right shoulder back from the top of the swing, however—such as shifting the weight and swinging the arms correctly—the shoulders return to open at impact rather than returning square.

Coming over the top from outside in (the diving-right-shoulder syndrome) is undoubtedly the most common cause of slicing and pulling the ball. The action also causes looking up by pushing the head up as well as throwing the clubhead from the top with upper body action and falling away from the ball.

Since the shoulders and hands are connected by the arms in between, whatever the shoulders do affects the arms, which in turn affects hand action—and since the hands are the only part of the body connected to the club, whatever the hands do determines clubhead action.

E: *Stresses the importance of grip and positions in hitting straight shots.* Unintentional shots such as slicing, pulling, hooking, and pushing (and all the others) are the nemesis of every golfer. They occur less frequently among proficient golfers but all too often are accepted as a necessary though frustrating "part of the game" by others. Since consistently hitting the ball straight is generally the result of many years of effort, encountering these particular shots on occasion should be acceptable but you should never let them become chronic problems.

Although incorrect positions or swing movements cause mishits by not returning the clubhead on the correct swing path, slicing or hooking also occurs when the clubhead returns on target but with the clubface open or closed. In that case an incorrect grip may have precluded the ability of the hands to square the clubface at impact—especially with right-hand involvement. To be *able* to hit with the right hand and square the clubface at impact, you must first establish an accurate grip and square clubface at address.

Combined with a square clubface at address, an accurate grip aligns the back of the left hand, the palm of the right hand, and the clubface directly toward the target. Good hand action then returns the hands and clubface back to square when the right hand hits the ball. Incorrectly positioning the hands, however (or just one hand for that matter), too far right or too far left will open or close the clubface at impact because the hands return to square but turn the clubface.

To identify an incorrect grip at address, square the clubface,

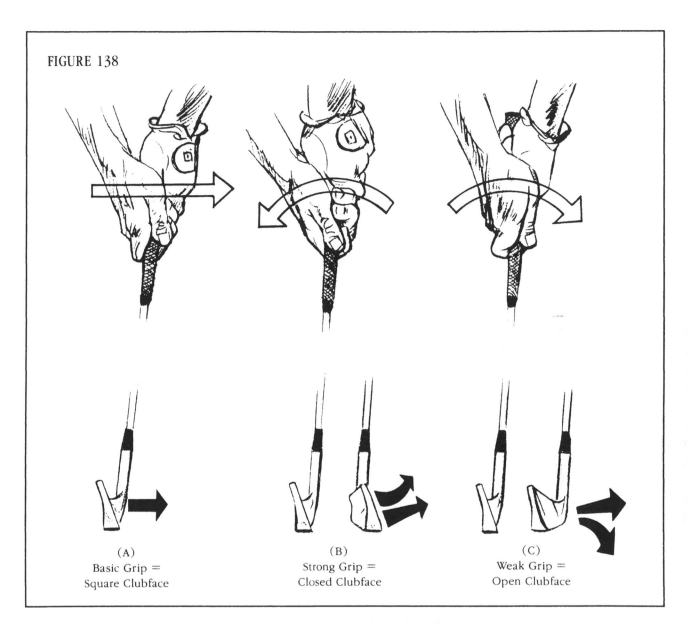

FIGURE 138

(A)
Basic Grip =
Square Clubface

(B)
Strong Grip =
Closed Clubface

(C)
Weak Grip =
Open Clubface

You can identify an incorrect grip at address by squaring the clubface, taking the grip, then turning your hands into the position they naturally return to at impact.

assume the grip, then turn your hands into the natural hitting position they return to at impact—with the back of the left hand and the palm of the right facing directly toward the target. The basic grip keeps the clubface square (A), an incorrect grip with the hands too far right in a "strong" position closes the clubface (B), and positioning the hands too far left in a "weak" position opens the clubface (C)—which is exactly what happens at impact. (Figure 138)

Although slicing or hooking the ball can be the result of changing only the grip at address, any intentional shots such as these—which include spinning the ball to a lesser degree by drawing the ball left or fading the ball right—are generally accompanied by open or closed positions at address as well as by swinging across the target lines when approaching the hitting zone. (See page 34.)

Any golf shot—good or bad, correct or incorrect, intentional or unintentional—occurs because you've used fundamentals either correctly on purpose or incorrectly as a result of not understanding the golf swing. Therefore understanding how golf shots are made intentionally can help you avoid positions and movements that cause the curved shots unintentionally. Nonetheless, shotmaking, per se, is still for experienced golfers.

Straight Shots—Swing Path from Inside to Square to Inside
(Figure 139)

The most important consideration in hitting any golf shot is first determining the primary target, or where to hit the ball, and then making alignments based on that location.

Although it may not seem so to those with chronic problems, lining up to hit a straight shot is easier than lining up to slice or hook, because the primary target is also the landing area (1); the clubface is just squared to that target for the line of flight (2), and the feet are then positioned parallel to form the directional line (3). The clubhead then swings away from the ball, following the target lines that constitute the swing path, and returns from inside to square to inside to hit the ball straight (4).

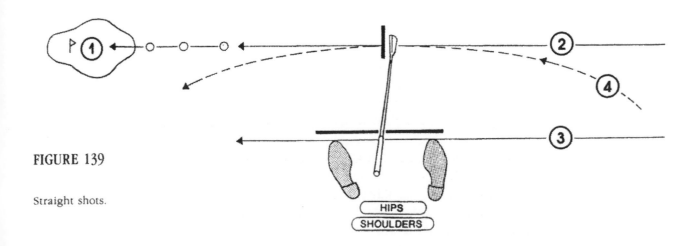

FIGURE 139

Straight shots.

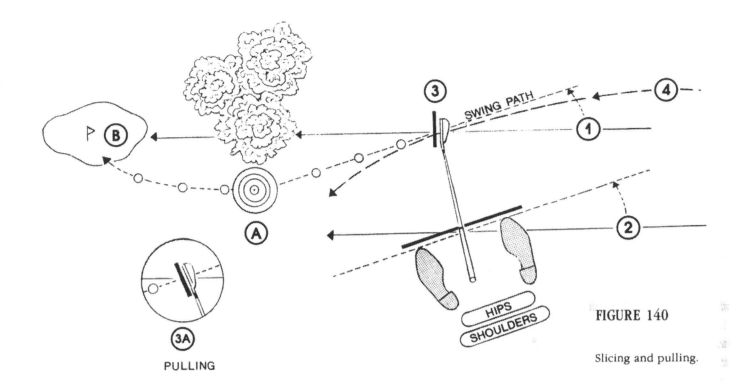

FIGURE 140

Slicing and pulling.

PULLING

Slicing and Pulling—Swing Path from Outside to Inside
(Figure 140)

Slicing: When you're setting up to slice the ball, first determine a secondary target by how far left to start the ball (A) so it will curve back to the primary target, or the landing area (B). Both target lines—the line of flight (1) and the directional line (2)—then remain parallel to each other but turn to the left to aim directly toward the secondary target. The clubface, however, is then turned to aim squarely toward the primary target. This opens the clubface to the directional line (3).

Although the clubface is no longer aligned square to the directional line, the line of flight is now used as a guideline for the swing path on which your clubhead travels, thereby enabling you to swing parallel to the line of your feet. With the clubface open in relation to the swing path, swinging parallel to the directional line will return your clubhead from outside in with the clubface open. This swings the club across what are ordinarily square target lines to spin the ball at impact (4). A weak grip then helps keep the clubface open through impact to spin the ball through the secondary target and toward the landing area.

Pulling: Pulling results from the same things that cause slicing except that the clubface returns square to the directional line at impact; consequently, when you set up to slice, too strong a grip may result in pulling (3A).

FIGURE 141

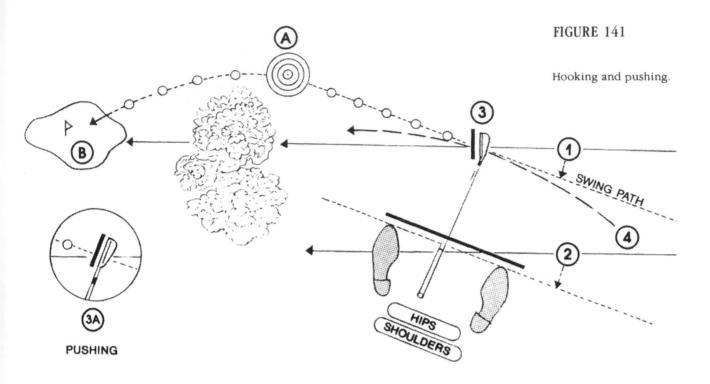

Hooking and pushing.

PUSHING

Hooking and Pushing—Swing Path from Inside to Outside
(Figure 141)

Hooking: The secondary target in hooking is determined by how far right to start the ball (A) so it will curve back to the primary target, or landing area (B). Both target lines—the line of flight (1) and the directional line (2)—then remain parallel to each other but turn to the right to aim directly toward the secondary target. The clubface, however, is then turned to aim squarely toward the primary target. This closes the clubface to the directional line (3).

Although, just as in slicing, the clubface is no longer aligned square to the directional line, the line of flight is used as a guideline for the swing path on which your clubhead travels, thereby enabling you to swing the clubhead on the line of your feet.

With the clubface closed in relationship to the swing path, swinging parallel to the directional line will return your clubhead to the hitting zone from inside out with the clubface closed. This swings the club across what are ordinarily square target lines to spin the ball at impact (4). A strong grip helps close the clubface more quickly to spin the ball through the secondary target and toward the landing area.

Pushing: Pushing results from the same things that cause hooking, except that at impact the clubface returns square to the closed directional line (3A); therefore, when you set up to hook the ball a weak grip may result in pushing.

Though knowledge and practice help experienced golfers become more proficient in manipulating the ball, to *prevent* slicing, pulling, hooking, pushing, etc., as chronic problems in golf, most golfers should continue to work on basics to try to hit the ball straight.

Working with fundamentals helps in many ways: establishing square positions; improving the golf grip; keeping the club on plane with the clubface square; and hitting from inside to square to inside (through the toe-up positions) to hit the ball straight. Extending the right arm through the hitting zone—toward the toe-up position—allows you to hit the ball straight by keeping the clubhead swinging on the right swing path.

Chapter Twenty-Two

Starting the Downswing

Every position and movement from the start of the swing is designed to build up power through the backswing and downswing and then to release it through the hitting zone by starting the downswing with the feet, legs, and hips. Data fed into the mental computer before the backswing starts, however, determine the start of the downswing. The movement is programmed from the moment the clubhead is positioned behind the ball.

Starting the downswing with lower body action delivers power at impact by shifting your weight from right to left, pulling your arms down from the top, turning your lower body, and releasing your hands and the clubhead through the hitting zone. Returning the club with upper body action keeps your weight on the right, expending power before reaching the hitting zone by throwing your arms and clubhead upward and outward from the top of the swing and releasing your hands too soon.

Downswing action is a reflex action—a "moment of truth"—when positions at address and movements through the backswing are proved to be right or wrong by how the downswing starts. The downswing starts with either the upper or lower body as a result of what precedes the action. Although it is important to understand the reflexive coil-recoil action of the backswing and downswing, one of the intrinsic values of understanding the overall swing is knowing that reflex action starts from the beginning of the swing rather than by conscious thought or action from the top of the swing.

Mistakes quickly show up through the backswing and are indicated by an inability of the feet, legs, or hips to initiate the downswing. The smallest correction before the backswing starts may correct the entire golf swing by promoting reflex action of the lower body the moment the backswing starts.

The initial movement from the top of the swing—whereby some part of your lower body shifts your weight back to the left to pull your arms, hands, and the clubhead down from the top—is so important at impact that there has been a continuing search down through the years for one key move or one key thought to *make* the downswing work. Golf instructors promote this endless search by inadvertently using terms that advocate various moves *from* the top of the swing to start the downswing action, such as:

> *Start your hips back toward the target.*
> *Turn your hips to the left.*
> *Start your hips back before completing the backswing.*
> *Start your left hip back.*
> *Start your right hip back in a "cross-lateral" shift.*
> *Pause at the top to start your hips back first.*
> *Wait for the clubhead.*
> *Leave the clubhead at the top when the downswing starts.*
> *Let your hips pull your arms down.*
> *Drive your knees toward the target.*
> *Drive your right knee toward the target.*
> *Pull your arms down from the top.*
> *Pull down with the last three fingers of your left hand.*
> *Push against your right foot.*
> *Shift your weight.*
> *Keep your head behind the ball and move your lower body.*
> *"Clamp" your left heel down.*
> *Stay behind the ball.*
> *Keep your shoulders behind the ball.*
> *Swing through the ball.*
> *Bring your right shoulder under.*
> *Keep your right shoulder back.*
> *Swing your legs toward the target.*
> *Start your left knee toward the target.*
> *Start your right knee toward the target.*
> *Start your right elbow toward your left knee.*
> *Start your right elbow and your left knee toward the target.*

Although any of these "solutions" may be used effectively—and each contributes a good swing thought—by continuing to focus attention on action from the *top* of the swing, golf instructors create a universal impression that the downswing starts *from* the top rather than from the beginning of the swing. Actually, all of the actions listed should occur—and do occur—when the swing is sound, and almost any swing thought may be used to start the lower body first. This can only happen, however, when rhythm, timing, and accuracy throughout the swing make coordination possible when the swing thought is used.

The most important point is that whatever happens at the top of the swing must be the result of a key swing thought at the beginning of the swing, because starting the downswing from the top of the swing changes timing and rhythm. As important as positions and movements are in promoting reflex action, positions must still have time to coordinate. When the backswing is sound, rhythm and timing become the primary factors in moving the lower body first in the downswing action.

The advantages of a well-grooved, well-timed swing that uses personalized swing thoughts cannot be overestimated. They are important to the swing and may be applied to anything specific that promotes a good golf swing. They may also be used to start the downswing. How and where these thoughts are applied, however, has great impact on the swing by influencing timing and rhythm. A change in timing or rhythm at the top of the swing caused by sudden swing thoughts either prevents reflex action from moving the lower body first or causes the lower body to react adversely by moving too quickly or shifting to the right.

Golfers who have stubbed the clubhead going back and have experienced the difficulty in stopping the swing for overs have experienced the dogged determination of reflex action to finish the swing by the quick return of the clubhead. As quick and persistent as reflex action is in the downswing movement, however, the application of any swing thought at the top of the swing is faster—and much too fast to coordinate with a rhythmic swinging movement. The quick response of muscles to thoughts or actions at the top of the swing, moving faster than reflex action, changes timing and rhythm and prevents smooth coordination; thus the importance of having a downswing thought before the backswing starts. When you find one move that starts your lower body first, you must have that key thought in mind before you start the backswing so that you can maintain rhythm and timing in the reflex movement.

When positions are correct and the backswing is sound, almost any swing thought from the start of the swing may help or improve the downswing, but few work effectively from the top. The key is to think

> The key is to think of the downswing action during the waggle and maintain that thought through the backswing.

of the downswing action during the waggle and maintain that thought through the backswing.

Any key thought used to trigger the downswing—applied before the backswing starts—alerts specific positions at address to prepare for coordination with the downswing action. In turn, positions involved affect backswing movements, which react accordingly. For instance, if pushing off against the inside of the right foot is a conscious action that you find starts good lower body action, planning the action during the waggle alerts and reinforces your right foot and knee for the down-swing action, subconsciously reinforcing your entire right side in the setup procedure. The preplanned action then contains your weight inside your right foot, maintaining timing and rhythm by promoting the action continuously from the beginning of the swing. The same key thought at the top of the swing, however, kicks the whole swing out of phase, changing timing and rhythm with a sudden burst of power from your right foot. Unless your right foot and knee are prepared for the action, the weight may move across your right foot on the backswing, whereupon any attempt from the top of the swing to push against your right foot pushes against the *outside* of the foot, rather dramatically flinging you backward, flailing your arms down first.

Although one of the more important movements in golf, the down-swing is also the most commonly difficult—so much so that you should search for key swing thoughts to help you improve the downswing action. Because your swing is unique in its weaknesses and strengths, and so many things affect the swing, you must find thoughts that fit your own golf swing. Not only are key swing thoughts different for every golfer, but they may vary from day to day for the same golfer—that's part of the challenge of golf. Remember that great golfers are separated from mediocre golfers just by the ability to do such basic things as find useful swing thoughts and know how and where to use them.

Chapter Twenty-Three

Practicing the Short Swing

Practicing the short swing below the shoulders and between the toe-up positions conditions the mind as well as the muscles and helps you develop confidence in letting your feet and legs motivate the movement of your hands and arms on the downswing.

All of the tools used for a full golf swing are also used in the short swing: the grip, position of address, waggle, forward press, toe-up positions of the clubhead, wrist break, and hitting with the right hand. Along with positions and movements, the short swing teaches balance, timing, and rhythm as keynotes of coordination.

You should practice the short swing when you're learning, analyzing, or correcting your swing. When you're learning golf, it's easier to develop fundamental positions, rhythm, and coordination in a smaller, controlled swing area, which is not as demanding as the full golf swing. When you're analyzing or correcting your swing, using a shorter swing makes it easier to sense and feel swing action, check suspected trouble areas, and minimize thought applied to *full* swing action while grooving corrected basics. In any instance, you should practice the short swing by methodically applying fundamentals in sequence with continuous movement, checking positions for accuracy while you build good swing action.

Learning golf and practicing the short swing are similar in principle to learning to drive: in both cases you use basic learning techniques to slowly develop both feeling and skill. Just as it would be foolhardy to jump into a car, switch on the ignition, and acclerate with no driving skills, you should take a patient attitude toward learning golf. To handle a car with proficiency, you must practice basics to develop reflexive skills; to develop a higher level of control in golf, you practice golf fundamentals to acquire proficiency and confidence.

Just as the three-quarter swing through the wrist break lets you develop feeling for the full golf swing, a one-quarter swing (without the wrist break) helps you develop feeling for first starting the backswing and then starting the downswing reflexively as your lower body responds to the coil-recoil action. Keeping your hands below hip level also strengthens your grip, contributing to the development of touch and feel with the hands, which is an important asset in golf.

When you apply fundamentals with deliberate accuracy, rhythm in a smaller movement combines with a firm grip and a little right-hand hitting action in the swinging movement to start your lower body forward and pull the arms and clubhead down. The same pause felt at the top of a full golf swing—which represents good timing—occurs in the miniature short swing as coordination combines with a slow backswing to delay hand action until the hands are pulled back down by the weight shifting left.

Practice the miniature movement of the short swing until the reflexive coil-recoil action of your lower body is ingrained by feeling, at which time, as long as you retain the feeling, you can gradually lengthen the swing. At any point where reflex action leaves the swing, however, or the action is forced to work, you should start the procedure again to regain the reflexive feeling.

An accurate grip and setup are of particular importance when practicing any part of the golf swing. The smallest, most insignificant positions within these larger units may independently play predominantly important roles by promoting coordination. Nothing should be overlooked as a contributing influence on the ultimate result.

Although you can establish and check your grip in the setup, it will also be reflected in your ability to hit consistently accurate shots; and accuracy should be an integral part of any practice session as further indication that the grip is correct. When practicing, incidentally, you can accomplish much *without* hitting balls to focus your attention on the swing path and on the coil-recoil action of the backswing and downswing.

PART V
Completing the Swing

Chapter Twenty-Four

Fundamental No. 15:
Completing the Follow-Through

Once their hands have passed through the hitting zone, golfers tend to let momentum complete the swing, relegating the follow-through to just an incidental result rather than a contributing force in the swing. It is a mistake, however, to believe that after the ball is hit nothing more can be accomplished to promote the shot. To complete the shot with any degree of finesse, you must regard and practice following through to the top of the swing as an essential part of the whole.

The Procedure

Extend the short swing into a completion of the swing by letting your hands swing on into a high finished position over your left shoulder. Let your weight shift entirely to the left side, rolling on across your left foot, and let your body turn by turning your stomach toward the target. Let your right foot come up on its toes, with the sole of your shoe facing away from the target, and hold the balanced position. (Figure 143)

FIGURE 143

The follow-through—
front view.

Being up on your toes is a fundamental position that allows
you to maintain good balance after completing the swing.

Importance of the Procedure

Effective completion of the follow-through:
A. *prevents you from quitting on the shot*
B. *keeps the swing on plane*
C. *teaches you feeling for a balanced follow-through*

A: Prevents you from quitting on the shot.

Following through completely is, ideally, the automatic result of a well-executed swing. So much emphasis is placed on just hitting the ball, however, that once the ball is on its way, very few golfers make a concentrated effort to really finish the shot. Consequently most golfers are quitting on the shot before the swing is finished. If you are unable to follow through to finish the shot completely, you are losing power through impact.

When you finish the shot by intentionally following through with your hands high over your left shoulder, you continue shifting your weight and accelerating the clubhead through the ball with maximum clubhead speed. Although the follow-through is regarded as an inevitable product of what precedes the action, you should never take it for granted so much that you consider it *only* the result of a well-executed swing.

Making certain that your body completes the turn by *practicing* following through tends to correct small mistakes made through the swing by pulling the swing together. Combined with hitting into the follow-through with right-arm extension, practicing the follow-through prevents such things as getting stuck on the right side and failing to shift your weight by keeping your body turning and pulling your weight left.

B: Keeps the swing on plane.

Swinging your hands up toward the right shoulder in the backswing and up over the left shoulder in the follow-through while keeping your arms together promotes good timing and keeps the swing upright on the correct swing plane.

C: Teaches you feeling for a balanced follow-through.

Few golfers know what it feels like to really finish the swing in a balanced position because they have never been in that position, either accidentally or purposely. Muscles are very reluctant to go where they have never been before, and they must frequently be taught the feeling of coordination when the hands swing on to the top. Swinging into and holding the position in practice helps you develop muscle memory and feeling for the balanced position.

If you're unaccustomed to finishing the swing and maintaining balance, you may find it difficult at first to turn your stomach toward the target and swing onto your left foot and up on your right toes. Being up on your right toes, however, is a fundamental position that allows you to maintain balance after completing the swing. The position is important as an indication of balance throughout the swing as well as a complete weight shift.

Balance through the swing, which helps you swing into a balanced position, is determined at address by the sitting-down position. As mentioned before, the feeling for a balanced setup is similar in feeling to a boxer's stance, which puts strength in the legs and feeling in the feet. Practicing good balance at address and in the follow-through helps you maintain balance while swinging.

Chapter Twenty-Five

Developing the Natural Swing

Fundamentals have been presented one by one throughout this book for the purpose of learning, and every fundamental has been presented in a sequence which, when connected, forms a circle in a natural swinging movement. In the process of learning, however, many mental specifics—or single thoughts—have been created. When these are emphasized independently or taken out of context, they cause conscious thought. Although necessary at address or when studying or practicing the swing, conscious thought must not be allowed to interfere with the natural swinging movement.

Changing swing thoughts or the swing plan after the backswing starts is an ever-present problem in golf; it changes your timing and rhythm. By resisting the urge to try to make specific fundamentals work, however, you eventually learn to trust the subconscious and allow things to happen through understanding the swing and practice.

Golf is a unique mental as well as physical endeavor. Because of the mental aspect, teaching a natural golf swing without promoting conscious thought is an instructional challenge superseded only by the physical challenge of playing the game. Oddly enough, in order to teach golfers how to develop a natural, thought-free swing, it becomes important to conclude the instruction with advice on how not to *consciously* apply the very things being taught.

Applying Fundamentals Without Conscious Thought

To develop a natural golf swing and apply fundamentals without conscious thought, you need to understand:

A. *what makes the golf swing natural*
B. *what prevents a natural swing*
C. *how to avoid conscious thought*
D. *how to apply fundamental knowledge*
E. *the importance of practice*

A: What makes the golf swing natural.

Although some individuals are born with superb muscular coordination, which makes learning and playing golf less complicated, few are born with a natural golf swing. Professional golfer Sam Snead once said, "The game is so unnatural that if you try to play it naturally, you'll never play it as well as you should." In golf, the term *natural* means only that you've developed your own skills. How and to what degree these skills are developed, however, determines your level of proficiency.

Generally, you must learn and develop a natural golf swing through any or all of four methods: (1) personal desire and motivation; (2) emulation, which is imitation so as to equal or excel; (3) golf lessons; and (4) written instruction.

Personal desire and motivation

are, of course, the very foundation for learning the age-old game. Any form of instruction is effective with enthusiasm for playing, but personal desire alone will not develop a sound golf swing. The swing is too complex. When combined with other methods, however, desire and motivation are primary factors in helping anyone develop his or her own potential.

Emulation

can also help you develop your golf swing. Young people, in particular, are great imitators and have become exceptionally competent players by simply copying other golfers. Examples include young caddies who have emulated great golfers and children who have grown up in golfing families. And today, of course, with touring professionals, golf clinics, television, and videotapes as well as golf books and magazines, students can study positions and movements very closely.

Although a natural swing can be developed through this kind of observation, there are also disadvantages. A poor golf swing can be copied as well as a good one, and unless observation also includes explanation, you may not reach your own potential by learning about basics. Although emulating a fundamentally correct swing is an excellent learning technique, emulation is most effective when also accompanied by some other method of learning that helps you understand the swing as well.

Golf lessons

from a qualified instructor is the preferred method for developing a golf swing. Because the golf swing is not natural for most people, taking lessons is always recommended for beginners as well as for experienced golfers who want to improve. All of the other methods then enhance the learning process.

Although most golf instructors are qualified to teach, many believe that explaining more than what are referred to as simple basics makes learning too complex. Because of this, and because of limited time involved, they may explain basics through the address position but are then more likely to instruct some preferred method or swing technique. Fundamentals may be included but not always explained.

Although the above teaching method may have the advantage of producing a golf swing unencumbered by conscious thought, learning only swing technique prevents golfers from being able to analyze and correct the swing because all of the basic concepts are not understood. When problems do occur (and they will), among the fundamentals *not* understood may be the very one that might have corrected the problem.

Written instruction

covers every aspect of golf in an endless supply of books and magazines. Although this provides excellent material for anyone who wants to improve, most of it is written for people who already play golf and who have already developed a golf swing. Understandably, then, most instructional subjects cover things of interest to players, such as shot-making, strategy, course management, the mental aspect of golf, equipment, swing corrections, where to play and how to play, and, of course, personal revelations about how to make it all work. While basics are covered from time to time, instruction can hardly include the entire swing and so, therefore, is generally out of context.

Although many books and articles have been written to help people learn to play golf, they are seldom written on *how to develop a golf swing*, as this book is, but rather on *how to improve in golf* once the swing is developed. Many well-read players, therefore, without understanding basics, still don't understand the golf swing.

"The game is so unnatural that if you try to play it naturally, you'll never play it as well as you should."
—Sam Snead

When the swing is not fundamentally strong to begin with, written instruction should be used in conjunction with other methods. A desire to learn the game, combined with lessons from a qualified instructor who helps you understand basics, provides an opportunity to study, observe, and apply any instruction effectively. A solution for those who want to use instructional articles most advantageously is to clip out the articles as they appear in magazines, file them under beginner, intermediate, and advanced, and use them as needed according to one's own progress and ability. The best way possible to help develop a natural swing is to use all of the methods of learning.

B: *What prevents a natural swing.*

Walter Hagen—one of America's all-time great golfers who played in the early 1900s—once responded to the statement "You really have to be dumb to play that game" with "You don't have to be, but it helps," pointing out the desirable, although somewhat unrealistic, advantage of just *having* a natural golf swing. Such a comment indicates that knowledgeable golfers undoubtedly do recognize conscious thought as a threat to a rhythmic swinging movement, but the swing proficiency of an accomplished golfer also indicates that fundamentals are understood and applied and that conscious thought can be overcome—first by application of conscious thought, then by practice to turn it into concentration.

Part of the difficulty and frustration in golf stems from the very thing that appears to make golf easy: the ball is a stationary target. Unlike in other sports such as tennis, baseball, volleyball, soccer, and table tennis, where the ball is a moving target, a golf ball sits motionless on the tee or ground. Rather than simplifying things, however, this complicates the game.

Although returning a moving ball requires specific skills that relate to the individual sport, the reflex action involved allows limited time to become involved with such things as positions or movements, swing technique, or losing the ball in a hazard. Lacking time for apprehension—that is, tension—to restrict the swing, a moving ball is returned with less tension due to reflexive response. With unlimited time allowed for setting up to the ball in golf, however, there is also time to become too mentally involved— particularly when confronted with making a fairly difficult golf shot. It is difficult to hit over lakes and bunkers, for instance, when the mind interferes with a natural swinging movement.

Overcoming the mental obstacle of hitting a stationary target is partly a matter of trusting fundamentals, practicing setting up more quickly, then swinging. With practice, starting a rhythmic swinging movement from the moment the clubhead is positioned behind the ball helps you develop more confidence by allowing you to develop the same instinctive response involved in hitting a moving target.

C: How to avoid conscious thought.

Aside from the preceding advice, there are only two ways to develop the same uncomplicated reflex swinging movement used in hitting a moving object, thereby avoiding conscious thought. You must either just *have* a natural swing and *be* a confident golfer, thereby applying fundamentals without the complication of having to understand them, or develop a natural swing based on complete understanding of all of the fundamentals, then overcome conscious thought by turning it into concentration through application and practice. The irony of golf, however, is that there is no in-between. Very few golfers know either nothing *or* everything about the golf swing, and the little bit of knowledge that every golfer has is the very thing that causes conscious thought and prevents a natural swing. Therefore it is sensible to presume that expanding on your knowledge will help you develop actions that will help you avoid conscious thought and make the golf swing natural. Your store of knowledge should include certain facts:

1. Dedicated golfers *cannot* know too much about the golf swing. Knowing too little causes conscious thought by encouraging application of only things that are understood to compensate for missing fundamentals. The one basic not applied, however, may be the very one that prevents coordination.

2. Correctly applied fundamentals will produce a natural swing when they are all connected by a rhythmically smooth and continuous swinging movement—by putting the swing in motion from the moment the clubhead is positioned behind the ball.

3. When all of the fundamentals are applied correctly, rhythm and coordination, which result in good timing, are keynotes in a reflexive, coil-recoil action of the downswing.

4. Analysis and corrections should be made only when chronic difficulty occurs. Many things affect the swing, and anyone who is less than perfect will top or slice or mis-hit the ball at times. The object is to smooth the swing so you develop confidence and consistency by missing fewer shots.

5. When chronic difficulty does occur, stop overanalyzing, looking for a reason. Rebuild your swing in practice, checking every fundamental, and *practice what is right to correct what is wrong*. Use the short swing and slow down rhythm to correct positions and movements.

6. Fear of making the shot or taking too long to set up to the ball creates tension, which prevents you from swinging rhythmically and reflexively. Trust the fundamentals. Practice setting up more quickly. Use the same procedure and the same golf swing when practicing the same golf shot.

7. Practicing the waggle allows concentration and confidence to replace conscious thought and indecision—and nothing suffices like practice in developing a natural swing. You can groove confidence, as well as the swing, in practice by applying fundamentals directed at a reflexive swing technique. And confidence and concentration developed in practice are an integral part of golf.

As you develop proficiency in addressing the ball, sense and feel take over and replace conscious thought.

D: How to apply fundamental knowledge.

All of the chapters explaining the procedure for using fundamentals have also explained the importance of each fundamental to help you understand the golf swing. Although the instruction has been lengthy for the purpose of learning, the following pages present a review of the application of fundamentals, highlighting the essential requirements that lead to developing a natural swing:

Position of Address

Sight from behind the target to determine the target line; then assume the left-hand grip and stand upright with your feet together. Using only your left hand, comfortably extend your left arm so the arm and shaft are in a straight line with each other and square the clubface to the target. Now square your feet to the square clubface.

Keeping your feet parallel to the line of flight, move first your left foot and then the right to the width of the shoulders, thereby positioning the ball at address according to the shot being made and the club being used. Angle your left foot slightly open in relation to the square right foot and keep your hips square. Sit straight down to the ball by flexing your knees inward, flex your hips back to stick your seat out a bit, and let your left hand move slightly down and inward as your right hand extends to complete the grip.

Waggle

Complete the grip by waggling the clubhead up and down to secure your right hand. Make certain your hips and shoulders remain square and your right arm and shoulder are lower than the left each time the left arm extends and the clubhead returns to the ground. At this point your posture is upright, bent slightly from the waist with the chin up, and your weight is distributed equally between your feet, *off* your toes and on the inside of the feet. The entire position is square.

Conscious thought is needed for awhile in any learning stage. As you develop proficiency in addressing the ball, however, sense and feel take over and replace conscious thought. As you waggle positions into a coordinated relationship with each other, raising the clubhead up and down helps you position your right hand as well as coordinate positions. And conscious thought changes into concentration through a back-and-forth movement behind the ball as you put a good swing plan into effect.

Forward Press

Secure positions by rolling your elbows toward each other, again firming the left arm but positioning the right arm looser and slightly lower than the left. Firming the grip, while pressing your right hand forward, rocks your legs slightly forward, with the knees parallel, and straightens your left wrist to start the movement of the backswing.

Backswing

The forward rocking movement starts the backswing, whereupon keeping your left arm straight and your right elbow down while pushing your left shoulder forward combines with turning around the strong right leg position to push the clubhead away from the ball, into and through the toe-up position. Just setting out to hit the ball combines a swinging movement with a hitting action to start a coordinated, powerful swing.

As the clubhead is pushed on through to a completion of the shoulder turn, your shoulders turn your hips around the strong right leg by shifting your weight against the right instep and pushing slightly against the ball of your left foot. Keeping your left knee pointing ahead and letting your left heel lift as your leg swings inward puts the "swing" into golf with good footwork while promoting a coil-recoil action of the upper and lower body.

Downswing

A good swing thought at the beginning of the swing, combined with completing the shoulder turn, results in reflex action from the top of the swing, where rhythm and timing cause a pause at the top as the backswing transfers to the downswing. The coil-recoil action of the upper body against the lower body starts the lower body back first, whereupon pulling with your left arm, turning your lower body toward the target, and keeping your right shoulder back pulls the arms, hands, and clubhead down into the hitting zone.

Hitting Zone

Releasing the hands and clubhead down the target line is the result of every position and movement from the start of the swing coordinating through impact. (See page 211, Figure 131.) And when the swing itself is sound, just setting out to hit the ball, keeping your head in place, and hitting through the toe-up position helps square the clubface at impact.

Follow-Through

As your weight rolls on across your left foot, your right foot comes up on its toes, and your body turns squarely toward the target in a balanced, completed follow-through.

E: The importance of practice.

Relatively few golfers, even though dedicated to self-improvement, really know how to practice. Without understanding the swing, it is difficult to know *what* to practice because the swing is so complex; consequently, observing golfers on a practice range often resembles a paid-admission spectator sport, sometimes giving the impression that, while grooving imperfection, the object of hitting balls is to get rid of them as fast as possible with maximum muscular intent. Understanding the swing, however, or having professional guidance provides key objectives for productive practice sessions.

Although you should always try to develop a natural swing unencumbered by too much thinking, practice is where you should do your thinking. Practicing should be a mental game to develop natural instinctive ability in order to prevent golf from becoming either only physical or only mental when you actually play the game. Training the mind is a matter of first knowing *what* to think about and then practicing how and where to apply it.

What and how you practice should be determined by your ability and needs and your progress from beginning to professional golfer; it should not be based on just a sudden desire to attain the unattainable or on just *being* an accomplished golfer without making the required effort. A student golfer, for instance, is ill equipped to practice the finer technique of an expert and should practice swing specifics until the swing is fundamentally sound. A countless number of things can be practiced, but certain procedures should be followed in every practice session:

1. Knowing *what* to practice is a key to any practice session. It is essential in practice to have a positive thought in mind regarding what you are to accomplish.

2. Start practice by smoothing your swing with soft short iron shots, working up through the clubs to the driver. Add maximum power only when your swing is rhythmically smooth.

3. Rhythm should be an integral part of each practice session because rhythm promotes coordination, and good coordination results in good timing. Try using a rhythmic count, such as "back and through" or "one and two"; swing back on "one," pause on "annnnnd" at the top as your weight shifts left, and hit smoothly on through the ball and into the follow-through on "two." The speed of the count fits rhythm to the tempo of the swing, which may vary between fast and slow. Whatever the count and rhythm, however, keep it the same for each golf shot to develop consistency.

4. Always line up on a target, not only to practice accuracy but to develop confidence as well. Practicing distance without accuracy gives you a false sense of security on the practice range, which leads to insecurity on the course.

5. Although distance and direction are primary goals, take time to learn feeling and balance by learning to feel positions and movements throughout the swing.

Nothing is more gratifying for established golfers than to have a sound golf swing and be able to keep the swing intact through adjustment or correction. It is a continually rewarding experience. The golf swing, however, is as unpredictable as the weather and as capricious as the wind. It is not uncommon in golf for even the best of players to sense that the swing has a mind of its own, occasionally taking a diabolically preplanned, whimsical delight in just using the golfer as an outlet for its own self-expression.

Because of the complexity of the swing and its somewhat capricious nature, not even experienced professionals are always able to find and correct recurrent problems in golf, and they have long since learned that the problems must be corrected, because the swing cannot be forced to conform. Forcing conformity into the swing simply turns on its rebellious nature; and the more insistent the golfer, the more rebellious the swing.

When chronic problems do occur and cannot be resolved in practice, it is truly the mark of an expert to accept limitations and know when to call for help. A golf swing based on fundamentals is easily corrected by a knowledgeable teacher if you don't succeed on your own.

Even professionals seek professional help, simply because it is far easier to *see* a flaw than to *feel* one in the swing. Average golfers, however, particularly those who have built their swings on basics, should be just as selective as professionals in seeking professional help. Select professional instructors who have also built *their* knowledge on the use of fundamentals.

PART VI
Golf Swing Problems and Solutions

Chapter Twenty-Six

Understanding Golf Swing Problems

Down through the centuries golf has become the most personally challenging game involving the largest number of players throughout the world, partly because those who pursue the game accept the frustration as part of the challenge of playing.

Because of the dedication of so many to a game that is loved so much, golf continues to command the attention of those still searching for ways to lessen the frustration and increase the pleasure of golf; consequently, many hundreds of books have been directed toward this end. Regardless of how much time and effort is spent on behalf of beleaguered golfers, however, problems will always occur in golf. Oddly enough, that is part of its fascination.

Understanding the golf swing—which, admittedly, takes much time and effort—will help you overcome problems in golf by either preventing them or correcting them. Initially you prevent problems by using fundamentals to develop a sound, repeating swing, and you correct problems by using fundamentals to adjust or correct selective parts of the swing that relate to specific problems.

Although understanding the golf swing makes it possible to prevent or correct recurring problems, two factors still make it difficult to improve beyond a certain point. First, most golfers are unable to determine what constitutes a problem to begin with; second, few golfers understand what the underlying problems are that cause additional problems in golf.

Between obvious and underlying golf swing problems, the latter are more troublesome because they are often small, insignificant things that cause the more obvious problems but are often overlooked. Topping the ball, for instance, may obviously be caused by the weight shifting right rather than left through impact. But the underlying cause may be a fast backswing, which prevents you from being able to shift your weight correctly. Such factors are seldom corrected, however, because they are not generally recognized as causes.

So many things—positions and movements, timing and rhythm, dedication and practice, experience and attitude, and mental as well as physical ability—influence the outcome of the golf swing that you can't expect the cause of a problem such as slicing to be exactly the same from one golfer to another. Nor can the seemingly identical problem always be corrected with the same easy solution.

Every factor involved in golf affects each golf swing differently— and there may be one or several reasons for any poor outcome. Understanding the problem and knowing which fundamental—or which combination of fundamentals—will correct that particular problem, in that particular golf swing, at that particular moment is essential for both correction as a teacher and self-improvement as a golfer.

Two other things are important to remember about correcting your golf swing: First, preventing problems is still the best solution. Second, it is important to know what is right as well as what is wrong. Simply going back to basics by following the step-by-step procedure for rebuilding the swing—*without* in-depth analysis—will gradually eradicate even a major problem. And knowing what is right as well as what is wrong when looking for solutions simply eliminates factors that do not relate. Checking off areas that are known to be correct when compared with fundamentals leaves fewer things to consider as possible personal problems.

The troubleshooting guide in the next chapter is intended to help dedicated, and generally more analytically minded, golfers become more knowledgeable about golf swing problems. Although it will be helpful, it is not intended to be a panacea for every personal problem in golf. Remember that correction is still a matter of detection—identifying the real problem so you can isolate and correct it.

Chapter Twenty-Seven

Correcting Golf Swing Problems

Problem	Common Causes	Page/Reference
Alignment difficulty with	▸ Having no guidelines or procedure for attaining objectives at address	31–35, 37, 53(G) 105–110
	▸ Difficulty sighting the target line or difficulty with visual alignment due to incorrect head position	47(B), 206(C)
	▸ Incorrect grip	7–9
	▸ Positioning clubhead with right hand or positioning right foot first	49(E), 63(B)
	▸ Positioning feet before first squaring clubface	43, 57, 60(A)
	▸ Difficulty positioning and setting angle of feet	64(D)
	▸ Pushing square positions open while either completing grip or using forward press or waggle	39(B), 94(A), 115(A)
	▸ Waggling positions out of alignment	35
	▸ Insufficient practice	254(E)
Angle of Attack steep	▸ Loose left-hand grip	16(B), 174(1)
	▸ Quick wrist break before reaching the parallel shaft position	159–161
	▸ Fast backswing with lazy arms through the hitting zone	222(B)
	▸ Difficulty sweeping clubhead through hitting zone	206 (Fig. 127)
	▸ *See also Clubhead, throwing from the top*	

Apprehension	▸ *See Tension*	
Arms positioning incorrectly	▸ Incorrect or rigid left-arm extension at address	48(C), 53(H), 100(A)
	▸ Positioning right arm higher than left when positioning arms together	102(C)
swing action of, difficulty with	▸ Crowding arms at address by not extending left arm	49(D)
	▸ Positioning chin too low	41(D)
	▸ Tension due to incorrect left-arm procedure at address	53(H), 100(A)
	▸ Flying right elbow	138(F)
	▸ Bending left arm at top of swing	100(B)
	▸ Difficulty extending and accelerating arms due to not keeping arms together	102(D), 103(E)
	▸ Difficulty combining rhythm with tempo due to fast backswing	188–189
	▸ Misunderstanding hitting action	215–216, 218(A), 222(B)
	▸ Incomplete follow-through	245(A)
	▸ Having no guidelines for swinging due to insufficient short swing practice between toe-up positions	193–195, 199(A), 208(D), 223(C), 227(D), 239–240
	▸ *See also Weight shift, difficulty with, or reverse*	
Backswing fast	▸ Not understanding that the one fastest moment in swing must be reserved for impact	188–189
	▸ Having no key objectives in practice due to not understanding the golf swing	254(E)
	▸ Insufficient practice in developing concentration by developing the waggle	105–110
	▸ Misunderstanding hitting action and trying to hit too hard	81, 222(B)
	▸ Positioning hands behind the ball without using a forward press	49(E), 115(A)
	▸ Hitting only with the hands	143(G), 215–216
	▸ Difficulty developing timing and rhythm	145(H), 255(3)
incomplete	▸ *See Blocking out, backswing; Shoulder turn, incomplete*	
overswinging in, problem of	▸ Short left thumb	18(D)
	▸ Loose left-hand grip	16(B), 24(B), 174(1)
	▸ Stance too narrow	71(E)

	‣ Right knee and right foot positioned incorrectly	67(4), 176(4), 176(5)
	‣ Hips and shoulders turning together into backswing due to dipping or bending left knee	133(C), 143(G)
	‣ Swinging too fast	145(H)
	‣ Bending left arm at top of swing	100(B)
	‣ Flying right elbow combined with full shoulder turn	138(F), 176(3)
	‣ Insufficient practice in just shortening the backswing while practicing the follow-through	179
	‣ *See also Hands, letting go at the top*	
restricted	‣ Stance too wide	71(E)
	‣ Positioning chin too low	41(D)
	‣ Difficulty with left foot and left knee action	168(B)
	‣ Keeping right elbow in too tight on full golf shots	103(E), 138(F), 176(3)
	‣ Right thumb, as well as left, under shaft at top of swing	27(D)
	‣ *See also Swaying, back and forth*	
starting, difficulty	‣ Having no procedure to follow for attaining objectives at address	31–32
	‣ Not understanding beginning movement of swing	43
	‣ Difficulty changing conscious thought into concentration by developing key swing thoughts	106, 146(I), 235–238
	‣ Wasting concentration on fundamental procedure	35
	‣ Taking too long to set up to the ball	252(6)
	‣ Leaving out the waggle and forward press	118(C), 119(D), 252(7)
stopping, difficulty	‣ Starting too fast	145(H)
	‣ Stubbing clubhead going back due to pressing clubhead down too hard or positioning hands behind ball	162(D)
	‣ Quick reflex action of downswing	237

Balance establishing and maintaining, difficulty	‣ Having no procedure to follow for attaining objectives at address	31–32, 37, 53(G), 97(C)
	‣ Angle of feet incorrect	64(D)
	‣ Incorrect left arm extension at address	49(D)
	‣ Keeping the hips rolled under when addressing the ball	84(A)
	‣ Narrow stance	71(E)
	‣ Poor posture with chin too low and weight on toes	38(A), 41(C), 97(C)
	‣ Weight established too much left or too much right	63(C)
	‣ Head positioned incorrectly	209 (Fig. 129)
	‣ Knees not flexed inward	86(C)
	‣ Incorrect ball position	72(F)

	▸ Swinging too fast and trying to hit too hard	145(H), 222(B)
	▸ Poor footwork	168(B)
	▸ Insufficient practice swinging into a balanced position	245(C)
	▸ *See also Ball, falling away from*	

Ball
   difficulty hitting

	▸ Ball is a stationary target	250(B)

falling away from

	▸ Upper body, rather than lower body, starting down-swing	235–238
	▸ Incomplete shoulder turn	185(10)
	▸ Ball positioned too far back in stance	72(F)
	▸ Weight established on right foot	63(C)
	▸ Quick wrist break before reaching the parallel shaft position	159–161
	▸ Left knee dipping down or bending forward as soon as backswing starts	143(G)
	▸ Difficulty developing timing and rhythm due to swinging too fast	145(H), 222(B), 255(2), 255(3)
	▸ Misunderstanding term ''staying behind the ball''	227(D)
	▸ Angle of left foot closed and weight stuck on right side	69–70, 199(A)
	▸ Insufficient short swing practice	239–240
	▸ Insufficient practice swinging into the follow-through	245(A)
	▸ *See also Balance; Hands, hitting from the top; Weight shift, reverse*	

hitting behind

	▸ Incorrect or loose grip	16(B), 24(B), 174(1)
	▸ Ball positioned too far forward	72(F)
	▸ Positioning hands behind ball	49(E)
	▸ Bending the knees too much	84(A)
	▸ Quick wrist break before reaching the parallel shaft position	159–161
	▸ Bending left arm at top of swing	100(B)
	▸ Dipping or bending left knee as soon as backswing starts	143(G)
	▸ Weight stuck on right side	199(A)
	▸ Upper body starting downswing due to incomplete shoulder turn	185(10)
	▸ Insufficient practice swinging into follow-through	245(A), 245(C)
	▸ *See also Ball, falling away from; Hands, hitting from the top*	

hitting in front of or on top of	‣ Ball positioned too far back in stance	72(F)
	‣ Weak or collapsing left wrist through backswing	180(7)
	‣ Being lazy with arm action and hitting with the hands	222(B)
	‣ Coming over the top with the right shoulder and swinging from outside in	202(B)
	‣ Difficulty staying behind the ball	227(D)
	‣ *See also Swaying, back and forth*	
hooking	‣ Ball curving left due to clubhead returning either on the line of flight or from inside out but with clubface closed to swing path	202–203 (Figs. A & B), 232 (Fig. 141)
	caused by	
	‣ Having no guidelines for swinging due to insufficient short swing practice between toe-up positions	193–195, 208(D), 223(C), 239–240, 245(B)
	‣ Closed positions at address	33–34
	‣ Grip incorrect by being too strong	7–9, 26(C), 228(E)
''killing''	‣ Misunderstanding hitting action in golf	222(B)
lunging through	‣ *See Swaying, back and forth*	
positioning, difficulty	‣ Having no procedure to follow for setting up to the ball	31–32, 53(G), 72(F), 77(G)
	‣ Incorrect left arm extension at address	49(D)
	‣ Positioning feet before positioning clubhead	57
	‣ Positioning right foot first	63(B)
pulling	‣ Ball hit straight left of target due to outside-in swing path and clubface square to swing path	202–203 (Figs. A & B), 231 (Fig. 140)
	caused by	
	‣ Difficulty with alignment, which causes open positions or closed clubface at address	33–34, 46(A), 47(B)
	‣ Reaching too far to position clubhead	49(D)
	‣ Ball positioned too far forward	72(F)
	‣ Angle of left foot either too open or too closed	68–69
	‣ Positioning right arm higher than left, which tends to fly the elbow	102(C), 138(F)
	‣ Weight established or stuck on right side	63(C)
	‣ Starting clubhead sharply inside on flat swing plane	125(A)
	‣ Swinging too fast or trying to hit too hard	81, 145(H), 222(B)
	‣ Difficulty combining rhythm with tempo due to fast backswing	188–189

	Separation of arms while swinging	102(D)
	Right shoulder starting forward from top of swing	185(10), 202(B)
	Difficulty accelerating and extending arms through hitting zone	103(E), 222(B)
	Closed clubface at impact due to poor hand action	223(C)
	Having no guidelines for swinging due to insufficient short swing practice between toe-up positions	193–195, 199(A), 208(D), 227(D), 239–240, 245(B)

pushing

▸ Ball hit straight right of target due to swinging inside-out with clubface square to swing path   202–203 (Figs. A & B), 232 (Fig. 141)

caused by

▸ Closed positions or open clubface at address due to incorrect alignment   33–34, 46(A), 47(B)

▸ Positioning hands behind ball or positioning right arm higher than left, which pulls the clubhead back and loops it from the top   49(E), 102(C)

▸ Ball positioned too far back in stance   72(F)

▸ Pushing clubface open with waggle or forward press   115(A), 118(B)

▸ Flying right elbow   138(F)

▸ Angle of left foot closed   68–69

▸ Difficulty releasing due to insufficient short swing practice between toe-up positions   193–195, 199(A), 208(D), 223(C), 239–240, 245(B)

▸ *See also Blocking out, forward swing*

quitting on

▸ *See Golf shots*

scooping

▸ Cupping right hand under left rather than hands rolling over into toe-up position   223(C)

caused by

▸ Positioning hands behind ball   49(E)

▸ Weight stuck on right side   63(C), 199(A)

▸ Poor footwork due to keeping right heel down through hitting zone   208(D)

▸ Tension or apprehension resulting from lack of practice   252(6)

▸ Insufficient practice swinging into follow-through   245(A)

▸ *See also Ball, skulling*

shanking

▸ Hitting the ball dead right by hitting on the hosel; a result of pulling the clubhead sharply inward away from the ball, then looping or casting it to outside the line of flight, back through impact with the face wide open . . .

▸ . . . swinging sharply from inside to outside with the face wide open and the hosel leading the clubface through impact

caused by

▸ Having no guidelines for swinging correctly due to insufficient practice between toe-up positions   193–195, 223(C), 239–240

▸ Positioning right arm higher than left   102(C)

▸ Pulling clubhead away from ball and looping from the top   49(E)

▸ Pulling clubhead around in a flat swing plane rather than swinging the clubhead upright   125(A)

▸ Open clubface at impact due to fear of shanking   226

▸ Tension caused by fear and apprehension due to fear of shanking again   252(6)

▸ Incorrect left arm extension at address that causes reaching too far—*or* playing the ball too close   49(D)

▸ Inexperienced golfers incorrectly practicing high cut shots   80

▸ Having no short swing guidelines for either hand action or swing path   239–240

(*NOTE:* Shanking the ball is generally preceded by pulling; therefore, correcting problems that relate to pulling helps eliminate shanking.)

skulling

▸ Hitting grounders by hitting top half of ball on upswing with leading edge of short iron

caused by

▸ Ball positioned too far back in stance   72(F)

▸ Positioning hands behind ball   49(E)

▸ Incorrect setup for short shots   77(G)

▸ Left knee dipping down or bending forward into backswing   143(G)

▸ Cupping right hand under left and bending left wrist inward   223(C)

▸ Keeping right heel down through impact   213(E)

▸ Weight stuck on right side due to insufficient practice between the toe-up positions   199(A), 208(D), 239–240

▸ *See also Ball, topping; Looking up*

skying

▸ Ball skied or popped up due to chopping down with the woods and hitting under the ball with the top of the clubhead

	‣ Incomplete shoulder turn or shoulders coming over the top	185(10), 202(B)
	‣ Collapsed left wrist at top of swing with *right* thumb, as well as left, under shaft	27(D), 180(7)
	‣ Separation of arms while swinging	102(D)
	‣ Poor hand action due to insufficient practice between toe-up positions	208(D), 239–240, 245(B)
	‣ *See also Ball, pulling; Swaying, back and forth*	
toeing	‣ Incorrect left-arm extension at address	48(C), 49(D)
	‣ Standing too upright with heel of clubhead off ground	88(E)
	‣ Poor hand action due to insufficient short swing practice between the toe-up positions	199(A), 208(D), 223(C), 239–240, 245(B)
	‣ Positioning hands behind ball	49(E)
	‣ *See also Clubface, hitting on heel or toe of*	
topping	‣ Hitting grounders by hitting top half of ball with bottom of clubhead on the upswing	
	caused by	
	‣ Positioning hands behind ball by positioning club with right hand or positioning right foot first	49(E), 63(B)
	‣ Ball positioned too far left *or* too far right	72(F)
	‣ Loose left-hand grip	16(B), 174(1)
	‣ Angle of left foot closed	69–70
	‣ Addressing ball with hips rolled under and knees too bent	84(A)
	‣ Dipping or bending left knee as soon as backswing starts	143(G)
	‣ Quick wrist break before reaching the parallel shaft position	159–161
	‣ Swinging too fast and trying to hit too hard	145(H), 222(B)
	‣ Weight stuck on right side due to insufficient short swing practice	199(A), 239–240
	‣ Weight on right through impact due to weight established too much left or too much right	63(C)
whiffing	‣ Standing stiff-legged and reaching too far	48(C), 49(D), 88(D)
	‣ Weight firmly established on either left or right foot	63(C)
	‣ Misunderstanding hitting action in golf	138(E), 215–216, 222(B)
	‣ Left knee dipping down or jutting forward through backswing	143(G)
	‣ *See also Ball, falling away from*	

Blocking Out			
backswing		▸ Open positions at address that prevent shoulder turn and pivot	39(B), 55(I)
		▸ Positioning right arm higher than left	102(C)
		▸ Poor posture with chin too low and weight on toes	41(C)
		▸ Flying right elbow	138(F)
		▸ *See also Swaying, back and forth*	
forward swing		▸ Closed positions at address	33–34
		▸ Angle of left foot closed	68–69
		▸ Ball positioned too far forward	72(F)
		▸ Poor posture with chin too low and weight on toes	41(C)
		▸ Swinging flat-footed	213(E)
		▸ Misunderstanding hitting action	222(B)
		▸ Insufficient practice in clearing left side and releasing into a balanced follow-through	199(A), 208(D), 245(C)
		▸ *See also Swaying, back and forth*	
Casting		▸ *See Clubhead*	
Chin Position			
incorrect		▸ *See Head position*	
Clubface			
closed		▸ *See Ball, hooking; pulling*	
hitting on heel or toe of		▸ Incorrect left-arm extension at address	48(C), 49(D)
		▸ Positioning clubhead with heel or toe up by leaning over too far or standing too upright	88(E)
		▸ *See also Ball, shanking; toeing*	
hooded		▸ Square clubface at address but setting or pressing hands beyond straight arm–shaft position	52–53, 115(A)
		▸ Ball positioned too far back in stance	72(F)
		▸ *See also Ball, smothering; Swaying, back and forth*	
open		▸ *See Ball, pushing; shanking; slicing*	
Clubhead			
accelerating, difficulty		▸ Difficulty coordinating swinging with hitting	222(B)
		▸ Inability to combine rhythm with tempo due to fast backswing	188–189
		▸ *See also Clubhead Speed*	

casting	▸ Throwing clubhead outward from top of swing, beyond target lines, and back through hitting zone from outside in	
	caused by	
	▸ Standing too far from ball with weight on toes	49(D)
	▸ Loose grip	16(B)
	▸ Bending left arm at top of swing	100(B)
	▸ Right shoulder coming over the top	202(B)
	▸ *See also Hands, hitting from the top*	
dropping at the top	▸ Weak or loose left-hand grip	16(B), 16(C), 174(1)
	▸ Short thumb	18(D)
	▸ Fast backswing	145(H)
	▸ Bending left arm at top of swing	100(B)
laying off	▸ *See Swing Plane, flat*	
looping	▸ Target lines not parallel	34
	▸ Positioning right arm higher than left	102(C)
	▸ Positioning hands behind ball and pulling clubhead away with fast backswing	49(E), 115(A)
	▸ Starting clubhead too much inside or too much outside on backswing	125(A)
	▸ Right shoulder diving forward from top of swing	202(B)
overcontrolling	▸ Right-hand grip stronger than left or separation of hands while swinging	24(B), 26(C)
	▸ Tightening tips of forefingers	19(E), 28(E)
	▸ Positioning hands behind ball	115(A)
	▸ Cocking the hands sharply upward at start of swing	159–161
	▸ Misunderstanding hitting action in golf and hitting only with the hands	138(E), 215–216
	▸ Swinging too fast and trying to kill the ball	145(H), 222(B)
	▸ Incomplete shoulder turn	185(10)
	▸ *See also Hands, hitting from the top; Tension*	
picking up	▸ Difficulty with left-arm extension at address and through the backswing	48(C), 100(B), 103(E)
	▸ Pressing the hands too far beyond a straight arm–shaft position	115(A)
	▸ Cocking the hands sharply upward before reaching parallel shaft position	138(E), 159–161

positioning, difficulty	▸ Having no procedure to follow for establishing positions in sequence	31–32, 49(D), 53(G)
	▸ Not knowing how or where to position ball	72(F)
releasing, difficulty	▸ *See Releasing*	
stubbing	▸ Pressing clubhead down too hard or positioning hands behind ball	162(D)
throwing from the top	▸ Loose left-hand grip	16(B), 174(1)
	▸ Fast backswing	145(H)
	▸ Bending left elbow	100(B)
	▸ Incomplete shoulder turn	171(D)
	▸ Insufficient practice in moving lower body first from top of swing	199(A)

Clubhead Speed		
difficulty developing	*Problems could be caused by any of the following:*	
	▸ Incorrect or loose grip	7–9, 16(B)
	▸ Poor posture, balance, and weight distribution due to poor procedure	37, 38(A), 84(A)
	▸ Short extension of arms while swinging or flattening the swing plane	103(E), 125(A)
	▸ Difficulty coordinating swinging with hitting	138(E), 143(G), 215–216, 222(B)
	▸ Bending left elbow caused by fast backswing	100(B), 145(H)
	▸ Inability to combine rhythm with tempo due to fast backswing	188–189
	▸ Moving the swing center	67(2)
	▸ Incomplete shoulder turn	66(1), 185(10)
	▸ Separation of arms while swinging	102(D), 245(B)
	▸ Collapsed left wrist at top of swing	180(7)
	▸ Difficulty starting lower body first from top of swing	235–238
	▸ Having no guidelines for swinging correctly due to insufficient short swing practice between the toe-up positions	193–195, 199(A), 208(D), 223(C), 227(D), 239–240
	▸ Incomplete follow-through	68–69, 245(A)
	▸ Insufficient practice	189–190, 254(E)
	▸ Grooving or adjusting swing to ill-fitting clubs	88(E)
	▸ *See also Concentration; Tension*	
Coming over the Top	▸ *See Shoulders*	

Concentration, poor	▸ Knowing too little about the golf swing	250(B), 251(C)
	▸ Having no procedure to follow for setting up to the ball	31–35
	▸ Inability to turn conscious thought into concentration	146(I)
	▸ Wasting concentration on fundamental procedure	35
	▸ Difficulty programming the downswing before the backswing starts	235–238
	▸ Insufficient practice in developing the waggle	105–108, 252(7)
	▸ Change in disposition and attitude	189

Confidence lack of	▸ Not understanding the use of fundamentals	1–3, 109
	▸ Having no procedure to follow for setting up to the ball	31–32
	▸ Taking too long to set up to the ball to hit a stationary target	250(B), 252(6)
	▸ Inability to accept an occasional poor shot	251(4)
	▸ Analyzing the swing while playing rather than grooving the swing in practice	252(5)
	▸ Insufficient practice in grooving instinctive reflexive responses by learning to waggle	105–110, 239–240, 252(7)
	▸ Developing false sense of security by practicing distance without accuracy	255(4)
	▸ Infrequent practice	189–190

Conscious Thought interference from	▸ Difficulty grooving natural instinctive responses by:	
	1. Learning to waggle	105–110
	2. Learning the use of key swing thoughts	146(I)
	3. Programming the downswing	235–238
	4. Practicing	252(7), 254(E)
	▸ Knowing too little about the golf swing	250(B), 251(C), 162(1)
	▸ Changing swing thoughts or swing plan after the backswing starts	247
	▸ *See also Confidence, lack of*	

Consistency addressing ball with, difficulty	▸ Having no procedure to follow for stepping up to the ball the same way every time	35, 37, 53(G), 105–106
	▸ Having no sequence to follow for positioning ball and clubhead correctly in relation to feet	47(B), 49(D), 60(A), 72(F)
	▸ Insufficient practice in developing the waggle	105–110, 252(7)

| swinging with, difficulty | ▸ Having no guidelines or checkpoints throughout the golf swing | 3 |
| | ▸ Incorrect grip | 7–9, 228(E) |

	▸ Not understanding the purpose or use of waggle	105–106
	▸ Bending left or flying right elbow	100(B), 138(F)
	▸ Separation of hands or arms while swinging	24(B), 102(D)
	▸ Difficulty with timing, rhythm, and tempo due to fast backswing	145(H), 188–189
	▸ Difficulty coordinating swinging and hitting	222(B)
	▸ Overanalyzing	251(4), 252(5)
	▸ Insufficient practice	239–240, 254(E)
	▸ *See also Concentration, poor; Swing path, difficulty with*	
Coordination **poor**	▸ Knowing too little about the basic golf swing	1–2, 3–4, 251(1)
	▸ Trying to attain unknown objectives with positions established at random	31–32, 37
	▸ Incorrect or loose grip	7–9, 16(B)
	▸ Tension caused by taking too long to set up to the ball	252(6)
	▸ Insufficient practice in learning how to waggle	105–106, 252(7)
	▸ Bending left arm or separating arms while swinging along with difficulty coordinating swinging and hitting	100(B), 102(D), 215–216, 222(B)
	▸ Fast backswing, which prevents good timing, rhythm, and tempo	145(H), 188–189, 255(3)
	▸ Having no guidelines for swinging correctly due to insufficient practice between toe-up positions	193–195, 199(A), 208(D), 227(D), 239–240, 245(B)
	▸ Angle of feet incorrect	66(1), 68–69
	▸ *See Shoulder turn, incomplete*	
Crossing the Line	▸ *See Swing plane*	
Downswing **starting correct,** **difficulty**	▸ Difficulty programming the downswing before the backswing starts	235–238
	▸ Right foot angled open and right knee not flexed inward	66(1), 67(4), 168(A), 176(5)
	▸ Difficulty combining swinging and hitting due to misunderstanding hitting action	143(G), 215–216, 218(A), 222(B)
	▸ Bending left elbow	195
	▸ Swinging too fast	145(H)
	▸ Moving the swing center	206(C)
	▸ Incomplete or incorrect shoulder turn	171(D), 185(10)
	▸ Weight stuck on right side	199(A)
	▸ Insufficient short swing practice	239–240
	▸ Difficulty completing the follow-through	245(A)
	▸ *See also Weight shift*	

Dropping the Clubhead at the Top	▸ See Clubhead	

Elbow(s) bending left	▸ Left arm not firmly extended at address	48(C), 100(B)
	▸ Pulling clubhead away with hands instead of using shoulder turn	49(E), 174(2)
	▸ Quick wrist break before reaching the parallel shaft position	161
	▸ Fast backswing combined with lazy arms through hitting zone	145(H), 222(B)
flying right	▸ Positioning arms incorrectly or separating arms while swinging	102(C & D), 138(F), 245(B)
	▸ Positioning right arm higher than left	102(C)
	▸ Swinging the hands into the backswing with the clubface closed	223(C)
	▸ Leaving out the hitting action	218(A)

Extension difficulty with	▸ See Swing arc, narrow or restricted	

Feet difficulty positioning	▸ Having no procedure to follow for setting up to the ball	31–32, 57
	▸ Positioning feet before squaring clubface	43, 46(A), 60(A)
	▸ Postioning right foot first	63(B)
	▸ Having no guidelines for:	
	1. Where to position ball	72(F)
	2. How far to stand from ball	49(D)
	3. How wide the stance should be	71(E)
	4. Setting angle of feet	64(D)

Firing and Falling Back	▸ See Ball, falling away from	

Flying Right Elbow	▸ See Elbow(s)	

Follow-Through incomplete	▸ Angle of left foot closed	68–69
	▸ Positioning chin too low	41(D), 206(C)
	▸ Difficulty coordinating swinging and hitting due to fast backswing	145(H), 215–216, 222(B)
	▸ Quitting on the shot caused by backswing too long on short shots	80
	▸ Insufficient practice swinging into a balanced follow-through	245(C)
	▸ See also Ball, falling away from	

Footwork		
poor	▸ Poor posture, balance, and weight distribution due to:	
	1. Incorrect procedure	15(A), 37, 97(C)
	2. Reaching too far to position clubhead with weight on toes	38(A), 49(D)
	3. Weight established too much left or too much right	63(C)
	4. Incorrect sitting down position	41(C), 86(C), 88(D)
	▸ Angle of feet incorrect	64(D)
	▸ Incorrect ball position	72(F)
	▸ Keeping feet and legs inactive by swinging only with hands and arms	143(G), 215–216
	▸ Difficulty coordinating swinging-hitting action due to swinging too fast	145(H), 215–216, 222(B)
	▸ Swinging flat-footed by keeping heels on ground	168(B), 213(E)
	▸ Difficulty coordinating left-foot and left-knee action	169(C), 185(13)
	▸ Swaying across right foot with right knee moving beyond instep	176(4 & 5)
	▸ Consciously maneuvering feet and legs while excluding other basics	119(D)
	▸ Incomplete follow-through	245(C)
	▸ Insufficient short swing practice between the toe-up positions	193–195, 199(A), 208(D), 239–240
	▸ *See also Weight shift*	

Frustration		
	▸ Inability to establish and swing through positions that promote coordination	3
	▸ Forcing conformity into a swing that is not fundamentally sound	255
	▸ Swinging too fast and trying to hit too hard	145(H), 222(B)
	▸ Inability to understand and accept the unique challenge of golf	147, 259
	▸ Trying to hit a stationary target	250(B)
	▸ Insufficient practice	189–190, 254(E)
	▸ *See also Conscious thought, interference from; Tension*	

Golf		
difficulty playing	▸ Not understanding that the golf swing is not natural but can be developed	1, 248(A)
	▸ Not understanding the importance of developing a golf swing based on fundamentals	3–4
	▸ Difficulty hitting a stationary target	250(B)
	▸ Inability to concentrate by not developing key swing thoughts	146(I)
	▸ Insufficient practice	254(E)

Golf Shots		
erratic	▸ Incorrect grip	228(F)
	▸ Flying right elbow	138(F)
	▸ Target lines not parallel	60(A)
	▸ *See also Swing plane, change in*	
fat	▸ *See Ball, hitting behind*	
quitting on	▸ Angle of left foot closed	68–69
	▸ Difficulty hitting (on through) short shots due to backswing too long	80
	▸ Insufficient practice releasing through hitting zone and swinging into the follow-through	199(A), 245(A), 245(C)
	▸ *See also Follow-through, incomplete; Tension*	

Golf Swing		
analyzing, difficulty	▸ Not understanding the golf swing so as to recognize what the underlying problems are that cause additional problems	1–2, 259–260
	▸ Learning only swing technique without understanding basics	249
	▸ Analyzing full swing rather than just going back to basics for correction in the short swing	239, 252(5)
	▸ Overanalyzing due to inability to accept occasional imperfection	147, 251(4)
developing natural, difficulty	▸ Not understanding that the golf swing is not natural but can be developed	1, 248(A)
	▸ Missing important step-by-step procedure for developing swing	187–188
	▸ Insufficient practice	254(E)

Grip		
incorrect or loose	▸ Not understanding importance of grip in overall swing efficiency	7–9
	▸ Not knowing where the pressure points should be	13(Fig. 9), 16(B & C), 23(Fig. 21), 174(1)
	▸ Tightening thumbs and tips of forefingers	19(E), 28(E)
	▸ Keeping the clubhead on the ground to secure right hand grip	24(A & B)
	▸ Right hand not drawn downward over left thumb	23(Fig. 22)
	▸ Either hand turned too far left or too far right with right hand, in particular, too far under shaft	26(C), 228(E)
	▸ Loosening right-hand grip while positioning right arm	102(C)
	▸ *See also Hands, letting go at the top*	

Hand Action
poor

▸	Incorrect or loose grip	7, 26(C)
▸	Tension caused by tightening tips of forefingers	19(E), 28(E)
▸	Starting clubhead sharply inside on flat swing plane	125(A)
▸	Incorrect wrist break due to positioning hands incorrectly	154(B)
▸	Bending left wrist inward through backswing	180(7)
▸	Misunderstanding hitting action	138(E), 215–216, 218(A), 222(B)
▸	Swinging too fast and trying to hit too hard	145(H), 222(B)
▸	Swinging hands around rather than upright toward the shoulders	176(3), 245(B)
▸	Incomplete follow-through	245(A), 245(C)
▸	Overswinging	177(6), 183(8)
▸	Weight established too far left, too far right, or on the toes	38(A), 63(C)
▸	Having no guidelines for swinging due to insufficient short swing practice between toe-up positions	193–195, 199(A), 208(D), 223(C), 227(D), 239–240
▸	*See also Arms; Hands*	

Hands
hitting from the top

▸	Loose left-hand grip or grip too tight	16(B), 28(E), 174(1)
▸	Overcontrolling clubhead due to incorrect right-hand grip	26(C)
▸	Difficulty coordinating swinging-hitting action due to fast backswing	145(H), 215–216, 222(B)
▸	Early wrist break with hands controlling clubhead	159–161
▸	Bending left arm at top of swing	100(B)
▸	Bending or dipping left knee downward or forward rather than letting the left leg swing inward	143(G)
▸	Incomplete shoulder turn	171(D), 185(10)
▸	Angle of left foot closed with weight stuck on right side	69–70, 199(A)
▸	Insufficient practice in starting lower body first from top of swing	235–238, 239–240
▸	*See also Ball, falling away from*	

letting go at the top

▸	Weak or loose left-hand grip	16(B & C), 174(1)
▸	Fast backswing	145(H)
▸	Collapsed left wrist at top of swing	180(7)
▸	Separation of hands while swinging	24(B)

overactive

▸	*See Clubhead, overcontrolling*

positioning, incorrectly	▸ Difficulty positioning hands correctly due to following poor procedure	24(A), 49(D), 85(B)
	▸ Positioning right foot first	63(B)
	▸ Positioning hands behind ball without using a forward press to straighten left wrist	51(Fig. 43), 115(Fig. 78)
	▸ Pressing the hands beyond a straight arm–shaft position	117 (Fig. 79)
	▸ Overswinging	183(8)
	▸ *See also Grip, incorrect or loose; Posture, poor*	
pulling clubhead away from ball	▸ Positioning hands behind ball and not using a forward press, which causes knees and shoulders to move laterally rather than turn rotationally	49(E), 115(A), 130(B)
	▸ Positioning right foot first	63(B)
	▸ Not understanding difference between pushing and pulling in a swinging movement	145(H)
releasing, difficulty	▸ *See Releasing*	

Head Position
incorrect

	▸ Chin-on-chest position due to poor procedure, leaning over too far, looking straight down at ball rather than cocking the chin to the right, or wearing bifocals	15(A), 41(C), 206(C)
	▸ *See also Posture, poor*	
moving	▸ *See Looking up; Swaying*	

Hips
open alignment of

	▸ Having no procedure or guidelines at address for setting up square	31–35
	▸ Pushing positions open while securing right-hand grip	94(A)
	▸ Positioning right foot first	63(B)
	▸ Angle of right foot too closed	68(5)
	▸ Hips slipping open while setting up to the ball	39(B)
	▸ Pressing hands too far forward with either waggle or forward press	115(A), 118(B)

Hitting from the Top ▸ *See Hands*

Key Swing Thoughts
difficulty using

| | ▸ Difficulty turning conscious thought into concentration | 106 |
| | ▸ *See also Concentration, poor* | |

Knees		
incorrect action of	▸ Bending knees forward at address rather than flexing them inward	84(A), 86(C)
	▸ Incorrect use of forward press	118(C)
	▸ Poor footwork due to conscious effort made to either lift the left heel or keep it down	168(B)
	▸ Left knee dipping down or jutting forward through backswing	143(G)
	▸ Knees and hips moving laterally as the backswing starts	130(B)
	▸ Right knee swaying beyond right instep due to knee not flexed inward	176(4)
	▸ *See also Footwork, poor*	

Laying Off	▸ *See Swing Plane, flat*	

Left Arm Bending	▸ *See Elbow(s)*	

Legs		
inactive	▸ Incorrect procedure that prevents good posture and balance at address	37, 97(C)
	▸ Allocating the swing to just the hands and arms	143(G)
	▸ Insufficient short swing practice between the toe-up positions	193–195, 199(A), 208(D), 239–240
	▸ Difficulty developing the forward press and waggle	105–110, 118(C)
	▸ Insufficient practice in swinging into the follow-through	245(A), 245(C)
	▸ *See also Footwork, poor*	

Looking Up		
	▸ Positioning chin too low	41(D), 206(C)
	▸ Reverse weight shift caused by dipping left knee downward	143(G)
	▸ Right shoulder coming over the top	202(B), 228
	▸ Weight stuck on right side due to swaying across right foot	67(2), 199(A)
	▸ Insufficient short swing practice in keeping head steady	239–240
	▸ *See also Hands, hitting from the top*	

Overswinging	▸ *See Backswing, overswinging in, problem of*	

Pivot		
difficulty with	▸ Open hips at address	39(B)
	▸ Poor posture and balance due to incorrect procedure	41(C), 41(D)
	▸ Incomplete shoulder turn	171(D)
	▸ Hips turning too far by dipping left knee at start of swing	133(C)

	‣ Difficulty programming downswing before the backswing starts	235–238
	‣ Weight stuck on right side due to insufficient practice moving lower body first from top of swing	199(A)
	‣ Keeping right heel down through hitting zone	213(E)
	‣ *See also Swaying, back and forth*	

Position of Address difficulty establishing	‣ Having no procedure to follow for obtaining objectives at address	31–32, 37, 53(G), 57
	‣ Positioning clubhead with grip already completed without understanding procedure	91–92
	‣ Difficulty sighting the target line	47(B)
	‣ Insufficient practice in developing the waggle	105–110
	‣ Taking too long to set up to ball	252(6)

Positions overestablishing or overcorrecting	‣ Not understanding that even small adjustments or corrections make big differences in overall results	65, 101

Posture poor	‣ Having no procedure to follow for setting up to the ball	31–32, 53(G), 97(C)
	‣ Leaning over too far or reaching too far to position the clubhead	15(A), 49(D)
	‣ Keeping the hips rolled under at address rather than flexed back a bit, and positioning chin too low	41(C), 41(D), 85(Fig. 62)
	‣ Establishing poor positions by using unsuitable clubs	88(E)
	‣ *See also Balance, difficulty establishing and maintaining*	

Quitting on the Shot	‣ *See Golf Shots*	

Releasing difficulty	‣ Incorrect ball position	72(F)
	‣ Poor footwork and legs inactive	143(G), 197, 204
	‣ Quick wrist break	161
	‣ Hands swinging around rather than upright toward the shoulders	245(B)
	‣ Difficulty pulling with left arm and extending right arm	128
	‣ Difficulty combining swinging with hitting due to fast backswing	215–216, 218(A), 222(B)
	‣ Angle of left foot closed	68–69
	‣ Insufficient short swing practice between the toe-up positions	193–195, 199(A), 208(D), 223(C), 227(D), 239–240

	‣ Insufficient practice swinging into follow-through	245(A), 245(C)
	‣ *See also Blocking out, forward swing; Weight shift, difficulty with*	
early	‣ *See Hands, hitting from the top*	

Rhythm
difficulty developing

	‣ Taking too long to set up to the ball	252(6)
	‣ Changing swing thoughts after the backswing starts	247
	‣ Insufficient practice	189–190, 255(3)
	‣ *See also Timing, difficulty with*	

Shoulder Turn
difficulty with

	‣ Having no guidelines or procedure at address for attaining important objectives, which results in	31–32, 37, 97(C)
	1. Weight on toes	38(A)
	2. Stance too wide	71(E)
	3. Angle of feet incorrect	61(1), 68–69
	4. Positioning chin too low	41(D)
	5. Open hips at address	39(B)
	also	
	‣ Incorrect left-arm extension at address with right arm higher than left	49(D), 102(C)
	‣ Positioning hands behind ball without using a forward press	49(E), 115(A)
	‣ Left shoulder starting downward rather than forward at the start of the swing	130(B)
	‣ Fast backswing	145(H)
	‣ Moving the swing center	183(9), 206(C)
	‣ Bending the left elbow or separating arms while swinging by flying the right elbow	100(B), 138(F)
	‣ Keeping the right elbow in too tight on backswing	103(E), 176(3)
	‣ Right shoulder starting forward from top of swing rather than staying back and coming down	202(B)
	‣ Insufficient practice in starting lower body first from top of swing	235–238
	‣ *See also Swaying, back and forth*	

incomplete

	‣ Not understanding importance of completing shoulder turn	171(D), 185(10)
	‣ Right foot angled open and/or right knee not flexed inward	66(1), 176(5)
	‣ Loose grip at address or separation of hands while swinging	16(B), 24(B)

▸ Pulling clubhead away from ball		130(B)
▸ Keeping clubhead on line of flight too long		129–130
▸ Positioning right arm higher than left, which causes separation of arms while swinging as well as flying the right elbow		102(C), 102(D), 138(F)
▸ Bending left elbow at top of swing		100(B)
▸ *See also Tension*		

Shoulders
coming over the top

▸ Right shoulder starting forward from top of swing rather than staying back and moving downward		185(10), 202(B)
caused by		
▸ Positioning right arm higher than left		102(C)
▸ Swinging the clubhead sharply inside on backswing		128 (Fig. 88)
▸ Separation of arms while swinging with right arm not returning close to body on downswing		102(D), 208(D)

positioning, incorrectly

▸ Positioning right arm higher than left		102(C)
▸ Trying to position shoulders without having a basic procedure		32, 95(B)
▸ Shoulders open at address due to:		
1. Incomplete left-arm extension		55(I)
2. Pushing positions open while completing the grip		94(A)
3. Opening shoulders along with opening stance for short irons		80

Spinning Out

▸ Angle of left foot too closed *or* too open		68–69
▸ Shoulders and hips turning together from top of swing due to insufficient practice between toe-up positions		199(A), 208(D)
▸ Keeping right heel down through impact		213(E)

Stance
closed or open

▸ Having no procedure to follow for setting up square		31–33
▸ Difficulty sighting target line		47(B)
▸ *See also Feet, difficulty positioning*		

Swaying
back and forth

▸ Open positions at address		39(B), 55(I)
▸ Moving head due to leaning over too far and positioning chin too low		41(C & D), 183(9), 206(C)
▸ Positioning right arm higher than left		102(C)
▸ Positioning hands behind ball and not using a forward press		49(E), 115(A)
▸ Right foot angled open and right knee not flexed inward		66(1), 67(2), 176(4)
▸ Incorrect ball position		72(F)

‣ Fast move away from ball	145(H)
‣ Keeping clubhead on line of flight too long	129–130
‣ Knees and shoulders moving laterally into backswing due to dipping left knee and shoulder down and inward into backswing	130(B)
‣ Inability to turn *around* the right leg on backswing due to right knee not flexed inward and poor footwork	86(C), 168(A), 185(13)
‣ Flying right elbow with clubface closed through backswing	138(F)
‣ Insufficient short swing practice in staying behind the ball while clearing the left side and hitting through the ball	199(A), 227(D), 239–240
‣ *See also Weight Shift, difficulty with*	

up and down

‣ Difficulty keeping head steady due to incorrect procedure such as:	
1. Leaning over too far or bending the knees too much	15(A), 84(A)
2. Positioning hands too high or low	154(B)
3. Weight established either too far left or too far right	63(C), 86(C)
‣ Left knee jutting forward or dipping downward into backswing	143(G)
‣ *See also Clubhead, picking up*	

Swing Arc
narrow or restricted

‣ Positioning chin too low	41(D), 206(C)
‣ Breaking the wrists too soon	159–160
‣ Keeping right elbow in too tight	176(3)
‣ Short extension of arms at address and through the swing	48(C), 208(D)
‣ Flat swing plane	125(A)
‣ Incomplete follow-through	68–69, 245(A), 245(C)
‣ Insufficient short swing practice	210(Fig. 130), 239–240
‣ *See also Posture, poor*	

Swing Center
moving

‣ *See Swaying*	

Swing Path
difficulty with

‣ Open or closed positions at address	33–34
‣ Poor posture due to incorrect procedure	15(A), 97(C)
‣ Opening shoulders along with opening stance for short irons	80
‣ Having no guidelines for swinging correctly due to insufficient short swing practice between the toe-up positions	125(A), 193–195, 202(B), 208(D), 239–240, 245(B)

Weight Distribution incorrect		
	‣ Having no procedure to follow for setting up to the ball	31–32, 37, 53(G), 97(C)
	‣ Positioning right foot first	63(B), 63(C)
	‣ Knees not flexed inward	86(C), 176(5)
	‣ Weight established on toes due to leaning over too far or reaching too far	38(A), 41(C), 49(D)
	‣ Waggling or pressing hands too far forward at address	117(Fig. 79)
	‣ Keeping the hips rolled under at address rather than flexed back a bit	84(A)
	‣ *See also Feet, difficulty positioning*	

Weight Shift difficulty with		
	‣ Poor posture due to incorrect procedure	15(A), 97(C)
	‣ Angle of feet incorrect	64(D)
	‣ Incorrect ball position	72(F)
	‣ Positioning hands behind ball	49(E)
	‣ Weight established either on the toes or too much left or right	38(A), 63(C)
	‣ Weak right side due to right knee not flexed inward	168(A), 176(4), 176(5)
	‣ Leaving out the running start and forward rocking movement	118(C), 119(D)
	‣ Poor footwork and legs inactive,	143(G), 197, 204
	‣ Swinging too fast	145(H)
	‣ Overswinging as result of loose left-hand grip or bending left arm	16(B), 100(B)
	‣ Incomplete shoulder turn	185(10)
	‣ Change in timing due to sudden downswing thought at top of swing	237
	‣ Insufficient short swing practice between the toe-up positions and into the follow-through	193–195, 199(A), 239–240, 245(A)
	‣ *See also Follow-through, incomplete; Weight Distribution, incorrect*	

firing and falling back in		
	‣ *See Ball, falling away from*	

reverse		
	‣ Weight incorrectly shifting left as backswing starts, then shifting right as the downswing starts	
	caused by	
	‣ Inability to coordinate swinging and hitting due to swinging too fast	145(H), 215–216, 222(B)
	‣ Trying to prevent swaying by firmly establishing the weight on either the left or right foot	63(C)

▸ Raising left heel straight up or bending left knee straight forward on backswing rather than letting left leg swing inward	168(B)
▸ *See also Ball, falling away from*	

Wrist Break incorrect		
	▸ Incorrect grip	7
	▸ Not understanding how or where the wrists should break	149
	▸ Starting the backswing with the left wrist bent inward due to:	
	1. Positioning clubhead with right hand	49(E)
	2. Positioning right foot first	63(B)
	3. Not using a forward press	115(A)
	▸ Bending left wrist inward through backswing—often due to swinging too fast	145(H), 180(7)
	▸ Left wrist bent inward at impact with right hand cupping under due to closed clubface through backswing	225 (Fig. 137)
	▸ Failure to clear left side through impact	208(D)

Index

Coil-recoil action, 171(D). *See also* Downswing

Concentration, 35
developing, 146(I), 251(C), 252(7), 189–90
use of waggle in, 105–10

Confidence
addressing ball with, 97(C), 105, 108
building and developing, 31–32, 147, 187–88, 250(B), 251(4)
grip importance in, 9
practice in, 189–90, 255(4)
short swing practice in, 239–40
waggle in, 252(7)
hitting short shots with, 80
hitting with, 215–16

Conscious thought
cause of, 247, 251(1)
how to avoid, 251(C)
use of key thoughts in, 146(I)
overcoming, 105–10, 250(B), 252(7)
importance of, 235–38
useful, 254(E)

Consistency
addressing ball with, 35, 72(F)
purpose of waggle in, 105(1)
grip and set-up importance in, 240
swinging with, 108, 172(E), 251(4)
arms together in, 102(D), 138(F)
timing and rhythm in, 145(H), 188–89, 255(3)

Coordination, 1, 31–32, 171(D), 248(A)
essence of, 145(H)
feet and legs in, 185(12)
grip and set-up importance in, 7–9, 240
muscle memory in, 245(C)
reflex action in, 235–38
starting backswing, 121
swinging and hitting with, 67(2), 218(A), 222(B), 227(D)
practicing, 195, 255(3)

sense and feel in, 169
short swing practice in, 239–40
wrist break in, 162(C)
timing in, 170, 188–89. *See also* Timing
waggle importance in, 105–10
weight shift in, 66(1), 199(A)

Cut shots. *See* Golf shots

Directional line
establishing, 32–34
angle of feet in, 64(D)
open stance in, 78–79
procedure for, 46(A), 58–59, 60(A)
maintaining, 39(B), 78–79, 94(A)
use of, 123 (Fig. 84), 125(A), 151 (Fig. 101C), 198 (Fig. 123), 208(D)

Downswing
coil-recoil action in, 133(C)
keynotes in, 251(3)
shoulder turn importance in, 171(D), 185(10)
planning ahead for, 106
reflex action in. *See* Downswing, coil-recoil
reviewing, 253
starting correct, 235–38
footwork in 66(1), 176(4)
moment of truth in, 235
search for one "key move" in, 236
short swing practice in, 193–95, 239–40
timing in, 67(4)
weight shift in, 67(3), 69, 177(5), 199(A)
See also Backswing, completing

Elbow(s)
positioning rolled inward, 98–104
procedure for, 99
swing action of, 102(D), 103(E), 176(3), 218(A)
See also Arms

Emulation, 248

Extension, 103(E)
importance of, 125(A)
toe-up positions in, 198 (Fig. 123)
See also Arms, positioning; swing action of

"Feel." *See* Golf, sense and feel in

Feet
action of. *See* Footwork
positioning, 56–81
alignment in, 32–34, 46(A), 60(A)
angle in, 64(D)
left foot first in, 63(B), 63(C)
procedure for, 58–59
See also Stance

Follow-through
blocking out, 182A
completing, 68–69, 242–46
importance of, 245(A)
procedure for, 243–45
short shots in, 78–79
reviewing, 254
toe-up position in, 196–213. *See also* Clubhead

Footwork
angle of feet in, 64(D)
right foot importance in, 67(3), 177(5)
follow-through in, 68–69, 245(C)
forward press in, 119(D)
heels in, 168(B), 185(13), 213(E), 244
procedure for, 167 (Fig. 110B), 197, 216 (Fig. 133B), 243–44
sitting down position in, 84(A)
swing action in, 143(G)
timing in, 145(H)
weight distribution for, 38(A), 63(C), 86(C)
weight shift in, 199(A)
See also Feet, positioning

Forward press, 112–19
procedure for, 114
purpose of, 115(A)
reviewing, 253
See also Legs, swing action of

Tempo
  practicing, 255(3)
  understanding, 188–89
  See also Timing
Terminology
  alignment, 32–33
  hitting zone, 227(D)
  stance, 64(D)
  swing, 125(A)
Thumbs
  positioning. *See* Grip
  swing action of. *See* Hand action
Timing
  critical moments in, 121, 170
  extension importance in, 126
  footwork in, 67(3), 67(4),
    143(G)
  hitting action in, 222(B)
  key to, 226
  practicing, 201, 255(3)
    short swing in, 195, 239–40
    throwing action in, 220–21
    shoulder turn and pivot in,
      133(C)
    tempo, rhythm and
      coordination in, 145(H),
      188–89, 251(3)
    use of waggle in, 105(3)

weight shift in, 199(A)
wrist break in, 162(C)
See also Downswing starting
    correct
Torque, 66(1), 135–36, 171(D). *See
    also* Downswing, coil-recoil
Touch. *See* Golf, sense and feel

Vardon, Harry, 7

Waggle, 35, 105–10
  planning ahead in, 106, 227(D)
  purpose of, 105
  reviewing, 252(D)
  use of, 24(A), 94(A), 162(D),
    189–90, 252(7)
  See also Forward press
Weight distribution
  establishing, 38(A), 49(D),
    63(C), 86(C)
    forward press in, 119(D)
  protecting, 53(G), 63(B), 97(C),
    118(B)
  short iron, 81
  See also Short irons
Weight shift
  backswing, 168(A)
  balance for, 38(A), 84(A)

maintaining, 145 (H)
downswing reflex action in,
    235–38
follow-through importance in, 69,
    245(A)
footwork in, 63(C), 67(4),
    143(G), 168(B), 177(5)
  angle of feet in, 67(3), 69
  See also Footwork
hitting action in, 222(B)
importance of, 199(A)
practicing, 200 (Fig. 124),
    239–40
use of key thoughts in, 238
width of stance for, 71(E)
See also Weight distribution
Whiffing, *See* Ball
Wrist break, 148–64
  firm left arm in, 100(B)
  hands in, 138(E)
  importance of positions in, 149,
    154(B)
  procedure for, 150–51
  straight left wrist in, 49(E),
    85(B), 115(A), 152(A),
    180(7)
  waggle in, 162(D)